D1394648

LENIN IN ZÜRICH

Alexander
SOLZHENITSYN

Lenin in Zürich

CHAPTERS

TRANSLATED BY

H. T. Willetts

THE BODLEY HEAD
LONDON SYDNEY
TORONTO

Russian text first published by
YMCA Press, Paris, under the title
ЛЕНИН В ЦЮРИХЕ
World copyright © 1975 Alexander Solzhenitsyn
English translation copyright
© 1976 by Farrar, Straus & Giroux, Inc.,
New York, and The Bodley Head, Ltd
ISBN 0 370 10607 5
Printed and bound in Great Britain for
The Bodley Head Ltd,
9 Bow Street, London WC2E 7AL
by William Clowes & Sons Ltd, Beccles
Set in Monophoto Imprint
First published in Great Britain 1976

CONTENTS

AUTHOR'S PREFACE

Chapter 22 of 'Knot' I, which was omitted from the published version of that work (*August 1914*), and the chapters from 'Knots' II and III on Lenin in Zürich during the First World War, were written or begun while I was still in the USSR. Unexpectedly finding myself in Zürich, I came across much important additional material. As a result, the scope of these chapters has been considerably enlarged, and there seemed to be some point in publishing them as a separate book, rather than making them wait for publication of the 'Knots' themselves, which will not be in the very near future.

August 1914

22

Yes, yes, yes, yes! It's a vice, this habit of plunging recklessly, of rushing full steam ahead, intent only on your goal, blind and deaf to all around, so that you fail to see the childishly obvious danger beside you! Like when he and Yuly Martov, the moment their three years of Siberian tedium were over, and they were on their way abroad at last, carrying a basket of subversive literature and a letter with the plan for *Iskra* in invisible ink, chose that of all times to be too clever, too conspiratorial. The rule is to change trains en route, but they had forgotten that their train would pass through Tsarskoye Selo, and were detained by the gendarmes as suspicious persons. Luckily the police with their salutary Russian sluggishness gave them time to get rid of the basket, and took the letter at its face value because they could not be bothered to hold it over a flame—and that was how *Iskra* was saved!

Later, in a year of tense struggle between the 'majority' of twenty-one and the 'minority' of twenty-two, the whole Party had let the Japanese war slip by almost unnoticed.

This other war he had neither written nor thought about. He had not reacted to Jaurès's appeal. Why? Because the *reunion movement* had spread like a plague, until in the last few years it had infected the whole of Russian social democracy. Nothing could be more dangerous and damaging to the proletariat than this epidemic: 'conciliation', 're-unification'— cretinous nonsense, the ruin of the Party! Then the leaders of the ditherers' International had seized the initiative. Let them make peace between us! Let them unify us! They summoned

us to their sordid little unification conference in Brussels[1].
How to wangle out of it? How to dodge it? Engrossed in this
problem he had hardly heard the pistol shot at Sarajevo!
When Austria declared war on Serbia, he had hardly noticed.
Even Germany's declaration of war on Russia had meant
nothing to him. Reports were put about that the German
Social Democrats had voted for war credits. Obviously a
trick. Take more than that to fool us. Just trying to create
confusion in the socialist ranks. Yes, yes—once you get up
steam you are carried helplessly along. It is difficult to stop,
to collect your wits. Yes, he had had ten days to consider the
ambiguity of his situation, right on the Russian frontier, to
get clear of Poronin now that the damned place was no good
to anybody, to escape altogether from the Austro-Hungarian
trap. What work could he do in a country at war? He should
have made a dash for the blessed haven of Switzerland—a
neutral country, a safe country where there were no restric-
tions, policemen were intelligent, and laws were laws. But
no! He hadn't stirred. His mind was still on old pre-war problems. Suddenly Russia was at war with Austria, and the very
next evening, in pouring rain, a sergeant of gendarmes was
knocking at his door.

In a general way, of course, he had known that war must
come! He had foreseen it, foretold it. But not at this precise
moment, not this year. So he had missed his chance. And
landed in a mess.

Hanecki's clean-shaven, pleasant, rather delicate face is
calm enough now, but how he raged at the judge in Nowy
Targ! How he galloped about in that old cart! Hanecki didn't
abandon me in my time of trouble.

Along the platform to the engine and back. To the engine
and back again.

Still a hellish long time before the train was due to leave.
Almost half an hour. Anything might happen yet. Although
there on the station, with a gendarme reassuringly pacing the
platform, nobody was likely to attack him.

Looked at dialectically, a gendarme is sometimes a bad
thing and sometimes a good thing.

The engine had a big red wheel, almost the height of a
man.

However wary you are, however circumspect, however suspicious, in seven long years the abominable tranquillity of an essentially petit-bourgeois existence will make you drowsy. In the shadow of something big, you lean against a massive iron wall, without looking at it carefully—and suddenly it moves, it turns out to be a big red engine wheel, driven by a long, naked piston rod, your spine is twisted and you are underneath! With your head banging against the rails, you belatedly realise that yet again some stupid danger has taken you unawares.

But why had it happened to him, the moment the war began? At first he had laughed. What could they suspect him of? As far as the Austrian police at least were concerned, he was immaculate. (He had only moved to Cracow because he had heard from Hanecki that the Austrian government would support all anti-Tsarist forces.) Then his lodgings were searched. He had Russian addresses and conspiratorial notes (they were a nuisance, always getting into the wrong hands), but these the blockheaded sergeant had missed altogether, pouncing instead on a manuscript about the agrarian problem. Too many figures! Must be in code! He had confiscated the manuscript. A pity, but never mind. The police always rub the wrong way and find a pimple on the smoothest back. Lenin's only worry was the Russian addresses, but the sergeant poked and pried till he finally found a Browning and some cartridges! Lenin looked at Nadya in amazement. He didn't recognise the beastly revolver, had no memory of it, had never handled it, didn't know how to fire it, nor would it ever have occurred to him to use such a crude weapon. Where had it come from? (It turned out that some over-zealous Russian comrade—silly fool—had pressed it on them, and Nadya, like a nitwit, had accepted it.)

You live your own life, never seeing yourself as others see you. Then suddenly in the eyes of a policeman you are someone who has taken up residence near the Russian frontier, has visitors from Russia, receives money from Russia, and quite large sums at that, does a lot of walking in the mountains, no doubt making sketch plans. Everyone in Nowy Targ had been warned to detain suspicious persons who might be making road maps or poisoning the wells. A spy! With a revolver into

[13]

the bargain! Please report on time for the morning train, we're going to Nowy Targ.

An endless chain of stupidities! A wall of stupidity! The silliest, most elementary, blindest of oversights—just like that time at Tsarskoye Selo. (Or that other time in 1895—when they were all ready to publish their paper, but came to grief before they could get the first issue out.) Yes, yes, a revolutionary must always be ready to go to gaol (though it's cleverer to stay out), but not for such a silly reason! Not in this humiliating way! Don't let them tie your hands just at the wrong moment! That stinking cell in the Nowy Targ police station! Mouldy old Austria-Hungary! Perhaps he would be court-martialled?

No accidental setback, no defeat, no dirty, underhand trick on the part of your enemies is ever so galling as your own miscalculations, however slight. They nag at you day and night, especially in a prison cell. Because they are *your own* mistakes —you cannot be objective about them, cannot live them down or forget them, cannot get away from the thought that it need never have happened! It need never have happened! But it has happened because of your own bungling! The blunder is all *yours*! Pace the flagged floor from wall to wall, toss on your creaking wire bed for eleven long days and eleven long nights —you won't run away from it, won't sleep it off. It nags and burns like an ulcer. It need never have happened! It need never have happened! You brought it on yourself! You've dropped yourself in it!

Still twenty-three minutes until the train leaves, only the first bell has gone. If only we could be off!

Hanecki—Kuba to his Party comrades—looks very much at his ease, every inch the businessman, with his ingeniously trained wisp of moustache and his cool, steady stare—an irresistible charmer. In that critical situation he had not backed away, not gone soft, not surrendered, but behaved like a bulldog sinking its teeth in a policeman's trousers. The minute the search was over, Lenin had cycled straight over to him, not to Grishka Zinoviev, and he had not been mistaken. So as not to lose face, he had tried to make light of it, turn it into an amusing if tiresome little story. (But inside he felt stunned: after all, there was a war on, who was going to waste time on enquiries? They would just shoot him! There was nothing to stop them polishing him off—and because of one silly slip the whole Party would go down the drain, and the socialist world revolution with it!) But Kuba had seen the danger at once! He hadn't encouraged Lenin's show of unconcern, hadn't tried to reassure him, but had showered him with names. Social Democrats! Members of Parliament! Public figures! People who must be written to immediately, told the facts, pestered, urged to intervene!

That same evening, from Poronin, Hanecki had sent his first telegrams and Ulyanov had wired to the Cracow police, requesting confirmation of his unqualified loyalty to the Austro-Hungarian Empire. In the morning, Lenin had still not returned from Nowy Targ, and Hanecki—since there was no train in the middle of the day—had jumped into a cart and raced off to see the police chiefs and the investigating magistrate (at some risk to himself; he might easily have been arrested, as Grishka was shortly afterwards). He'd dispatched letters by the dozen in all directions, gone straight off to see people in Cracow—he could spin any bureaucrat a yarn at a moment's notice—and then wired Vienna. In his place any Slav would have wearied, relaxed his efforts, given up, but Hanecki was indefatigable, he could not have gone to more trouble for his own brother, he had not let up for a moment. On his return from Cracow, he had even forced his way into the gaol to visit Lenin, who had given him one further commission; to obtain for him permission to leave for Switzerland.

Spurred on by Hanecki's urgent telegrams, the Social Democratic deputies Victor Adler and Diamand had appealed to the Austrian Chancellor and the Ministry of the Interior, giving written guarantees that the Social Democrat Ulyanov was a worse enemy of the Russian government than the Chancellor of Austria-Hungary himself. The Cracow police had been given their instructions: 'In present circumstances Ulyanov may be of great service to us.' Even so, they had taken eleven days—until August 6th—to release him. How they hated letting go!

Even after his release the week in Poronin had not been at all quiet. What you could drum into the Austrian Chancellor and other aristocratic Austrian imbeciles was less readily understood by Galician peasants, who were as obtuse as peasants the world over, in Europe, in Asia, or in Alakayevka. To the benighted inhabitants of Poronin, this foreigner, although now at large, remained just what he had been—a spy! It was staggering! Beyond all understanding! Peasant women coming out of church, whether or not they had seen Nadya and were doing it for her benefit, had deafened the whole street with their din. If the authorities had let him go, they would poke his eyes out for him! Cut out his tongue! Nadya had come home pale and trembling all over. Her fright was contagious. They might very well poke his eyes out, he wouldn't be a bit surprised! There was nothing to stop them cutting his tongue out either! Nothing could be simpler: they would come along with their pitchforks and knives ... Never in his life had Lenin been exposed to such enormous danger. Nobody had ever treated him like this ... History after all recorded many such obscene outbursts of mob fury! There were no guarantees against it even in civilised countries. You were safer even in gaol than amongst an ignorant rabble.

To feel alarm in the face of threats means that you are prepared, not that you are panicky.

So his last days and hours in Poronin had been darkened and troubled. For two years this safe, peaceful little town had been couched to spring. They had kept to the house, been unable to eat or sleep, started feverishly packing. Lenin had tried to pick out the most important papers and books, but he was not master of himself, he could not concentrate, and besides he had amassed tons and tons of paper. (It was only that spring that they had moved there from Cracow to settle permanently.)

How could he have been so slow, lingered so close to the Russian frontier? Cossack raiders could have carried him off in a flash.

Here on the platform by the neat green train, in the presence of the gendarme and the station personnel, there could be no mob violence, and at last he felt at ease. They were all more cheerful on this cheerful, sunny, cloudless morning. No military freight was being loaded, no newly mobilised soldiers were on the move, the platform and the train looked just as they always did in the summer holiday season. But tickets were freely available only as far as Nowy Targ, and passengers for Cracow needed a police permit.

For this reason the carriages were half empty. Nadya and his mother-in-law had already taken their seats and were looking out of the window. A few comrades had come to see them off and stood looking up at them. Vladimir Ilyich had taken Kuba's arm and they were walking backwards and forwards along the platform, both of them short men, both of them broad, only Lenin was big-boned and Kuba merely fat.

When a man displays such remarkable abilities you must listen carefully to what he says, however visionary it may seem to be. He had known Kuba a long time, ever since the Second Congress, but solely in connection with Polish affairs. It was only that summer that he had shown a new side of himself and become indispensable. He was worth his weight in gold: extraordinarily efficient, and tight-lipped in all serious matters—no outsider would ever get a word out of him. They had spent the months of June and July walking about the plateau near Poronin and discussing Kuba's pyrotechnic schemes for making money. Possibly because of his bourgeois origins, Hanecki had a remarkable financial flair, an extraordinary grasp of money matters—a quality as valuable as it was rare in a revolutionary. He had argued, correctly, that money was the Party's arms and legs, without money any party was helpless, just a lot of hot air. If even parliamentary parties needed a great deal of money—for their electoral campaigns—it was infinitely more important to an underground, revolutionary party, which had to organise hiding places, safe meeting places, transport, literature and weapons, train its fighters, support its professionals, and when the time was right carry out a revolution.

He was preaching to the converted! These were things which all Bolsheviks had understood ever since the Second Congress and their first steps as an independent party: without money you can't move an inch, money is all-important. They had started by squeezing donations out of fat-headed Russian merchants, like Mamontov, or Konovalov ('give them a bun'), and Savva Morozov had kicked in a thousand a month to pay the expenses of the Petersburg committee, but others had shelled out irregularly, in a fit of businessman's benevolence or 'intellectual' sympathy. (Garin-Mikhailovsky had just once given ten thousand.) Then you had to start begging again. A surer way was to take it for yourself. Perhaps screw a legacy out of somebody, as they had from Shmidt, the factory owner, or marry off Party members to heiresses, or swindle the Lbov gang out in the Urals by taking their money and not delivering the promised weapons. Or you could be more systematic about it and develop military techniques: they had planned to print false money in Finland and Krasin had obtained the water-marked paper. Krasin again had made bombs for the expropriations. The 'exes' had gone off extraordinarily well: then because of Plekhanov's and Martov's squeamishness the Fifth Congress had banned them, but it was impossible to call a halt, and Kamo and Koba had triumphantly grabbed another 340,000 from the Treasury in Tiflis. But success went to their heads, and comrades had started changing crisp Tsarist five-hundred-rouble notes in Berlin, in Paris, in Stockholm. They should have been content with less. The Tsarist ministry had circulated the serial numbers, and so Litvinov was caught. So was Sara Ravich, in Munich, and a note she was trying to smuggle out of prison was intercepted. After their homes had been searched, thirteen Geneva Bolsheviks had been picked up, and Karpinsky and Semashko would have been put away for a spell if the liberals in Parliament hadn't helped. But worst of all, obscenest of all, Kautsky, with his false, hypocritical, sneaking devotion to principle, had started squawking like an old hen. What a vile trick: setting up a 'socialist court' to try the Russian Bolsheviks, and ordering them like a half-wit to burn the all-powerful five-hundred-rouble notes! (Lenin had only to see a picture of that hoary-headed holy man in his goggling glasses, and he retched as though he found himself swallowing a frog.) It's all right for you, the German workers are well off, they pay large dues, your party is legal, but what about us? (Of course they hadn't been such fools as to burn all of it.) Then they did another stupid thing, and made the malicious old man financial arbitrator between Bolsheviks and Mensheviks. They had to make a tactical pretence of accepting reunion, which meant pooling their funds—and the Mensheviks hadn't a bean. Since it was impossible to conceal the whole Shmidt inheritance, they had given part of it to Kautsky, as arbitrator—and later on, when the new split came, he would not hand it back to the Bolsheviks.

This last summer Hanecki had captured Lenin's imagination with his plans to found a trading company of his own in Europe, or take a partnership in some existing firm, and make guaranteed monthly remittances to the Party out of his profits. This was not a Russian pipe-dream: every move had been worked out with impressive precision. Kuba hadn't thought of it himself, it was the brain-child of the elephantine genius Parvus, who had been writing to him from Constantinople. Parvus, once as poor as any other Social Democrat, had gone to Turkey to organise strikes, and now wrote frankly that he had all the money he needed (if rumour was right, he was fabulously wealthy) and that the time had come for the Party too to get rich. He had put it neatly. Their best hope of overthrowing capitalism was to become capitalists themselves. Socialists must start by becoming capitalists! The Socialists had laughed at him. Rosa, Klara and Liebknecht had let him know how they despised him. But perhaps they had been in too much of a hurry. Sarcasm wilted in the face of Parvus's solid financial power.

It was partly because of Hanecki's schemes that the war had caught them napping.

They discussed them further in these last few minutes, and made arrangements to keep in touch. They would in any case be seeing each other soon; Zinoviev would follow on after Lenin, and then Hanecki, as soon as he obtained exemption from Austrian military service.

... There went the second bell. Lenin hopped nimbly on to the step. Hatless, almost completely bald, in his shabby suit, with his sharp features, his habit of looking uneasily over his shoulder, and his neglected beard, he really did look rather like a spy. Hanecki wanted to tease him about it, but he knew that Lenin couldn't take a joke and refrained.

But what did he look like himself if not a spy, with his sad, wary eyes, and the shiny suit which did not go with his businessman's face?

The stationmaster stood stern and stiff in his tall red and

black cap. There were three rings on the bell. The guard sounded his horn and started running.

People waved good-bye, and they waved back through the open window.

All in all, life in Poronin hadn't been too bad. A quiet, steady life, not like the mad rush of Paris. For all his homeless wanderings about Europe, he had never become a European. He found it easier to act if his surroundings were simple and narrow. They had lived through so many anxious moments here. So many joys.

So many disillusionments.

Malinovsky.

The platform, the station and those left behind were snatched from sight. Even Hanecki, admirable and reliable comrade though he was, would be missing from the next stage of his life. At some future stage he might very well become again the most important and useful of men, and desperately urgent letters with double and treble underlining would be dashed off in the small hours, but for the time being he had done a splendid job and ceased to exist.

There was an infallible law of revolutionary struggle, or perhaps of human life in general, which no one had yet put into words but which Lenin had often noticed at work. At any given time one or two people emerged to take their place at his side, people who for the moment were intellectually closer to him, more interesting, important and useful than anyone else, people who particularly stimulated him to confide in them, to discuss things with them, to act in concert with them. But hardly any of them retained this position for long, because situations change every day, and we must change dialectically with them, change instantly, or, rather, anticipate change— that is the meaning of political genius. It was natural that one after another, encountering the whirlwind that was Lenin, should be drawn immediately into his activities, should carry out his instructions at the prescribed moment and with the prescribed speed, by whatever means and at whatever personal sacrifice. Natural, because all this was done not for Vladimir Ilyich but for the compelling power which manifested itself through him, and of which he was only the infallible interpreter, who always knew precisely what was right just for today, and indeed by the evening was not always quite what it had been in the morning. Once one of these transitional people grew obstinate, ceased to understand why his duties were necessary and urgent, began to mention his mixed feelings or his own unique destiny, then it was just as natural to remove him from the main road, dismiss him, forget him, abuse and anathematise him if necessary—but even when he dismissed or damned someone Lenin was acting in obedience to the power which drew him on. The exiles on the Yenisei had occupied this position of intellectual intimacy for a long, long time, but only because there was no one geographically nearer. From afar he had imagined that Plekhanov would take their place—but after a few short meetings a cold, cruel lesson had put an abrupt end to that. Martov had been close—indeed dangerously, undesirably close—for years on end. But he too had had to give way. (From his bitter experience with Martov he had learnt once and for all that there can be no such relationship between human beings as simple friendship transcending political, class and material ties.) Krasin had been a close friend while he was making his bombs. So had Bogdanov while he was fund-raising for the Party, but when this abruptly ended he had misjudged the sharp slope before him, while aspiring to set the course, and come crashing down. Meanwhile, new loyal followers were sucked into the whirlwind—Kamenev, Zinoviev, Malinovsky ...

Only those who saw the Party's needs in correct perspective could hold their places and march at his side. But when the urgent need of the moment changed, the perspective usually changed too, so that all those recent collaborators remained helplessly rooted in the dull, stationary earth, like so many signposts, receding from view until they vanished and were forgotten, though sometimes they loomed sharply at a new turning in the road, this time as enemies. There had been fellow spirits who were close for a week, a day, an hour, for the space of a single conversation, a single report, a single errand—and Lenin open-heartedly lavished all his fervour, left the impress of his own sense of urgency on them, so that each one felt himself to be the most important person in the world; then, an hour later, they were already receding, and he would soon have clean forgotten who they were, and why he had needed them. Thus, Valentinov had seemed close when he first arrived from Russia, though he had aroused misgivings with his stupid remark that some bit of metalwork he had made meant more to him, when he was working in a factory, than the political struggle. He had soon shown his true nature: he had lacked the stamina to stand up to Martov and become no better than a Menshevik himself.

The train was rolling down the incline, struggling round the mountain bends. Paths and cart-tracks ran down the slopes, and higher up, beyond farmhouses, ricks and standing crops, the mountain road was still visible. You could run up it with your eyes. In all his walks around Poronin he had never been there.

He sat down at last. He should be thinking, or working, not sentimentalising.

His womenfolk, reading his looks and his movements aright, did not pester him with trifles or fidget unnecessarily, but sat quietly in their seats.

All those exhausting years, from 1908 on, after the defeat of the revolution, had been one long story of desertions and dismissals. One after another they had left: the Vperyod group, the Recallists, the Ultimatists, the Machists, the God-Builders ... Lunacharsky, Bazarov, Aleksinsky, Brilliant, Rozhkov, Krasin, Lyadov, Menzhinsky, Lozovsky, Manuilsky, Gorky ... The whole old guard, knocked together during the split with the Mensheviks. There were moments when it seemed that there would be no one left, that the whole Bolshevik Party would consist of himself, a couple of women, and a dozen third-raters and washouts who used to come to Bolshevik meetings back in the Paris days; that if he got up to speak at a general meeting he would have not a single friend there and would be shoved off the platform. They went away, one after another—and what iron certainty it needed not to start doubting himself, not to waver, not to run after them and make it up, but, with his clear prophetic insight, to stand firm and wait for them to return of their own accord, to come to their senses ... and those who didn't could go to hell.

In 1906 and 1907 defeat was not yet total, society was still on the boil, milling round the rim of the maelstrom. Lenin had sat in Kuokkala, waiting in vain for the second wave. But from 1908, when the reactionary rabble had tightened its grip on the whole of Russia, the underground had shrivelled to nothing, the workers had swarmed like ants out of their holes and into legal bodies—trade unions and benefit clubs—and the decline of the underground had sapped the vitality of the emigration too, reduced it to a hothouse existence ... *Back there* was the Duma, a legal press—and every émigré was eager to publish *there* ...

That was why the outbreak of war was such a marvellous thing! He was overjoyed by it!! *Back there*, all those Liquidators would be suppressed immediately, the importance of legal activity would sink sharply, whereas the importance of the emigration and its strength would increase! The centre of gravity of Russian political life was shifting back abroad!

Lenin had sized up the situation while he was still in gaol at Nowy Targ. (Nadya, have we gone through Nowy Targ yet? I must have missed it.) There in his cell, fighting down his anxiety, trying not to let a personal mishap overshadow the general good fortune, he had absorbed and begun processing the fact that all Europe was at war. The result of this process in Lenin's brain was always the birth of slogans ready for use: the creation of slogans for present needs was the ultimate purpose of all his thinking. That, and the translation of his arguments into the Marxist vernacular: his supporters and followers would not understand him in any other language.

What emerged he had revealed after his release to Hanecki before anyone else: the thing to realise was that now the war had begun they should not wish it away or try to stop it, but take advantage of it. They must rise above the sanctimonious notion, sometimes insinuated even into proletarian heads, that war was a disaster or a sin. The slogan 'Peace at any price' was for psalm-singing hypocrites! What line should revolutionary democrats everywhere follow in the present situation? The first need was to refute the fairy-tale that the Central Powers were to blame for starting the war! The Entente would take refuge in the story that they were 'innocent victims of aggression'. They would even pretend that the *rentiers*' republic must be defended in the interests of democracy. These excuses must be stamped on, trampled underfoot! The propaganda line must be that *all* governments were equally to blame. What mattered was not who was to blame, but how to turn the war to the best advantage. 'They're all to blame'—only if that were accepted could they go on working to bring down the Tsar's government.

This is a lucky war! It will greatly benefit international socialism—with one sharp jolt it will cleanse the workers' movement of the accumulated filth of peacetime! Instead of the previous division of Socialists into opportunists and revolutionaries—an ambiguous distinction which leaves loopholes for enemies—it will make unmistakably clear the real line of cleavage in the international movement—that between patriots and anti-patriots. We are the anti-patriots!

It meant the end of the International's shabby schemes for reuniting Bolsheviks and Mensheviks. They had planned a further attempt at reconciliation—at the Vienna Congress in August—but by July five fronts were ablaze! There wouldn't be another peep out of them. The rift now yawned so wide that there could be no thought of reconciliation! Yet earlier in July they had had him by the throat: 'We see no differences sufficient to justify a split!' 'Send a delegation to talk peace!' Talk peace with the Menshevik scum! Ah, but now, now that you've voted war credits, your International is dead! It will never get on its feet again, it's a corpse! You'll keep up your skeleton's dance for a long time yet, but we must declare for all to hear: you're dead! Inessa's trip to Brussels was our last meeting with you, we've had enough!

At this point, his mother-in-law suddenly realised that they had left a suitcase behind! They hastily checked and counted the baggage under the seats and on the overhead racks. It wasn't there! How disgraceful! They might have been escaping from a burning building! Vladimir Ilyich was upset. Without order in the family and the home, work was impossible. It might sound comic, but an orderly household was itself a contribution to the Party cause. He didn't dare tell the older woman off. She could give as good as she got, and anyway they respected each other—he even gave her little presents to keep on the right side of her. But he reprimanded Nadya. What could you expect from her, though, when she couldn't sew on a button or remove a stain properly? He

[24]

could do better himself! She wouldn't even give him a clean handkerchief unless he asked.

He never forgave a mistake. No matter who made it, he would remember it as long as he lived.

He turned his head to the window.

The train was gradually winding its way down from the mountains. Engine smoke, sometimes grey, sometimes white, swept past the windows. He was sick of mountains, too, after all these years of emigration.

With Nadya, it was like water off a duck's back. All right, we've forgotten a case. We can't go back for it, can we? We'll write from Cracow, and they'll send it on.

Nadya had a firm rule, often applied in the past. If she took Volodya's share of the blame on herself, he would cool off and come round. What vexed him most was to be found equally at fault.

He looked his age as he sat there gloomily, with his un-trimmed beard and moustache and his anxiously arched ginger eyebrows, staring absently, unseeingly through the window. Nadya knew his changes of expression so well. Just now, she must be careful not to cross him, not even to speak to him, or distract him by exchanging a word with her mother. She must just let him sit there, sink into himself, bathe his hurts in soothing silence, recover from the frantic days in Nowy Targ, the threats in Poronin, the lost case. At such times, whether he took a solitary walk or sat silently thinking, after half an hour or an hour of meditation his brow would clear and the angry little wrinkles would be smoothed from around his eyes, leaving long deep creases.

A split in the international socialist movement was long overdue but only the war had brought it into the open and made it unavoidable. It was absolutely marvellous! It might seem that the proletarian front had been weakened by the mass betrayal of Socialists: not so—it was *good* that they had betrayed! It was now so much the easier to insist on his own distinct line.

Whereas, a month ago, he hadn't known what to say or how to wriggle out of it! An inspiration—instead of going to Brussels himself he would send Inessa, leading a delegation!! Inessa!!! With her excellent French! With her incomparable

[25]

poise—cool, calm, slightly disdainful. (The Frenchmen in the presidium will be at your feet immediately. And the Germans won't understand you too well—and that's just fine! Every time a German speaks, call for a translation!) What a clever move! They would be at their wits' end, those ultra-Socialist donkeys ... Get on with it at once! Write and ask her. Will she go? Can she go? A holiday with the children on the Adriatic? Rubbish, find somebody to look after the children, we'll pay the expenses out of Party funds. Writing an article on free love? Without being rude (a woman can never give one hundred per cent of herself to the Party, she's always up to some nonsense) your manuscript can wait. I'm sure you're one of those who are at their best and bravest doing a responsible job single-handed. Rubbish, rubbish, I don't listen to pessimists! ... You'll cope magnificently! ... I'm sure you have cheek enough for it! ... They'll all be furious I'm not there (that makes me happy!) and they'll probably want to revenge themselves on you, but I'm sure you'll show your claws in no uncertain fashion! ... We'll call you ... let's see ... Petrova. Why reveal your real name to Liquidators? (I'm 'Petrov' too—you should remember, if nobody else does. So, through our pseudonyms, we shall face the public united in one person—openly yet secretly. You will actually be me.) My dear friend, I do beg you to say yes! Will you go? ... Of course you will! ... Of course you will! ... Yes, indeed, we must rehearse thoroughly. And be mighty quick about it. You must simply lie to the Liquidators: promise them that *maybe*, later on, we'll accept a majority decision. (But *of course* we shall never really accept anything! *Not a single one* of their proposals!) Then tell some fib about the children being ill, and say that you can't stay on any longer. We must convince the European Socialists, petit-bourgeois scum that they are, that the Bolsheviks are the most serious of the Russian parties. Slip them the bit about trade unions and benefit clubs—that has a tremendous effect on them. When they ask questions—cut them short, avoid answering, fight them off! Take the offensive at all times! Get Rosa talking, show them that she has no proper party behind her, that Hanecki's opposition is the real party. You've got it now! You'll go! ... Warmest best wishes! Very truly[2] ... Your own ...

[26]

Then Hanecki had spoilt things. He'd delivered an ultimatum—not altogether unreasonable: 250 crowns for the Brussels trip, or he wouldn't go. But Party funds must be used carefully. (And Hanecki isn't the only one! There are plenty of people we could make use of, but we mustn't throw our money around ...) So in Hanecki's absence the lousy Polish opposition had betrayed and voted with Rosa and Plekhanov for the rotten, idiotic conciliation scheme.

... All the same, you saw it through better than I could. Apart from the fact that I don't know the language, I should certainly have blown up! I couldn't have stood that farce! I should have called them a lot of crooks. But you carried it off calmly, firmly, you foiled all their tricks. You have done the Party a great service! I'm sending you 150 francs. (Probably not enough? Let me know how much more you spent and I'll send it.) Write to me. Are you very tired? Are you very angry with me? Why is it 'extremely unpleasant' for you to write about the conference? Maybe you are ill? What is wrong with you? Do reply, or I shall have no peace.

Inessa was the only human being whose moods he sensed and responded to even at a distance. Indeed, at a distance the pull was stronger.

One thing to remember: with wartime censorship he must adopt a less intimate tone. It might give an opening for blackmail. Socialists must be prudent.

Their correspondence had been interrupted by the war, and now her letters would go to Poronin. Still, there was every reason to believe that once she had sent her children off to Russia Inessa would return to Switzerland. Perhaps she was there already.

The women were quietly discussing how they were going to manage in Cracow. Nadya suggested that her mother and Volodya should stay with the luggage while she called on Inessa's old landlady. It would save trouble if they could move in that very day.

As she said it, her eyes travelled to the window, brushing Volodya's cheek. He remained impassive, didn't turn his head, made no comment, but all the same the tightening of his temples and the lowering of his eyelids assured Nadya that he had heard and approved.

[27]

It was convenient and quick, it would save them having to look, true enough. But still, there was no particular need for them to stay in Inessa's room. It was just that Volodya disliked the unfamiliar, and anyway it was only for a short time. These were the best excuses she could offer her mother.

She had always felt humiliated in her mother's eyes. The feeling was less painful now than it had been, but it was still there.

However, Nadya had schooled herself to follow rigid rules. Volodya must not be deflected from his path by so much as a hair's breadth. She must do everything to make his life easier, and never hamper him. She must always be there, but ready at any moment to efface herself when she was unwanted.

She had made her choice, and she must stick to it. She had shouldered the burden and must bear it. She must not permit herself a single hard word about her rival, although there was plenty she could say. She must always welcome her warmly, like a girlhood friend—so as not to spoil Volodya's good humour, or his standing with his comrades. She must join in their rambles and their reading sessions—*à trois*.

When it had all started—indeed, earlier, when Inessa, then a Sorbonne student with a red feather in her hat (no Russian woman revolutionary would have had the nerve to wear it), although she had two husbands and five children behind her, had first walked into their Paris apartment—before Volodya was half out of his chair, Nadya had seen vividly what was to come. Seen, too, her powerlessness to prevent it. And that it was her duty not to try.

Nadya had volunteered to remove herself. She would not be an obstacle in the life of such a man—there were obstacles enough already. More than once she had been on the verge of leaving him. But Volodya, after some thought, had told her to stay. He had made up his mind. Once and for all.

She was needed, then. Certainly, nobody else would get on so well with him. Resignation was made easier by the realisation that no woman could claim such a man all to herself. It was enough of a vocation that she, amongst others, was useful to him. No less than the other one. Indeed, in many ways she was closer to him.

So she had stayed, determined never to stand in his way,

never to show her hurt. Indeed, to train herself not to feel it, so that the hurt would burn itself out and die down. Instead of treating it gently she had prodded and inflamed the wound so as to cauterise it. So if there was some practical advantage in staying in what not so long ago had been Inessa's room, then that was where she would stay, without fretting about all the time Volodya had spent there in the past.

But with her mother there to see it . . .

It would soon be Cracow. Volodya was brightening up. Obviously, he had made some headway in his thinking.

No, the trip to Brussels went off splendidly, you mustn't regret it. My one regret is that you had no time to strike up a correspondence with Kautsky, as I told you to . . . (You would have written under your own name, but I would have discreetly drafted the letters for you.) What a low character he is! I hate and despise him more than anyone on earth. What filthy, rotten hypocrisy! . . . It really is a pity we couldn't get that game going, we'd have had some sport with him!

Volodya had cheered up, and even whistled a little tune. Completely forgetting the lost case, he suggested eating, and took out the pocket-knife which he always carried.

They spread out a napkin and produced a chicken, hard-boiled eggs, a bottle of milk, Galician bread, butter in grease-proof paper, salt in a little box.

Volodya even made a bit of a joke about his mother-in-law being a capitalist and a blot on his revolutionary biography.

Seriously, though, they must get their financial affairs settled, and swiftly. They had a lot of money in a Cracow bank—who could have expected war so soon?—a legacy from Nadya's aunt in Novocherkassk, her mother's sister, more than 4,000 roubles. And now it was bound to be confiscated as enemy alien property. What a blunder! At all costs he must find someone smart enough to squeeze the money out of them. Then convert it into something safe—into gold, or maybe some of it into Swiss francs. And they must take it with them.

Then—to Vienna without delay. They must hurry up the visas and testimonials for Switzerland, and get there quickly. Austria-Hungary was a belligerent, anything might happen. His mother-in-law had a legal Russian passport, and so had

Nadya, except that hers had expired. But Lenin had none at all.

One thing to be said for the opportunists' International was that it never refused help to anyone in difficulties. And in every country it had what amounted to ministers of its own. On this occasion, Kuba had insisted that he should pay courtesy calls on Adler and Diamand, thank them all over again in person for obtaining his release (although he had already telegraphed his heartfelt gratitude), and, whatever happened, keep a civil tongue ... Volodya smiled wryly, with specks of white and yolk round his mouth. It was certainly a tricky corner for him—having to go and make himself agreeable to mouldy old revisionists, petit-bourgeois scum. After all, it was only fair: if loyalty to political principles was beyond them they could at least help him to live. That provided a concrete, practical platform for a temporary tactical understanding with them. Even in Switzerland he wouldn't be able to do without this bunch. He wouldn't be admitted without sponsors—and who else would sponsor him? (Robert Grimm is an overgrown schoolboy—I met him in Bern last year, when you, Inessa, were in hospital.)

Ridicule left not a scratch on Lenin, no humiliation could get him down, he never felt ashamed—but all the same it was not easy for a man of forty-four to humble himself to younger men, to be so dependent on other people, to have no strength of his own.

If they hadn't left Geneva for Paris in 1908, they would not now have to fight their way into Switzerland, they would have been firmly and safely established there—with their own printing press, with connections, with all they needed. What had possessed them to move to Paris? ...

(If they hadn't gone to Paris—he would not have met Inessa.)

Only last year, when you went to Kocher for treatment, Inessa, and we discovered what a good doctor is (Volodya had read up on goitre himself, and checked the treatment), we should have had the sense to stay in Bern right then. Why not? If a revolutionary has to outlive Tsarism, and he is no longer twenty-five, his health counts as one of his weapons. It is also Party property. The Party's funds should be used ungrudg-

[30]

ingly for its maintenance. He should live where there are excellent doctors, indeed as close as possible to the most eminent men in the profession—and that could only mean in Switzerland. You wouldn't go to Semashko for treatment—that would be too silly! ... As doctors our revolutionary comrades are a lot of donkeys. You wouldn't trust one of them to poke about inside you.

You're still far from well, Inessa. You ought to be closer to Kocher.

Yes, but, Volodya, the atmosphere in Switzerland is dreadfully petit-bourgeois, remember how stuffy we always found it! Remember how they all shied away from us after the Tiflis 'ex'. In their country, you see, the law is sacrosanct, and they will not stand for crimes against property! ... And they call themselves Social Democrats!

All very true, but in Switzerland you'll never be in a fix like mine in Nowy Targ. Getting Semashko and Karpinsky out was child's play.

And what libraries they have! What a pleasure it always is to work there—and now, with a war on! No other place is so civilised and so comfortable.

A clean, well-scrubbed country, pleasant mountains, friendly guest-houses, limpid lakes with water-fowl on them.

The settling tank of the Russian revolution.

And because it was a neutral country the only place from which he could keep up his international contacts.

When he thought about it, when he reflected, what a joy it was—all Europe involved in a war such as it had never known before! The war which Marx and Engels had expected, but not lived to see. Such a war was the surest way to world revolution. The spark which they had fanned in vain in 1905 would burst unaided into a conflagration! There would never be a more propitious moment!

A presentiment quickened within him; this is it, the event you have lived to interpret and complete! Twenty-seven years of political self-education, books, pamphlets, party squabbles. An apathetic and ineffectual spectator during the first revolution. Regarded by everyone in the International as a disturber of the peace, an impertinent sectarian, leading a feeble, constantly dwindling little group calling itself a party.

All the time, without knowing it, you were waiting for this moment, and now the moment has come! The heavy wheel turns, gathering speed—like the red wheel of the engine— and you must keep up with its mighty rush. He who had never yet stood before the crowd, directing the movement of the masses, how was he to harness them to that wheel, to his own racing heart, check their impetus and put them into reverse?

Cracow.

They put their coats on and collected their things.

Lenin got ready absent-mindedly, only vaguely aware of their arrival and of what must be done.

They carried the baggage themselves, without a porter.

They were deafened by the noise: they had grown unused to crowds. And this was a different, wartime crowd. There were five times as many people on the platform as there should have been on a working day, and they were five times more worried, and all in a hurry. Nuns, who shouldn't have been there at all, elbowed the travellers, thrusting holy pictures and printed prayers on them. Lenin hastily drew back his hand as though from something dirty. A goods van stood incongruously at a passenger platform, and people were carrying into it an endless succession of big boxes labelled 'Fleapowder'. Soldiers, civilians, railwaymen and passengers jostled each other. Slowly and with difficulty they elbowed their way along the densely thronged platform. There was a big streamer on the station wall, with a slogan in red letters on yellow fabric:

JEDEM RUSS—EIN SCHUSS![3]

This had nothing at all to do with them, but he couldn't suppress a shudder.

The station hall was packed and stifling. They found a shady spot on a raised place against the side wall, at an angle to the square. The crowd there was denser than ever, and there were a lot of women. They settled Nadya's mother on a bench, with the luggage all round her, and Nadya went off to see Inessa's landlady. Vladimir Ilyich ran to buy newspapers and came back reading them as he walked, bumping into people, then perched himself on a hard suitcase, gripping the pile of papers between his elbows and his knees.

There was nothing particularly cheerful in the news. Reports on the battle in Galicia and on East Prussia were equally evasive, which meant that the Russians weren't doing too badly. But there were battles in France! War in Serbia! Who amongst the older generation of Socialists would ever have dreamt of such a thing?

The Socialists would be completely at a loss. They couldn't rise above their calls for peace. Those who weren't 'defenders of the fatherland' could think of nothing better than blethering and yapping about 'stopping the war'.

As though anyone could. As though anyone had the strength to seize the racing engine wheel with his bare hands.

Piss-poor, slobbering pseudo-Socialists with the petit-bourgeois worm in them would try to capture the masses by jabbering away 'for peace' and even 'against annexations'. And everybody would find it quite natural: against war means 'for peace', doesn't it? ... They must be hit first and hit hard.

Which of them had the vision to see and the strength of mind to embrace the great decision ahead: not to try and stop the war, but to step it up! To transfer it—*to your own country*!

We won't say so openly, but we are *for* the war!

'Peace' is a slogan for fatheads and traitors! What is the point of a hollow peace that nobody needs, unless you can convert it immediately into *civil war with no quarter given*? Anyone who does *not* come out in favour of civil war must be branded as a traitor!

The main thing is a sober grasp of the balance of forces, a sober assessment of alliances. It is no good standing like silly priests between the embattled armies, arms raised, sleeves flapping. Germany must be seen from the start not as just another imperialist country, but as a mighty ally. To make a revolution we need weapons, troops, money, so we must look for someone with an interest in giving them to us. We must find channels for negotiation, covertly reassure ourselves that if difficulties arise in Russia and she starts suing for peace, Germany will not agree to peace talks, will not abandon the Russian revolutionaries to the whim of fate.

Germany! What power! What weapons! And what resolution she had shown in striking through Belgium! They knew that there would be howls of indignation, but didn't let it

[33]

worry them! If fight they must, then fight they would! How resolute are the orders of their high command! Not a hint of Russian shilly-shallying there. (They had shown the same decisiveness in grabbing him and slinging him in Nowy Targ gaol. And still more in releasing him.)

Germany will undoubtedly win this war. And so she is the best, the natural ally against the Tsar.

The carrion crow in the Russian coat of arms is trapped at last. You're caught by the foot, you'll never pull free! This war was of your own choosing! Now you'll be cut down to size! Shorn of everything as far as Kiev, as far as Kharkov, as far as Riga! We'll thrash the imperial spirit out of you! Die, damn you, die! All you're good for is oppressing others. Russia will be completely dismembered. Poland and Finland must be detached. And the Baltic lands. And the Ukraine. And the Caucasus. Die, damn you!

There was a hubbub on the square and the crowd surged in their direction, as far as the platform barrier, where the police held them back. What was going on? A train had pulled in. A hospital train. Perhaps the first such train, after the first major battle. A path was cleared through the crowd, to give the file of waiting ambulances room to turn round. Hefty, grim-looking orderlies quickly passed stretcher after stretcher from the train to the ambulances. Women pressed forward from every side, trying to struggle through the crowd, eagerly, fearfully craning to catch a glimpse of grey faces barely visible amongst bandages and sheets, dreading to discover their men. There were shrieks of recognition or relief, and the crowd closed in tighter and pulsed like a single being.

Though the raised place where the Ulyanovs were sitting was some distance away, they could see it all. But Lenin, to get a better view, rose and went nearer to the parapet.

There weren't enough ambulances and stretchers, and instead of waiting some of the wounded were leaving the platform on their own feet, supported by nurses—pale figures in grey hospital smocks or blue greatcoats, with thickly bandaged heads, necks, shoulders, arms, some walking gingerly, some firmer on their feet—and now the waiting crowd would not be held, but swarmed towards them, shrilly, joyfully yelling, embracing and kissing dear ones and strangers alike, taking them over from the nurses, carrying their kitbags, while above them, over all those heads, borne aloft by male hands, mugs of frothy beer and white plates of roast meat floated out from the restaurant.

By the parapet, refreshed and excited, stood the man in the black bowler, with his untrimmed reddish beard, his brows knit in concentration, his eyes sharp and eager, and he too had one hand raised, with the fingers splayed as though holding a great beer mug, he too swallowed painfully as though he had been in the trenches and parched for want of that drink. His probing gaze widened and contracted, widened and contracted as he seized on every detail in the scene which might be turned to use.

A joyful inspiration took shape in his dynamic mind, one of the most powerful, swiftest and surest decisions of his life. The smell of printer's ink from the newspapers, the smell of blood and medicaments from the station hall evaporates—and suddenly, like a soaring eagle following the movements of a little golden lizard, you have eyes only for the one truth that matters, your heart pounds, like an eagle you swoop down on it, seize it by its trembling tail as it is vanishing into a crevice in the rock—and you tug and tug and rise into the air unfurling it like a ribbon, like a streamer bearing the slogan: CONVERT THIS WAR INTO CIVIL WAR! ... And this war, this war will bring all the governments of Europe down in ruins!!!

He stood by the parapet, looking down on the square with his hand raised, as though he had taken his place for a speech but was not quite ready to begin.

Daily, hourly, wherever you may be—*protest* angrily and uncompromisingly against this war! But ...

(The dialectic essence of the situation.) But ... will it to continue! See that it does not stop short! That it drags on and is *transformed*! A war like this one must not be fumbled, must not be wasted!

Such a war is a present from history!

October 1916

38

Their meetings in the Stüssihof restaurant were known as the Skittle Club, although there was no skittle alley.

'... The Swiss government is the executive committee of the bourgeoisie ...'

'Skittle Club' was somebody's idea of a joke: their politics made no sense, but plenty of noise.

'... The Swiss government is a pawn in the hands of the military clique ...'

But they had cheerfully adopted the name. We'll knock the capitalists down like ninepins!

(He had educated them. He had cured them of religion. He had implanted in them an appreciation of the historical role of violence.)

'... The Swiss government is shamelessly selling out the masses to the financial magnates.'

It was some years now since Nobs had started the discussion table in the restaurant on the Stüssihof square. He had brought together the younger people, the activists. Then Lenin had gradually started coming.

(How many humiliations he had had to endure in this conceited country! The Social Democrats in Bern had always looked down on him. When he had moved to Zürich last spring he had tried to get the Russian émigrés together for lectures—but the few who came at all had soon drifted away. Then he had transferred his attentions to the young Swiss. Some men of forty-seven might think it beneath their dignity —fishing for baby-faced supporters and working them over one by one, but if you could wrest a single one of them from the opportunist Grimm it was time well spent.)

'... The Swiss government is toadying to European reaction and encroaching on the democratic rights of the people.'

Across the table sits simple-minded, broad-faced Platten, the fitter (since he had broken his arm he had been a draughtsman, but fitter sounded more proletarian). His big face is busy absorbing what is said—it is all so difficult. His brow is knotted and his soft ripe lips pursed with effort, helping his eyes and ears not to miss a word.

'... Swiss Social Democrats must show complete lack of confidence in their government ...'

The table has been made longer for a jolly Swiss gathering. No cloth covers its planed surface pitted with knot-holes, polished by a century of elbows and plates. All nine of them have arranged themselves on two benches, giving themselves plenty of room, and one place is blocked by a pillar. Some have ordered snacks, some beer, just to keep up appearances, and because the Swiss always do. (Everyone pays for himself.) A lantern hangs from the pillar.

That elongated, triangular face under the unruly lick of hair, the keenest face there, belongs to Willi Münzenberg, the German from Erfurt. He is very quick on the uptake, and in fact it's all much too slow for him. His long restless hands reach out for more. These are the clichés he rings out himself at public meetings.

(He'd had luck with the younger people in Zürich. There were half a dozen of them here—all youth leaders. Not like in 1914, when he had sent Inessa to see the Swiss leftists—Naine was fishing, Graber helping his wife to hang the washing out —and nobody wanted to know.)

'... We must learn not to trust our governments ...'

Lenin is at the corner of the table by the pillar, which conceals him from one side. Nobs is at the far end, diagonally opposite, as far out of range as possible, watchful, ingratiating, catlike. He started it all—does he now regret it? In years he is one of them—they are all around thirty—but in party status, in self-importance and even in girth he has ceased or is ceasing to belong.

Over every table hangs a lamp of a different colour. The

[40]

one over the Skittle Club is red. A reddish light plays on
every face—Platten's broad open features, the black quiff and
starched collar of the self-assured and foppish Mimiola,
Radek's unkempt and tousled curls, his irremovable pipe, his
permanently parted wet lips.

'... In every country stir up hatred of your own government! This is the only work worthy of a Socialist ...'

(Work with the young was the only thing worth doing.
There was nothing humiliating about it. It was simply taking
the long view. Grimm wasn't so very old, come to that—he
was eleven years Lenin's junior—but he already had a hand-
hold on power. He wasn't stupid, but theory was over his
head. He didn't want an armed rising, yet he had leftish
hankerings. When Lenin had entered Switzerland in 1914,
mentioning Greulich's name, and established himself there
with Grimm as his sponsor, they had met and talked far into
the night. Grimm had asked: 'What do you think the Swiss
Social Democrats should do in the present position?' To see
what he was made of, Lenin had answered in a flash: 'I would
immediately declare *civil war*!' For a moment Grimm was
scared. But then he had decided that it was just a joke.)

'... The neutrality of Switzerland is a bourgeois fraud and
means submission to the imperialist war ...'

Platten's brow is convulsed, his eyes strained and bewildered. How difficult, how terribly difficult it is to master the
lofty science of socialism! These grandiose formulas somehow refuse to fit in with your own poor limited experience.
War is a fraud, and neutrality is a fraud—so neutrality is just
as bad as war? ... But a sideways glance at your comrades
shows you that they understand it all, and you are ashamed to
admit that you don't, so you pretend.

(It was not just facile phrase-mongering. He had brought
forth these ideas in a fit of inspiration on his journey across
Austria, written a definitive summary of them when he
reached Bern, introduced them into a Central Committee
manifesto, then defended them in his tussle with Plekhanov
at Lausanne. You could know your Marxism inside out, and
still not find the answer when a real crisis burst upon you: the
man who finds it makes an original discovery. In the autumn
of 1914, when four-fifths of Europe's Socialists had taken a

[41]

stand in defence of the fatherland, while one-fifth timidly bleated 'for peace', Lenin alone in the ranks of world socialism had pointed the way for the others: *for war!*—but a *different* war!—and immediately!!)

Lenin too has a mug of beer in front of him. The Swiss politician at the tavern table is a species he can't endure, but this is the ritual. Bronski looks sleepy and imperturbable as always. But Radek, with the black whiskers that run from ear to ear under his chin, with his horn-rimmed glasses, his quick glance and his buck teeth, restlessly switching his eternally smoking black pipe from corner to corner of his mouth— Radek has heard it all before, and now finds it too elementary, too tame and too slow.

'... The petty ambition of petty states to stand aloof from the great battles of world history ...'

Platten is quietly floundering, trying not to give himself away. The idea of world revolution is easy to understand but it is so difficult to apply to his Switzerland. His mind consents. Since they have avoided the universal bloodbath, they mustn't sit calmly by but summon the people to class battles. But his heart is unreasonable: it is good that in those houses clinging to the mountain ledges peasants can live at peace, that the men are all at home, that grass is mown in the meadows four times in a summer, however steep the slopes may be, that the tall barns will be filled to the roof with the store of hay, that the tinkling of hundreds of little bells, sheep bells and cow bells, sounds from spur to spur, as though the mountains themselves were ringing.

'... The narrow-minded egoism of privileged small nations...'

The plodding walk of herdsmen. Now and then, the deafening crack of a stock-whip on the stony road, echoing through the folds in the hills. Water troughs at mountain springs, long enough for twenty cows to drink. Shifting winds over swaying grass, shifting mists steaming over wooded gorges, and when sunlight breaks through the rain there may be no room for the rainbow's arc, and it will stand upright like a pillar on the mountain. The quiet inscription on a hostel in the high wilderness: 'The motherland shelters her children with her forest cloak.'

'... Industry bound up with tourism ... Your bourgeoisie trades in the beauties of the Alps, and your opportunists help them at it ...'

Platten gives up his attempt at concealment, and innocently, trustingly, his face reflects his doubts.

Lenin has noticed! From where he sits at the corner of the table—the only older man amongst all those youngsters, looking well over fifty—he strikes home with a swift, shrewd, sideways thrust.

'... A republic of lackeys! That's what Switzerland is!'

The keynote of his harangue.

Radek guffaws happily, deftly switches his pipe—the fingering is different every time—and sucks in imposing quantities of damp smoke. Willi mischievously tries to catch Teacher's eye, his long hands writhing impatiently: encore! encore!

Platten isn't arguing. Platten is merely puzzled. Perhaps his country is like an ornate hotel, but lackeys are obsequious, fussing and fawning, while the Swiss are staid and dignified. Even ministers' wives don't keep lackeys, but beat their own carpets.

(But it had never been known for a letter to go astray in Switzerland, and the libraries were magnificently run: books were sent without charge and immediately to remote *pensions* in the mountains.)

'... Sops for docile workers in the shape of social reforms—to persuade them not to overthrow the bourgeoisie ...'

It has taken three weeks of effort to arrange this meeting and they have finally got them all together on the evening of Friday 21st—the eve of the Party Congress. Radek has been a great help, made himself very useful.

(When Radek was nice he was really nice, a super-pal. At present there was no living without him. And how well he spoke and wrote German! He took the sharpest bends in the road with ease—there was no need to waste time explaining. A scoundrel, but a brilliant one—such people were invaluable. But at times he was loathsome. In Bern they had avoided meeting, communicated through the post, and in February broken off relations for ever. At the Kienthal Conference he had spoken like an out-and-out provocateur.)

[43]

'... The Swiss people are more cruelly hungry every day, and risk being drawn into the war and killed in the interests of capitalism ...'

Nobs's sceptical amber cigarette-holder balances unaided on his nether lip.

(What a business it had been, starting without a single supporter in Europe the struggle for the renewal of the International, or rather its demolition and the construction of a new, Third International. At one minute scraping together any of the Bolshevik émigrés who would agree to come; the next, rallying with Grimm's help three dozen women—the International Conference of Socialist Women—and, since he could hardly attend in person to give them the guidance they needed, sitting for three days in the café of the Volkshaus while Inessa, Nadya and Zinka Lilina ran to report and ask for instructions.)

'... Will you go to the slaughter for interests which are foreign to your own? Or will you instead make great sacrifices for socialism, for the interests of nine-tenths of mankind?'

(Then there was the International Socialist Youth Conference. They had mustered fewer than a score, mostly people who had evaded the call-up and were sure to be against the war, and again he had sat in the same café for three days, while Inessa and Safarov trotted to him for instructions. This was when Willi had appeared on the scene.)

If you're twenty-seven, with ten turbulent years of the youth movement behind you—meetings, organisations, conferences, demonstrations ... And if, among your peers, you discover that you have a voice, courage, luck—people listen to you, you rise step by step as though to a platform where you can be seen better, and suddenly find yourself in demand as a public speaker, delegate, secretary ... And the Party leaders immediately try to draw you into their orbit, and urge you not to listen to that Asiatic with his wild ideas, yet it is from him and from the incendiary Trotsky that you always learn what is right and what matters!

'... "Defence of the fatherland" is a fraud on the people, and can never be "war for democracy". And Switzerland is no different ...'

Twenty-seven! The things he'd been through! His mother's

early death, beatings from his stepmother, beatings from his father, serving in his father's tavern, playing cards and talking politics with the customers, at the wash-tub under his stepmother's eye, always suffering because his clothes were ragged and his boots the wrong size, drawn into propaganda work while he was apprenticed to a shoemaker, emigration to Zürich when he was only twenty to work as a chemist's dispenser and join in all the class battles ...

In the reddish light from the lamp Münzenberg's devoted and determined face is trustful and expectant. The tempered strength of his will shows in the sharp jut of his narrow chin. His brows are knit in an eager frown of welcome for revolutionary ideas. He has already often done as Lenin said and the results have been good. He has rallied more than two thousand people for a 'youth day' on the Zürichberg, and led them through the city singing *The Internationale*, waving red flags and shouting 'Down with the war!' He has earned an invitation to Kienthal, and joined Lenin in signing the resolution of the left.

'... In Switzerland, too, "defence of the fatherland" is a humbugging phrase. It paves the way for the massacre of workers and small peasants ...'

Schmidt from Winterthur, an ungainly figure at the far end of the bench, is puzzled and peers past his neighbours to say: 'The war can't affect our country, we're neutral ...'

'Ah, but Switzerland may enter the war at any moment!'

Nobs chews his amber holder under his fluffy blonde moustache. He smiles like an amiable cat, but his eyes are mistrustful and a tuft of hair stands up like a question mark.

'Of course, refusal to defend the fatherland makes exceptionally high demands on revolutionary consciousness!'

(All his life he had been the leader of a minority, pitting himself with a handful of followers against all the rest, and aggressive tactics had been essential. His tactics were to whittle down the majority resolution as far as he could—and then still not accept it. Either you record our opinion in the minutes, or we leave! ... But you're in the minority, why are you dictating to us? ... Right—we're leaving! A breakdown! A public brawl! A disgrace! ... That was how it had been at all those conferences, and there had never been a majority that hadn't weakened. *The wind always blows from the far left!* No Socialist in the world could afford to ignore that fact. That was why Grimm was so unsure of himself, and why he had hurriedly called the Zimmerwald Conference.)

'... Not a single farthing for a regular army, not even in Switzerland! ...'

'Not even in peacetime?'

'Even in peacetime Socialists must vote against military credits for the bourgeois state!'

(Lenin had had to wait a long time for his invitation to Zimmerwald, and had been very depressed. Grimm might not summon him, and it would be quite unseemly to force himself on them. What sort of conference would it be anyway? A bunch of silly shits would get together and declare themselves 'for peace and against annexations'. *For peace*—he couldn't bear to hear those words! ... Meanwhile, he had discreetly used his influence to insinuate as many of his supporters as he could into the list of delegates. Those who were against their own governments—they would be the nucleus of a left International! ... But they could only muster eight: himself, Grishka and Radek, that was three, Platten, one Latvian and three Scandinavians. Still, the *whole* of the 'old' International, fifty years after its foundation, had barely filled the four waggons that carried the participants into the mountains so as not to attract the attention of the authorities, who in fact noticed neither the arrival of the delegates in Switzerland nor their dispersal. They had learned of it only from the foreign press.)

'But the special character of Switzerland ...'

'Special character nothing! Switzerland is just another imperialist country!'

Platten recoils. His brow is an open book. He struggles to bring the creases of astonishment under control. His unregenerate heart rebels: our Switzerland may be a tiny country, but surely it is a very special one? Since the three cantons were first united, have we ever annexed anybody? With intense mental effort he strives to accept these advanced ideas. His big, strong, helpless hands lie palm upwards on the table.

(Platten was good material to work on. Through Platten

[46]

alone he could bring the whole Zürich organisation into line. If only he would work harder at educating himself.)

'And so we, the Zimmerwald Left, are now completely unanimous: we *reject* defence of the fatherland!'

Some of the awkward squad still didn't understand.

'But if we reject defence of the fatherland are we to leave the country defenceless?'

'A radically incorrect formulation! The right way to put it is this; either we let ourselves be killed in the interests of the world imperialist bourgeoisie, or, at the cost of fewer casualties, we carry out a socialist revolution in Switzerland—the only way to deliver the Swiss masses from rising prices and hunger!'

(In Zimmerwald he had hardly spoken at all, but had directed his left-wing supporters from the shadows. That was the most effective way to deploy his forces. The speech-making could be safely left to Radek—he'd be witty, resourceful, relaxed, self-confident. His own duty as leader was to weld his small group more firmly together. An ordinary enemy is only half an enemy. But the man who used to be with us and suddenly wobbles off the line is doubly our enemy! We must hit him first and hardest! But it is better to anticipate trouble and prime your followers in caucus between sessions.)

'... The disgusting thing about pacifists is that they dream of peace without a socialist revolution.'

Radek is always cheerfully ready for marching orders. His pockets bulge with newspapers, books, all he needs for a day: if he has to hurry off to a revolution he can go as he is. How interesting he finds it all!!!

(But the rogue needed watching. He might change sides, might betray, at any minute. And he sometimes got things wrong—trying to reconcile Grimm and Platten, for instance, when it was important to keep them quarrelling.)

'... Revolution is absolutely essential for the elimination of war ...'

Just look at Bronski, dozing again. He might as well not be here at all. He is only ever needed to make the number up. When his vote is wanted, it will be there. And when required he will say—what is required. (Yes, he is stupid. But there are so few of us that every one may count.)

[47]

'... Only a socialist system can deliver mankind from war ...'

Difficult to say whether Nobs really approves. His eyes and his lips sympathise but his ears are still, and his brow un-ruffled. Yet he is editor-in-chief of the main left-wing paper, and effortlessly advancing to the commanding heights of the Party. They all have great need of him.

He needs them too, though. Nobs knows perfectly well that the wind always blows from the left. Small as their group is, it may change the course of the whole Swiss Party. Only he doesn't want them to be a millstone round his neck.

'... It is illogical for anyone who aims at ending the war to reject socialist revolution ...'

(When Liebknecht's letter was read to the Zimmerwald Conference, Lenin had sprung to his feet shouting: 'CIVIL WAR IS A SPLENDID THING!' Caution is all very well nine times out of ten, but the tenth time you must overstep the mark. Take the proletarian slogan—'Fraternisation'—to the trenches! Preach class struggle to the troops. Tell them to turn their bayonets against their fellow countrymen! THE AGE OF THE BAYONET IS AT HAND! It was risky, of course, for an émigré in a neutral country to carry on like this, but he had always got away with it. At Zimmerwald though, that foul German crook Ledebour had said: 'You can put your name to it here, because you're safe—why don't you go to Russia and *send* your signature?' That was the level of debate with such people!)

'... The Swiss Party is stubbornly stuck in the rut of strict legality and is making no preparation for revolutionary mass struggle ...'

From the counter with its two pot-bellied old barrels and its dozens of colourful bottles a waiter with blunt Swiss features is slowly carrying golden tankards and dark red glasses and tumblers to the tables. From the serving hatch another waiter brings yellow trays with thin brown slices of smoked sausage, and plates of roast meat or fish. Swiss bellies are un-hurriedly packing away inordinately lavish Swiss helpings, each enough for four. And at every glutton's elbow a second helping is keeping warm over a little flame.

'... The socialist reorganisation of Switzerland is perfectly

[48]

feasible and urgently necessary. Capitalism is completely ripe for transformation into socialism—here and now ...'

(At the last session of the Zimmerwald Conference, from midday on and all through the night, the left had raised a storm over each amendment, demanded at every turn that its dissenting opinion be recorded, and by these means shifted the resolution considerably to the left. They hadn't of course succeeded in putting through either the 'Civil War' or 'A New International' resolution. Still, the Zimmerwald Left had emerged as a new wing of the international movement, and Lenin was no longer a mere Russian sectarian, but its chief. The official leadership, however, had remained with the centrists, and the hero of the conference in newspapers throughout the world was Grimm. Though not much more than thirty, he was already on the Executive Committee of the International, because he was hand in glove with the opportunists. Lenin had been visiting or living in Switzerland for twenty years on and off, long before Grimm was ever heard of.)

Willi's thin, eager face. He agrees, agrees completely; but it is essential for him to understand exactly what must be done, and where to start.

'In Switzerland it will be necessary to expropriate ... a maximum of ... thirty thousand bourgeois at the very most. And of course to seize all the banks right away. And Switzerland will then be a proletarian country.'

From his place by the pillar, Lenin observes them obliquely, his domed brow inclined, bringing the full pressure of his mind and his hard gaze to bear on them, skilfully checking how much each of them has taken in. His thinning hair is a richer red in the light from the lantern.

'Strike at the roots of the present social order *by concrete action*. And *now*!'

That is the step which Socialists everywhere find so difficult. Nobs screws up his eyes as though in pain. Even the proletarian from Winterthur looks a bit down in the mouth. And Mimiola's high starched collar is choking him.

A fine fellow, our Ulyanov, but much too extreme. Nowhere on earth, let alone in Switzerland or Italy, would you find anyone so extreme.

[49]

It is hard, so hard for them.

Lenin's gaze slides rapidly, restlessly over all those heads, so different, yet all so nearly his for the taking.

They all dread his lethal sarcasm.

(When you can't force something through a narrow opening it often helps to pile on extra weight.)

He addresses the table at large, simultaneously pursuing each of the six Swiss into his thoughts. His voice is tense, but lacking in resonance—it seems always to get lost in his chest, his larynx or his mouth, and it slurs the r's.

'The only way to do it is to *split the Party*! It's a bourgeois affectation to pretend that "civil peace" can reign in Swiss social democracy!'

They shudder. They freeze.

But he goes on: 'The bourgeoisie has reared the social chauvinists to serve it as watch-dogs! How can you speak of *unity* with them?'

(Keep hitting the same spot, over and over again, varying the words just slightly—that's the first rule for propagandists and preachers.)

'It's a disease that affects Social Democrats not only in Switzerland, not only in Russia, but all over the world—this maudlin hankering after "reconciliation"! They're all ready to renounce their principles for the sake of a bogus "unity"! Yet short of a complete organisational break with the social patriots, it's impossible to advance a single step towards socialism!!'

However unresponsive they are, whatever they may be thinking, he has the assurance of a teacher confronting his class: the whole class may disagree, but Teacher is right just the same. His voice becomes still more guttural, more impatient, more excited.

'The question of a split is of fundamental importance! Any concession here is a *crime*! All those who vacillate on this are *enemies of the proletariat*! True revolutionaries are never afraid of a split!'

(Split, split, and split again! Split at all stages of the movement! Go on splitting until you find yourselves a tiny clique—but none the less the Central Committee! Those left in it may be the most mediocre, the most insignificant people, but if

they are united in a single obedience you can achieve anything!!!)

'It is high time for a split at the international level! We have
excellent reports on the split in the German Socialist Party.
The time has come to break with the Kautskyites in your own
and all other countries! *Break* with the Second International
—and start building the Third!'

(A method tried and proven at the very dawn of the century. He had pierced and slain the Economists with the death-
ray of *What Is To Be Done?*, his scheme for a band of professional conspirators. He had shaken off the clammy clinging
incubus of Menshevism with his *One Step Forward, Two Steps
Back*. He did not want power for its own sake, but how could
he help taking the helm when all the rest steered so in-
competently? He could not let his incomparable qualities of
leadership atrophy and go to waste.)

Yet the idea might have been born there and then, at the
table, might have been an instantaneous and irresistible revelation: *split* your party—and thereby ensure the victory of the
revolution!

Nobs, stiff with delicious fear, doesn't even murmur. If
you refuse, who knows, you may be the loser. Perhaps the
best place to be is right here, at this table?

Platten's paw has frozen on the handle of his tankard.

Mimiola has triumphed over his constricting collar, risen
clear of it. But he looks gloomy.

Willi wears a little smile of startled enlightenment. He is
ready. And he will carry the young with him. He will repeat
every word of it from the platform.

The heavy brow batters away at the breached wall.

'My book on imperialism proves conclusively that revolution is imminent and inevitable in all the industrialised countries of Europe.'

There are still a couple of them who want to believe, but
can't quite see it.

There you are, living in a room you've grown used to, and
one morning you go out into the street, with familiar buildings
all round you, and you start a revolution. But how?... Who is
going to show you how? There has never been anything quite
like it.

'Yes, but this is Switzerland ...'

'What of it? That was a glorious strike in Zürich in 1912! And what about this summer? Willi's marvellous demonstration on the Bahnhofstrasse! A baptism of blood!'

Yes, this was Willi's proudest boast.

'All those casualties!'

Even the 1st of August hadn't been as good as the 3rd, in honour of the fallen.

They hum and ha ... In Switzerland? ...

How can they disbelieve him? He treats every youngster as his equal, with perfect seriousness. Not like those leaders who snub their juniors once they get one foot on the ladder. He never grudges the effort spent on conversation with the young, wearing them down with questions, questions, questions, until he can slip a noose on them.

'Yes, but in Switzerland ...'

While they are clearing this little matter up Radek has found time to read two of the newspapers from his bulging pocket and leaf through a book. And still they don't understand!

Radek pokes the stem of his pipe at them. 'Your own Party Congress last year ... adopted a resolution on revolutionary action by the masses! What about that?'

Well, what about it? ... All sorts of resolutions are passed. Passing resolutions is easy enough.

'Then there's Kienthal!'

Five of those present had been at Kienthal, including Nobs and Münzenberg. Amongst the forty-five delegates they had been among the minority of twelve. They had threatened once again to wreck the meeting by walking out, had in fact left the hall and returned. So the majority had given way to the minority, and they had pushed the resolution further and further to the left: '*Only the conquest of political power by the proletariat can ensure peace!*'

True enough, but you can say anything in resolutions ...

'No, but here in Switzerland ...'

The most patient of men couldn't listen to these numbskulls without exploding! Then—he amazes himself with a fresh revelation, which comes out in a hoarse cracked whisper.

[52]

'Don't you realise that Switzerland is the most revolutionary country in the world???!'

They are all rocked back in their seats, clutching tankards,
plates, forks ... The lantern on the pillar sways in the wind of
his voice. Nobs grabs at his cigarette-holder as it falls from
his mouth.

?????????????????

(He saw it all! Saw the barricades that would soon rise in
Zürich, not perhaps on the Bahnhofstrasse where all the banks
were, but over towards the working-class district by the Volkshaus on the Helvetiaplatz!)

And with a caustic flash of the Mongol eyes, in a voice without depth or resonance, but with the cutting edge of a Kalmyk
sabre, catching only on the r's: 'Because Switzerland is the
only country in the world where soldiers are given weapons
and ammunition to take home!'

So ...?

'*Do you know what revolution means*? It means seizing the
banks! The railway station! The post office and telegraph!
The big enterprises! And that's all! Once you've done that,
the revolution is victorious! And what do you need to do it?
Only weapons! And the weapons are there!'

The things Fritz Platten hears from this man, who is his
fate and his doom! Sometimes his blood freezes ...

Lenin has abandoned persuasion and is rapping out orders
to these recalcitrants, these incompetent muddlers.

'So what are you waiting for? What more do you need?
Universal military training? Well then, the time has come to
demand it!'

He is improvising, thinking between sentences, picking his
way among his thoughts, but his voice never falters.

'Officers must be elected by the people. Any group of ... a
hundred can demand military training! With instructors paid
from the public purse. It is *precisely* the civic freedom of
Switzerland, its effective democracy, that makes revolution
immensely easier!'

Bracing himself against the table, he looks as though he
were about to spread his wings, fly up from the dining-room
of the Stüssihof restaurant and soar above the five-cornered,
enclosed, medieval square, itself no bigger than a good-sized

[53]

public hall, glide over the comic warrior with a flag on the fountain, spiral past the jutting balconies, past the fresco of the two cobblers hammering away on their stools three floors up, past the coats of arms on the pediments five floors up, and over the tiled roofs of old Zürich, over the mountain *pensions* and the over-decorated chalets of the lackeys' republic.

'Begin propaganda in the army *immediately*! Make the troops and young men of call-up age see that it is right and inevitable for them to use their arms to liberate themselves from hireling slavery! ... Put out leaflets calling for an *immediate* socialist revolution in Switzerland!'

(Rather rash words for a foreigner without a passport—but this was the one time in ten that made the difference between victory and defeat.)

'Take executive control of all working-class associations immediately! Insist that the Party's parliamentary representatives publicly preach socialist revolution! The compulsory take-over of factories, mills and agricultural holdings!'

What? Go and take people's property away from them, just like that? Without making a law? The Swiss duffers couldn't blink fast enough.

'To reinforce the revolutionary elements in the country, all foreigners should be naturalised without charge. If the government makes the slightest move towards war—create underground workers' organisations! And in the event of war ...'

Greatly daring, Münzenberg and Mimiola, leaders of youth, finished it for him:

'... refuse to perform military service!'

(Luckily Münzenberg and Radek, deserters from the German and Austro-Hungarian armies respectively, cannot be deported under Swiss law.)

Not one little thing have they understood! A mocking smile, but not an unfriendly one, passes over Lenin's face. There is nothing for it—down, down he comes, past the cobblers hammering away at their work with slavish diligence, over the blue column of the fountain, to alight with a rush in his old place in the restaurant.

'In no circumstances must they refuse; what can you be thinking of? In Switzerland especially! When they give you arms, take them! Demand demobilisation—yes, but without giving up your arms! Keep your arms and get out into the streets! Not a single hour of civil peace! Strikes! Demonstrations! Form squads of armed workers!!! And then *an armed uprising*!!!'

Broad-browed Platten is bowled over as though by a blow on the head:

'But with all Europe at war ... will the neighbouring powers ... tolerate a revolution in Switzerland? They'll intervene ...'

This is the nub of Lenin's scheme—the utter, unreproducible uniqueness of Switzerland.

'That's what is so splendid! While all Europe is at war— barricades in Switzerland! A revolution in Switzerland! Switzerland speaks three major European languages. And through those three languages the revolution will overflow in three directions and flood all Europe! The alliance of revolutionary elements will expand to include the proletariat of all Europe! A sense of class solidarity will be aroused in the three neighbouring countries! If there is any intervention, revolution will flare up throughout Europe!! That is why SWITZERLAND IS THE CENTRE OF WORLD REVOLUTION TODAY!!!'

Singed by the red light, the members of the Skittle Club sit fixed as the words chance to find them. The narrow triangle of Münzenberg's intrepid face is thrust forward into the glow. Nobs's fluffy moustache is also touched with the flame. Mimiola looks as if he was about to pull his tie off and lead his hot-blooded Italians over the ruins of Europe. Bronski in his sad, sly way is trying to look eager for battle. Radek wriggles, licks his lips, and excitement flashes behind his glasses: if that is the way of it, what fun he will have!

(The Skittle Club is the Third International in embryo!)

'You are the best part of the Swiss proletariat!'

Radek has a resolution ready and waiting for tomorrow's Congress of the Swiss Party. If only Nobs will print it ...

Hmmmmm ...

But who will put it to the Congress?

Hmmmmm ...

[55]

Since the restaurant would soon be closing, the party broke up.

There were three street lamps on the Stüssihof square, and lights shone from the windows of houses all round. You could easily read the plaque telling how in 1443 Burgomaster Stüssi had fallen in battle not far from here. His family home had stood for sixty years before that. That must be Stüssi, too, the comic Swiss warrior in armour and blue hose standing in the middle of the fountain. You could hear the thin jets of water splashing into the bluish basin. The air was dry and cold for this part of the world.

They were still talking as they took leave of each other and walked away over the smooth cobbles. The square seemed completely shut in, and unless you knew where to look for the crevices which were streets, you might wonder whether you would ever get out. Some of the company went off down a bumpy cobbled slope, and took the side street which led to the embankment. Others turned off at the beerhouse called the *Franciscan*. Willi, however, accompanied his teacher along the same street in the opposite direction, past the *Voltaire* cabaret on the next corner, where the arty set raved the night away, and on the narrow pavement they encountered prostitutes who were still waiting for customers. Past the *Voltaire* they turned steeply uphill, under an antiquated lamp on an iron post, along a street like a stairway, so narrow that with arms outstretched you could almost touch both walls at once, and there was hardly room to walk two abreast; up and up they went.

The heels of Lenin's stout mountain boots clattered on the cobbles.

Willi wanted his teacher to reassure him over and over again. He had not forgotten the fight on the Bahnhofstrasse that summer, but every trace had been swilled and swept away, the shop windows were as dazzling as ever, the bourgeoisie strolled around as comfortably as before, and the workers placidly obeyed their accommodating leaders.

'Yes, but the people aren't ready for it ...'

At a sharp turning in the alley, in the dim light of someone's sleepless upper windows, the voice from under the dark cap was quiet but sharp-edged as ever.

'Of course, the *people* aren't ready. But that doesn't give us the right to postpone the *beginning*.'

In spite of the platform victories behind him, the yells of assembled youth in his ears, Willi persisted.

'But we are such a small minority!'

Lenin stopped, and out of the darkness came something not revealed even to the select gathering at the Skittle Club.

'The majority is always stupid, and we cannot wait for it. A resolute minority must act—and then it becomes the majority.'

The Congress opened the following morning, across the river in the Merchants' Hall. Lenin, as leader of a foreign party, was invited to deliver greetings. Radek was also there, ostensibly representing the Polish Party. Two from 'our' side, speaking in succession.

On that first morning not all the delegates had arrived, and the audience was no larger than for a good lecture. (Lenin, in fact, was not used to large audiences; he had never known what it was like to address a thousand people at a time—except just once, at a mass meeting in Petersburg when he had lost his tongue.)

As soon as he looked out over the hall caution overcame him. Just as at Zimmerwald, just as at Kienthal, he had no overpowering urge to speak his mind fully—no, the full fervour of his conviction was naturally reserved for a closed meeting of his supporters. Here, of course, he did not call for action either against the government or against the banks. Standing before this nominally Social-Democratic but in reality bourgeois mass of self-satisfied, fat-faced Swiss, lounging at their little tables, Lenin sensed immediately that they did not and would not understand him, and that he had practically nothing to say to them. He somehow couldn't even bring himself to remind them of the highly revolutionary resolution which they themselves had adopted last year—and anyway it might spoil everything.

So his salutations would have been quite short, if he had not got painfully entangled with the Adler affair. (Two weeks

[57]

earlier Fritz Adler, Secretary of the Austrian Social-Democratic Party, had shot and killed the Prime Minister of
Austria-Hungary—killed the head of the Imperial government in time of war!) This assassination had captured everyone's imagination, there was a lot of talk about it, and before
making up his own mind about it Lenin had enquired carefully into the circumstances. Who had influenced Adler? (His
Russian Socialist-Revolutionary wife, perhaps?) Because he
was secretly preoccupied with this problem, a perpetual
source of disagreement with the Russian SRs here at the
Congress, he had devoted half of his speech to an irrelevant
discussion of terrorism ... He had said that the greetings sent
to the terrorist by the Central Committee of the Italian Party
deserved full sympathy, if the assassination were understood
as a signal to Social Democrats to abandon opportunist
tactics. And he had defended at length the opposition of the
Russian Bolsheviks to individual terror: it was *only* because
terror ought to be a *mass* activity.

Meanwhile the Swiss munched and swigged and mooed
and tippled—there was no understanding them.

But still, the Saturday session had gone well, and raised
his hopes. Platten was applauded by the majority, and Papa
Greulich, a seventy-five-year-old with a luxuriant grey mop
of hair, started joking about the Party 'adopting new pets'.
(Nothing to the round *Schweizerdeutsch* ruderies we'll heap
on you when the time comes! When we come to power,
we'll—hang you!) It had worked, it had gone off beautifully!
Lenin had cheered up and felt like an old warhorse in the
swirl of battle. Moreover, the circumspect Nobs had not
refused to put forward the Skittle Club's (i.e. Radek's) resolution: that the Congress should adhere to the Kienthal decisions. (The stupid Swiss might vote for it just to be in fashion,
without really knowing what the Kienthal decisions were—
and then they'd be caught! After that, you could bait your
hook with their own resolution and catch the lot of them!
Grimm as well!

Trivialities? No! That is how history is made—from one
hard-won resolution to the next, through the pressure of the
minority, you push and push every resolution—leftwards,
ever leftwards!

[58]

Then the next step. That Saturday evening, on the Skittle Club's initiative, by individual invitation, a separate, secret, private meeting of all young delegates was held away from the Congress building; they gambled on the normal sympathy of the young for the left. The plan was simple: to work out with their help a resolution (or rather submit a readymade one brought along by Radek) for them to put forward and force through Congress on the following day, Sunday.

At this private conference of young delegates Willi, of course, was in the chair—making lavish use of his commanding gestures, his bold, cheerful voice, and his tumbling hair—and Radek was at his side, smothered in curls, wearing his merrily militant spectacles, reading his resolution, explaining it, answering questions. (He was a good speaker, too—but his pen was beyond price.) Lenin, as he always preferred to, had sat inconspicuously among the rest, and contented himself with listening attentively.

All might have been well. The young delegates listened closely to their Russo-Polish comrade and seemed in agreement.

All might have been well, if something extremely unpleasant hadn't happened. They had not had the sense to lock the door. And through the unlocked door, unnoticed at first, came two malicious tale-bearers, two horrid old bags: Madame Blok, who was Grimm's friend, no less, and Martov's lady friend, Dimka Smidovich. Once these wretched females were in, there was no turning them out: they'd scream and make a scene! And the whole meeting could hardly move elsewhere! Anyway, they'd already seen and heard Radek speaking, and realised, of course, that a resolution for the Swiss Congress was being drafted by Russians.

What an infernal nuisance! What a colossal fiasco! Loathsome creatures with their filthy little intrigues! Of course, they'd rushed off to Grimm and whispered in his ear. And he, the brute, the rotter, the utter swine, had believed the silly bitches. He'd tried to start a vulgar brawl by printing vile innuendoes in his *Berner Tagwacht*, which were absolutely incomprehensible to ninety-nine per cent of its readers: '*A certain small group of foreigners*, who look at our workers' movement through spectacles of their own, and are utterly indifferent to Swiss affairs, are trying in a fit of impatience to provoke an artificial revolution in our country! ...'

Poppycock! Unmitigated hogwash! And that is what they call a working-class leader?

Then at the Congress they'd laughed down Nobs's resolution. When he proposed making it a rule for the future that only those opposed to national self-defence should be put up for Parliament, Greulich had been greatly amused: if we elect such deputies, he said, their hotheadedness may land them in the *skittle alley*.

The Congress had roared with laughter.

Consideration of the Kienthal resolution had also been postponed—until February 1917.

What a tragedy it all was! So much effort, so many evenings, so much conviction, lucid thought, and revolutionary dynamite had gone into it! And the result was—a heap of vulgar, stupid, opportunist debris, like dingy cotton-wool, like the dust of junk rooms.

In musty old Switzerland the bacillus of petit-bourgeois cretinism reigned triumphant.

And the bourgeois world still stood, unexploded.

44

The Ulyanovs lived exactly half-way between the cantonal and city libraries, and it was only slightly farther to the Centre for Socialist Literature: all were between five and seven minutes away at average walking speed. They all opened at nine, but today he was driven out of the house forty minutes earlier: stupidly, humiliatingly fleeing from that shock-headed ragamuffin, Zemlyachka's nephew, so as to spare himself, to avoid impertinent chatter which might enrage him and ruin his whole day.

Objectively speaking, there was no avoiding such figures in émigré revolutionary circles—slovenly, vacant-looking young men with unformed minds but ever ready to pronounce on any subject, just to show that they had opinions. They were everlastingly hungry and penniless. You might think that they would try to earn a bit by copying—there was a total lack of copyists in Zürich; think of all the trouble he'd had getting his lost *Imperialism* copied. But no, they could neither spell nor write legibly—and anyway they all wanted nothing less than an editorship, and immediately! Their constant preoccupation was where to find a free meal. On the Ulyanovs' budget this was an intolerable imposition: Zemlyachka's nephew was capable of wolfing two eggs, and four sandwiches for good measure. They had firmly banned him from the dinner table so he started appearing early in the morning, always with some flimsy excuse—returning or borrowing a book or a newspaper, but really with an eye to breakfast.

('Whatever you do, don't feed him,' he had told Nadya as he left the house just now. 'He'll soon stop coming.') It wouldn't be so bad if he meekly ate and then went away, but no, he thought it necessary to show his gratitude in a gush of pseudo-intellectual drivel, to elucidate fundamental questions and always in the same aggressive, know-all fashion.

These visits, that knowing, superior smile on the face of a milksop, made Vladimir Ilyich ill for the day. In general, any unexpected upset to his daily routine, especially an uninvited and untimely guest, any pointless waste of time, so exasperated and unsettled him that he was incapable of work. Nothing was more vexatious than expending your nervous energy and your cogency in argument, not at a conference, in a pamphlet, in debate with an important party opponent, but, for no good reason, on a lout who didn't even mean what he was saying. Most émigrés had to count their pennies, but a whole day frittered away was no loss to them. A single wasted hour made Lenin feel ill! Even if in retrospect some unforeseen meeting, conversation, or piece of business proved important and necessary, the unexpected always irritated him at the time.

But the émigré world has its own code of behaviour and you are defenceless against such visitors, you cannot simply show them the door or refuse to let them in: it would set malicious tongues wagging and seriously damage your reputation. You would instantly be accused of arrogance, lordliness, overweening conceit, 'leaderism', dictatorial pretensions ... the émigré world was a nest of vicious snakes, for ever writhing and hissing. So that whenever one of these impudent rogues saw fit to leave Russia—and even escaping from Siberia was the easiest thing in the world, so that everybody fled abroad, expecting to be kept at the Party's expense—you must not only welcome him but invent something for him to do. And within a year you might find the swine actually working on some journal, though probably only one number would ever appear.

Take that born trouble-maker Evgenia Bosh. Why didn't she go to Russia, as she was supposed to? There was absolutely nothing for her to do *here*, but she would try to invent something, and expected others to think up work for her. One of the plagues of émigré life was having to devise occupations for émigrés.

Of course, once the revolution began its ramifications would provide work for every one of these little boys and girls, indeed each of them would be indispensable, there would be only too few of them. But while there was no revolution, cramped and pinched as everyone was, these brats were unbearable.

It was an exhausting state of affairs. How long had it been going on? Was it nine years since they had fled from Russia, fled from defeat? Sixteen since that first unhappy meeting and clash with Plekhanov? Twenty-one since that stupid bungle in Petersburg? That tormenting state of mind when every sinew craves action, when you feel that you could move mountains or continents with the energy pent up and tense inside you, but there is nothing to exert your powers upon, no finger-tip contact with people, when parties, crowds and continents will not bow to your will but chaotically, senselessly whirl and collide, not knowing where they are bound—you alone know that!—while all your energy, all your plans go for nothing, and you burn yourself out converting half a dozen Swiss youngsters in the Skittle Club. Still, even they were something. Earlier on, when no one came to meetings except two Swiss, two Germans, one Pole, one Jew and one Russian, who sat telling each other jokes, things were really bad, it was pathetic, he was ready to call it a day!

Now that he had got down on to the Limmat Embankment without meeting Zemlyachka's nephew he could assume that he was safe. His self-defensive irritation gradually subsided.

Ragged grey clouds with whitish edges gave the day a cold, severe light.

Big plate-glass windows encroached upon the lake front, blatantly displaying on a background of silk and velvet all the ingenious handiwork of idleness—jewellery, perfumes, haberdashery, linen. The lackeys' republic was flaunting its luxury, untouched by the war, as provocatively as it knew how.

Moving away in disgust from these perverse fantasies in gold, satin and lace—he hated the things themselves, and still more the people who loved them—Lenin waited for a tram

[63]

to pass—a dog ran right in front of it but reached the other side unhurt—then crossed the road and set out along the river bank.

By the Fraumünster bridge he let a car, a hansom, and a cyclist with a long basket on his back go by. The City Library was right in front of him, and he would have liked to go in at once, but it was still closed.

If he went on he would have to make a detour: there was no way between the library and the water. The library building was the former Wasserkirche, so called because it jutted out into the water. Four hundred years ago, the resolute Zwingli had taken it away from the priests and handed it over for civic use.

There he stood in person, before the requisitioned church, on a black marble pedestal several steps high, with his snub nose, his book, and the point of his sword resting in the space between his feet. Lenin always spared him an approving glance. True, his book was the Bible, but all the same for the sixteenth century he had shown splendid resolution, today's Socialists could take a lesson from him. An excellent combination, the book and the sword. The book, with the sword as its extension.

Clausewitz: war is politics, with the pen finally exchanged for the sword. All politics lead to war, and that is their only value.

The river added dampness to the cold of the morning air. They said that it never froze. Somehow he always associated Russia with winter, and emigration with perpetual winterlessness. He leaned over the railings. Here, where the river mouth widened, there was an array of boats several rows deep along both banks—boats masted and unmasted, boats with cabins and boats with tarpaulin covers. The masts were swaying.

Kesküla was complaining that someone close to the Central Committee had stolen the money intended to pay for publication of a pamphlet. It would have to be paid again. Outrageous!

The water was dark, but quite clear. Grey stones could be seen on the bottom.

The three aspects of war according to Clausewitz: the

[64]

operations of reason belong to the government, free spiritual activity belongs to the commanders, and hatred to the people.

The neat square stones of the embankment pavement were thickly strewn with maple leaves (it was the custom not to sweep them up). That tree there—what was it?—had not yet lost its spiky cones.

Everything was getting frantically dear. They would soon have nothing to live on. The price of paper was rising faster than anything! Shlyapnikov was no good at all at extracting money from Gorky and from Bonch. He should wrench it out of them with pincers! Let them pay up and pay handsomely.

All his life his mother had helped him out from family funds. On his foreign travels or in Petersburg, however much he overspent, he had never had to think of earning money. He had been able to afford a balanced diet in gaol, to shorten his journey to Siberia, to avoid transit prisons. In emigration he could ask for money at any time, and by some miracle she had always managed to send it. But since the summer he had had no mother, and he would never be able to ask again.

A flock of black ducks with white heads bobbed on the lake, suddenly took off, scuffing the water, flew low over the surface, and settled. Then they flocked together again and swam sedately back to their old place.

But although Clausewitz seemed to have explained the basic laws of war in general, it was impossible to understand the law of the war now in progress. Or that of the war which must be started.

Surely the Swedes at least could make him a loan? Shlyapnikov must drop a hint to Branting: it would come more naturally from him, as Russia's representative.

A professional revolutionary ought to be relieved of the need to worry about his livelihood. Party funds should guarantee the leading members of the Central Committee a maintenance allowance for some time ahead.

The wives of solid Swiss citizens were crumbling bread and dropping it from the big bridge.

The ducks quickly gathered, and others—with green heads and yellow beaks—joined them. And yet others, with blue-grey plumage.

[65]

If we are to publish in *Letopis*, the alliance between the Machists and the Menshevik Organising Committee must be split. People around Gorky are intriguing against us.

Two or three ducks skimmed the lake, chasing each other and churning the water with wings and feet.

To think that he must look to Gorky for money and, what was more, humble himself before that incredibly spineless shilly-shallier, beg his forgiveness for assailing Kautsky, discard the most telling and enjoyable knocks in the whole book just to please him.

What would be nice now would be to go for a brisk row. They'd often talked about it, but never got round to it. Now it would have to wait till spring. Walking and scrambling about in the mountains or tramping the streets of Zürich were the only ways Lenin had of dissipating and soothing the ache of unused muscles. But he still felt it in his shoulders and the best thing for that was rowing.

Another great worry was the loss of his *Imperialism*, sent off in manuscript last summer. The most mysterious thing about it was that a responsible Post Office could find no clue as to how it had vanished. The British censorship had become ridiculous, and the French had lost all shame, so that it was not surprising if *Imperialism* had attracted attention—its author was no longer an ordinary émigré, one of the thousands here in Switzerland whom the police ignored. Perhaps he was already under surveillance? Perhaps he was being watched at this very moment, here on the embankment? His position was precarious. At the first—or anyway the second—hint from the Russian or the French ambassador he might be hauled before a military court or deported from Switzerland for infringing its neutrality. They would only have to listen in from a neighbouring table to one speech at the Skittle Club.

He stretched himself and trudged on downstream along the railings, near the water's edge, looking like the neediest of Zürich's inhabitants with his shabby bowler hat, his threadbare coat, and his waterproof shopping bag (his, though, held notebooks, abstracts, cuttings). Reaching the big bridge, he patiently let pass someone's opulent phaeton, a slow four-horse dray, and a one-horse tram with three big plate-glass windows and a uniformed driver up in front.

He would, therefore, have to burn dangerous drafts, give all important documents to respectable Swiss citizens for safe keeping, start signing himself '*Frei*' again, or something like that, and on occasions use invisible ink, even for letters between Zürich, Bern and Geneva. All this in a neutral country! Just like at home, under the noses of the gendarmes... And *Imperialism*, written out all over again, must be done up in the covers of a book so that it would get through.

He crossed the big bridge and came out on the broad paved way along the lake, which was also unswept and carpeted with brown maple leaves.

The air from this wider water was stronger, fresher, colder.

Swans, white and grey, were floating there. Or rather, not floating but sitting statuesquely on the water. In the shallows, now one, now another of them dipped its head to peck at something in the depths, its white behind sticking up, its feet treading the air. Then it lengthily shook the water from its snaky neck.

Behind, to the left, a pale sun was peeping from beyond the Opera House. But it was a cold sun, its light held no warmth.

It was soothing, all this water. All this space. The pressure in his chest eased. It was only when it released him that he realised how hard pressed and harassed he normally was.

The broad expanse of the lake. Scattered about it fishermen rode at anchor. On the other side, and to the left, the elongated, gently sloping wooded bulk of the Uetliberg stretched to the far end of the lake. There were white spots on it in places: a light snow had fallen on the high ground and had not melted.

A spacious lake, reminding him of Geneva.

The fresh, lapping waves of Lake Geneva would stay in his memory as long as he lived. That was where he had suffered the greatest disaster in his life: the shattering of his idol.

How young he had been, how full of youthful rapture, how infatuated when he had come to Switzerland for that first meeting with Plekhanov, to seek his recognition. It was then, sending 'Volgin' (Plekhanov) his declaration of friendship before leaving Munich, that he had first thought of signing himself 'Lenin'. All that was needed was that the old man should control his vanity, that one great river should

[67]

acknowledge the other, so that together they could encompass all Russia.

Young men full of vigour, who had served their time in Siberia, escaped great dangers and broken out of Russia were bringing these elderly, distinguished revolutionaries their plans for *Iskra*, for a journal, for working side by side together to fan the flames of revolution! It was incredible in retrospect, but he had still believed in a general reunification, including the Economists, had even defended Kautsky against Plekhanov. It sounded like a bad joke! They had naively supposed that all Marxists stood for the same things and could work in harmony. They had seen themselves as bearers of glad tidings; we, the young, are continuing what you began.

They had run up against something different: a calculating concern to retain power, to remain in command. The *Iskra* plan, and the fanning of flames in Russia, were matters of complete indifference to Plekhanov: all he wanted was to be sole leader. So he had cunningly represented Lenin as a comic conciliator, an opportunist, and himself as a rock-hard revolutionary. And he had taught Lenin where the advantage lay in a schism: the one who calls for a split is always on firmer ground.

How could he ever forget that night in the village of Vésenaz, when he and Potresov had disembarked from the Geneva steamer like whipped schoolboys, smarting and humiliated, when they had paced the village from end to end in the darkness, shouting their resentment, seething, ashamed of themselves—and all around them over the mountains and the lake an electric storm had walked the night sky, without breaking out in rain. They were so outraged that at moments they almost burst into tears. And an infernal chill had descended on his heart.

On that bitter night Vladimir Ulyanov was born again. Only since that night had he become what he was, become his true self.

This harsh lesson Lenin took to heart, never to forget it. He would never believe anyone again, never let sentiment tinge his dealings with others.

Somebody nearby started feeding the gulls, and they shot up from the water, greedily, impatiently swooping and wheeling, catching the bread in mid-air, screaming, fighting, even venturing on to the parapet, flying almost into the faces of Lenin and his neighbours. He waved one of them away and walked on.

How memory catches at chance coincidences, sentimental associations. Lake Geneva again, nothing more, had been between them before they had known each other, when he was beginning to come into his own, receiving the delegates to the Second Congress, carefully studying each one, testing him out, making a bid for his support, and she—was bearing her fifth child, to a husband younger than herself, and also reading for the first time *The Development of Capitalism* by somebody called Ilin, with no idea of what lay ahead.

Five years went by, and they still did not know each other, although she had been in Geneva several times. It was in Geneva too, at an unforgettable performance of *La Dame aux Camélias*, that he had been pierced with anguish, had first doubted the meaning of his life. At that very time her husband lay dying in Davos. Then, only a few months later, in Paris, she had come to him.

The wind, noticeably chillier here, crinkled the waters in a frown. He put his bag down by the embankment railings, raised his collar, and stood there peering down at the lake. It was already quite cold. Even according to the stupid Russian calendar it was October 25th, which meant November 7th European style. And Inessa was still freezing at her Sörenberg villa, doing her best to catch a chill. Or to make him angry.

Or to punish him.

She made him wait for her letters. She was denying him news of herself. Either she didn't answer at all, or else she wrote late. So that you had to choose your words carefully: of course, if you don't feel like answering ... or if you feel like not answering ... I won't pester you with questions ...

In all his personal relationships Lenin was careful to assert his superiority, was always on his dignity. But here it was impossible: he could find no vantage point. He could only hide his embarrassment in jokes. Only beg.

He must learn to meet silence with silence. To wait for her answer. But nothing could be more difficult: it was when you didn't see each other that you needed most of all to write, to share your thoughts! And anyway, there was business which could not wait.

It would be quite simple, here and now, without waiting for her answer, to write a few affectionate and unresentful lines. (No, they mustn't be affectionate, there must not be the slightest breath of affection; all letters in wartime were subject to censorship, and you had to write as though you were making a statement in a police station. Mustn't give them a weapon against yourself.)

Yes, he was at her mercy if she chose to punish him. He acknowledged dependence on no one in the world except Inessa. He felt it least when he was smarting from one of their fights. Most of all when they were together.

No, when they were not ...

Everything he had ever had in life—food, drink, clothes, house and home—had been not *for him*, indeed he had wanted nothing of all this except as a means of keeping himself going for the sake of the Cause. His month off in summer, his mountain walks in the Carpathians, or from Sörenberg up the Rothorn, the Alpine view before his eyes, the slab of chocolate eaten stretched out on the slopes of the Zürichberg, the smoked Volga sturgeon sent by his mother—none of this was self-indulgence, mere gratification of the flesh, it was a way of making himself mentally fit for his work. Good health was a revolutionary's main asset.

Only his meetings with Inessa, even their business meetings, were just for himself, for the sake of the foolishly happy, free and easy, lighthearted state of animal contentment in which they left him, although they could be a time-wasting and debilitating distraction.

All the men and women Lenin had ever met in his life he had valued only if, and as long as, they were useful to the Cause. Only Inessa, although she had entered his life through the Cause—and there was no other way, no outsider could have got near him—existed as if for him alone, complementing his existence with her own.

Inessa revealed to him things he would never have thought of, never imagined, and might have lived his life without discovering. In their arguments about free love he had an unbreakable net of logic for her vague ideas. Slip through it if you can! But it was hopeless. The dark water from the depths of the lake runs unhindered through the fisherman's net, and Inessa with her concept of free love was not to be caught in the net of class analysis. Slowed down for a moment, she slipped easily through the mesh. Her arguments were defeated but she was invincible.

Long ago, when the whole world was carefully measured, appraised and regulated, she had shaken his certainties, bidding him break bounds and follow her through a world which was the same yet unlike anything he had imagined, and he had gone with her, like a timid but delighted school-boy, anxiously clinging to her guiding hand, full of childlike, doglike gratitude towards her, worshipping her right down to the blue veins of her slender foot for all that she had revealed to him, and made to last as long as her love for him.

From where she was, from Sörenberg in the south-west, over the frowning autumn waters, even in the whistling November wind, he felt her love calling to him. He remembered the flutter of eyelids over half-closed eyes, the quick gleam of her white teeth.

Why was she punishing him? Why hadn't she come down to Clarens, where it was warmer? Last year the first snow had fallen on Sörenberg at the beginning of October. It had been very cold.

Over the roof of the theatre, which was dotted with mythological winged trumpeters, the sun suddenly shone out full strength. The sunlight was cold here, and orange-coloured where it had encroached on the heights of Uetliberg, but the lower slopes, where buildings towered around a grey-green dome with a belfry, were still in gloom.

Those were happy days—in Longjumeau, Brussels, Copenhagen, Cracow. In Bern too. Happy years. Seven of them.

He, who was incapable of wasting five minutes without finding idleness an exasperating burden, had spent hours on end with Inessa. He had not despised himself for it, not been in any hurry to pull himself together, but had abandoned himself completely to his weakness. It had reached the point where he had confided everything to her, wanted to tell her everything—much more than he would tell any man. How quick and fresh was her response and her advice! And how he had missed them in the last six months! Since April. Since Kienthal.

Had something snapped at Kienthal? He hadn't felt it at the time.

He had been forced to leave Bern: Grimm was the dominant influence there and he would never have been able to get together a circle of sympathisers. He had been right to go away. But how could he have imagined when he left that they would never meet again?

In Kienthal he had noticed nothing. In the thick of that wonderful six-day battle.

The one person whose feelings he could not afford to hurt: he might lose her for ever. This fear of upsetting a delicate equilibrium which he had experienced with no one else sometimes put him in a comic position. He had to humour her unfortunate passion for writing theoretical articles. Frank criticism was impossible, and he had to choose his words carefully or sometimes simply lie. 'What could I possibly have against publishing your article? Of course I'm for it.' Then, afterwards, he would pretend that unforeseen circumstances prevented it. Rebukes, and even political correction, had to be softened until they almost became praise. He had to endure her arbitrariness as a translator: at times, instead of translating his text, she would amend the sense, or even censor it, rejecting ideas which were not to her liking. No one could be allowed to do that! But to Inessa his reproaches were mild and courteous. His courtesy was a way of ingratiating himself. If he wrote a longer letter than usual, he would immediately apologise: 'I shouldn't be rambling on like this.'

But even his eagerness to please did not make him feel small. With Inessa, nothing was humiliating.

This was her way of punishing him, not writing. Not answering his letters.

Once she dug her heels in there was no persuading her.

A white steamer moved away from the landing stage, sending waves towards him. Two white swans, immune to the cold, their necks gracefully arched, apparently set in their pose for ever, were rocked by the waves.

He felt cold. He took his bag and walked on along the railings.

[72]

With Inessa beside him he had painfully bent his will to hers, but now that she was far away he could attain almost complete freedom from her.

Here in the severe light of an autumn morning, with sunshine chasing shadow over the cold lake.

For as long as he could remember he had been aware of a safety device in himself. Any setback, any waste of time, any display of weakness depressed the catch further and further, until suddenly it sprang back, flinging him into action with a force which nothing could withstand.

You must economise on idle sentiment or your work will stagnate.

With Inessa far away his natural caution was coming back to him. Caution forbade any additional stress in his life. A permanent union with Inessa? Life would be chaotic. She was too mercurial, too much a person in her own right, too distracting. Then there were her children—and a way of life quite strange to him. He could not, he had no right to let himself be slowed down and taken out of his way by those children.

The best solution was to live with Nadya, and he had been right to adopt it all those years ago. Yakubova had been more vivacious, and nicer looking, but could never have helped him as Nadya had. Nadya was much more than a fellow spirit: on the most trivial of subjects her thoughts and feelings never differed from his own. She knew how the whole world frayed and fretted and irritated him, and she herself not only did not irritate but soothed and protected him, took all his worries upon herself. However sharp his revulsions of feeling, however sudden his outbursts, she was there to share and soften them. And how quick she was to take her cue! When Radek was behaving like a swine she was curt and hard with him, and if he made some excuse to call she stopped him at the door. But when Radek became a model comrade, a congenial adviser, how warmly she welcomed him. If she had needed to rehearse, to make an effort, she might sometimes have gone wrong, but she merely felt for Ilyich with unwavering loyalty. Living with her made no excessive demands on his nerves.

Then again—and this was not to be ignored—Inessa was

not economical, not capable of living sensibly and modestly. She often behaved erratically. She would suddenly, for instance, take it into her head to dress in the latest fashion. Whereas Nadya had no equal for orderliness and economy. She understood instinctively that every extra franc in hand meant extra time for thinking and working. What was more, she never let her tongue run away with her—a rare thing in a woman—never boasted, never said a word to outsiders when she had been warned not to. For that matter, she knew when to keep quiet without being told.

In view of all this, it would ill become a revolutionary to be uncomfortably conscious in company that his wife was far from beautiful, not outstandingly intelligent, and a year older than himself. To succeed in the world he must be as free as possible from inner doubts and outside distractions, must narrowly concentrate all his efforts on his goal. For Lenin the politician his union with Nadya was all that reason could require.

True, there had always been the three of them. Leaving their homes in adjoining streets to meet in the forest round Bern; going for mountain rambles on Sörenberg to pick Alpine roses or mushrooms (although sometimes he and Inessa had gone off by themselves to remote mountain refuges); at some *pension*, where he and Nadya had sat reading in the shade, while Inessa spent hours at the piano; sitting on tree-stumps on the warm slopes, he and Nadya at their books as always, and Inessa gracefully sunning herself like a little girl out with her elders; best of all, those long hours when he had talked to both of them about his ideas, his plans, his future articles. How often he had taken in at a glance and marvelled at his incomparable, incredible, impossible good luck, wished that it would last for years. And it had lasted! If Nadya ever wrote a long, detailed, friendly letter, it was to Inessa. If there was one person whom she tirelessly praised to all their comrades, it was Inessa. Only in letters to Volodya's mother—her own mother saw how things were—in letters from daughter-in-law to mother-in-law, describing their life together and their walks, did she write as though there were just the two of them. Very tactfully.

Now their mothers had both died within a short time: hers

after an attack of influenza last spring, his that summer in Petersburg. The mail reached their mountain *pension* at Flums by packmule, so that the telegram announcing his mother's death had arrived late, on the second anniversary of the outbreak of war, which was also Swiss Union Day, one of those innumerable, chaotic Swiss festivals when beacons were lit, sky-rockets let off, and guns fired on every mountain top. They had sat together that evening looking at the beacons, and paid their last respects to his mother to the sound of those salvoes. It was probably easier like that, at a distance.

If you are both getting on for fifty, and your mothers, yours and hers, both die, it makes you still older. And brings you closer. Besides, you are both revolutionaries. So that perhaps ...

A motor boat was travelling diagonally across the lake, from that very direction, from Sörenberg, tossing its prow as it swiftly ploughed the water, leaving behind a triangular patch of foam and shattering the silence with its metallic coughing.

There was something about it, as it sped on, cutting a swift furrow through the water, pointing its pitiless beak, harshly chattering, which broke his train of thought, jolted his mind—and forgetting social analysis, forgetting logical argument, he suddenly saw very, very simply what he had never seen before.

If she stood for free love in theory, and could not be dissuaded, what reason was there to think that she did not practise it? ...

He had mentally reviewed, anticipated and enumerated for her benefit every point that could be made about relations between bourgeois and proletarians, but he had overlooked just one little thing: if they had not seen each other since Kienthal—and they were so near—if for half a year she had neither come nor summoned him, and had now almost stopped writing ...

Perhaps this summer she had been with someone else?

Why had he invariably pictured her alone, and never imagined that it could be otherwise?

On this side of the lake there was still wan sunlight, but on the other side thick grey clouds were streaming over Uetliberg, packing the valley with mist. The mountain, the lower slopes, the bell-tower were quickly swathed, and the mist crept on towards the Zürich shore.

What could be simpler? And how was it that he had examined the question from every angle—except this one?

No, it was impossible! His comrade and friend! After their glorious fight against the centrists at Kienthal!

He gripped the cold railings, and felt like howling—through the railings, across the lake, over Uetliberg, over all the mountains between them. Inessa! Don't leave me! Inessa! ...

He must write, immediately, swallowing his pride, write anything so long as it would bring an answer. Of course, the post office opened earlier than the library; why hadn't he thought of it before? It opened at eight: he should have gone there and written a letter. Now it was too late.

Yes, it was too late now. They were banging and clanging their bells like madmen, like idiots! As though every bit of old iron in the city was under repair. The bells of the Frau-münster clanged out over the post office, the double-belfried Grossmünster crashed out the hour up above the shop signs on every floor of Bellevue ... How many more churches were there in Zürich?

The mist and cloud had rolled over to his side of the lake and it was suddenly grey and cheerless.

He drew his watch from his waistcoat pocket with numb fingers. If they were banging on their buckets it must be nine o'clock. He hadn't been to the post office, he'd lost count of time, he'd come too far—however briskly he walked now he would reach the Cantonal Library well after opening time. A bad start. And he had set out with such good intentions.

Very well. The letter must wait. He must work now.

He bowled along, a short, stocky figure, scarcely troubling to avoid those in his path. There, nearby, was the City Library. He could go there, but he had the journals and books for today's work on call at the other one. He hurried as fast as he could along the loathsome bourgeois embankment, where the smells of delicatessen and confectionery wafted from doorways to tickle jaded appetites, where the shopkeepers had performed miracles of ingenuity to offer their customers a twenty-first version of sausage and a hundred-and-first

[76]

variety of patisserie. Windows full of chocolates, smokers' requisites, dinner services, clocks, antiques flashed by ... It was so difficult on this smart embankment to imagine a mob with axes and firebrands some day smashing all that plate glass to smithereens.

But—it must be done!

Everything here looked too solid and permanent—the houses, doors, doorbells, bolts.

Yes, it must be done!

From every corner of the city came the clanging of bells, frenzied and hollow.

45

Here, too, Zwingli had laid about him with almost proletarian resolution, setting a good example by bisecting the Predigerkirche midway between its spires. Half of it had been occupied for centuries past by a library. It was a source of particular satisfaction that both the main libraries of Zürich had triumphed over religion.

He went into the hushed room. Nine windows with pointed arches rose to a height of five or six storeys. At a still dizzier height, the ribs of the vaulted roof met in bosses.

All this soaring space was entirely wasted, except for a two-storeyed wooden gallery attached to the walls. On the walls, between bookcases, hung many sombre portraits—haughty municipal councillors and burgomasters in doublets and frilled shirts. He had never had time to look at them carefully, or read the inscriptions.

As he passed through the heavy doors Lenin saw that his favourite place in the gallery by the central window, and another which he found convenient, were both occupied. He was late. The day had begun awkwardly.

He signed the register, but the librarian with the glasses and the *ex officio* smile could not make out what had become of one of his three piles of books on reserve.

These petty vexations, one on top of another, could rob him of hours of working time.

The success or failure of a working day may depend on trivial events at its outset. Now he had started late. There was less than half a day, only three hours in fact, between opening time and the lunch break, and part of that was already wasted.

Imperialism had been fully drafted in twenty exercise books, written up, lost, and rewritten—but Lenin had taken out yet another heap of material on the same subject. He felt that something more was needed. Yet it was difficult to see what. He had had all his findings clearly in mind long before he reached his twentieth copybook. His prevision had become so acute of late that he knew remarkably early, before he sat down to write, what his conclusions would be.

Now it looked as though he must take out the sweetest knocks in the whole book. Stinking, slimy, sanctimonious old creature! Nowhere, in the whole history of social democracy, had there ever been a more loathsome and despicable humbug.

The missing pile was on Persia. He had already begun making extracts. Nobody had thought about socialism's Eastern front properly, and it needed study.

Never mind, his swipes at Kautsky would not go to waste— he would put them in somewhere else.

He was also drafting an important and detailed summary of policy for the Swiss leftists, so that they could systematically correct their failures at the Congress. But this could be more conveniently done in the Centre for Socialist Literature than here.

No, she had always helped, always translated for him. Any day now she would leave the mountains for Clarens, and might come to him. Why imagine the worst? He had not been thinking straight.

He had arrived feeling that he had also left something undone, overlooked something in his article against disarmament. He had finished it once (it was there in his bag), but doubt still nagged at the back of his mind. The main ideas were all there: disarmament is a counsel of despair; disarmament means renouncing any idea of revolution; those who look for socialism without revolution and dictatorship are no Socialists; we shall have women and children of thirteen and upwards fighting in Russia in the coming civil war. All true enough, but he was still left with a feeling that some statements were inadequately qualified. You must be super-cautious, never give your enemies a thing to quote against you. You must equip all dangerous sentences with protective subsidiary clauses, make sure that every sentence is defended at all points, hedged with qualifications, carefully balanced, so that no one can find a vulnerable spot. The article, then, would stand re-examination—and in fact he had already started. Here, for example, was something written in the heat of the moment: 'We support the use of violence by the masses.' They'd pounce on that! Tack a bit on—'... against their oppressors'.

But this was something he could do elsewhere, and time was going by.

He started looking over the theses for the Swiss leftists. Still a lot of work there. Everything had to be chewed up very small for them. House-to-house distribution of leaflets—to whom? To the poorest peasants and farm labourers. Which agricultural holdings should be subject to forcible expropriation? Let's say those over fifteen hectares. After what period of residence should foreigners qualify for Swiss citizenship? Let's say three months—and gratis, that's important. What is meant by 'revolutionary rates of taxation'? Too general. Must compile a table showing concretely what percentage is to be paid on property over 20,000 francs, property over 50,000 francs, and so on. How should people in guest-houses be assessed? Draw up a precise scale for them too—nobody ever seems to get down to practical details. A guest paying five francs a day is one of us—one per cent is enough—but anyone paying ten francs should be charged twenty per cent immediately.

His gorge rose as he thought of Grimm's and Greulich's latest dirty trick. Filthy opportunists, sneaking scoundrels—just you wait, we'll have you in the pillory!

He seemed unable to escape these vexations and distractions. It's always the same: let them get out of hand and it's impossible to concentrate, to work methodically, or even to sit still.

Then there was that frantic and still unsettled argument with the 'Japanese', which had wasted so much of his energy and was still interfering with his work. He had thought that after several articles and a couple of dozen letters the conflict was resolved, but it was still not quite dead!

[80]

He could never manage to concentrate all his efforts on a single major objective. He was for ever discovering enemies in secondary sectors which might at present look quite unimportant; but no front was ever unimportant—at some future moment these secondary fronts might be decisive. So that you must furiously round on those snapping at your flanks and show them your teeth. It wasn't just the 'Japanese' (Pyatakov and that Bosh woman of his, who had escaped from Siberia via Japan). Bukharin was siding with them too. They, who hadn't an ounce of brains between them, had reduced themselves with Radek's assistance to a state of collective stupefaction, to the ultimate in cretinism—if it wasn't 'imperialist economism' it was the self-determination of nations, or 'democracy'. These little rosy piglets, this younger generation of Party members, were so self-satisfied, so very sure of themselves, so ready to take over the leadership at any moment, and yet they were thrown by every sharp turn, not one of them had the trained skill and flexibility to swerve instantly to left or right, anticipating every fall with which the tortuous road of revolution threatened them.

Take democracy. Bukharin undervalued it in a primitive, adolescent fashion. He wrote openly that 'We shall have to dispense with democracy in the period of the seizure of power.' Not a bit of it! *In a general way* socialist revolution was impossible without a struggle for democracy, and the piglets should have their little pink snouts rubbed in this truth. But, of course, it must always be remembered that this was only true in a particular situation, in a certain sense, for a certain period. A different time would come when democratic aims *of any kind* would only be a *hindrance* to socialist revolution. (Double underlining here!) Suppose, for instance, when the battle is already raging, when the revolution is under way, we need to seize the banks—and they call on us to wait, to put the republic on a legal basis first?

Lenin had explained it over and over again, in letters many pages long, but they had turned up their noses. He had only bothered so much with these troublemakers and intriguers because the 'Japanese' had money for a journal. *Kommunist* could not have been started without their help. All the same, the alliance made sense only as long as Lenin had a majority

[81]

on the editorial board. (Equality with such fools was un-thinkable. To hell with them! It would be idiocy, it would ruin everything!) It was better to drag the fatheads through the mud. You wouldn't accept a peaceful solution, so we'll bash your ugly mugs in!

He had confined his argument with Bukharin to letters, and not let it come into the open. But he had been too furious to answer the letter Bukharin had written before his departure. Now he had gone off to America—probably he had taken offence.

To himself Lenin acknowledged that Bukharin was very clever. But his constant resistance was exasperating.

All opposition exasperated him—especially on theoretical questions, where it implied a claim to leadership.

Radek was another matter, and it would be well worth while thrashing the little shit as a lesson to the rest. Radek's lowest trick yet was surreptitiously egging on the piglets while hiding behind the Zimmerwald Left. (At Kienthal he had tried to make Lenin quarrel with all the leftists, and had caused him to fall out with Rosa.) Radek's political behaviour was that of a barefaced, impudent Tyszko-type huckster—the only politics such snotty-nosed guttersnipes had ever known. After the way he had slung Lenin and Zinoviev off the board of *Vorbote* the only thing to do was to punch him on the snout or turn your back on him. If you forgive this sort of thing in politics, people regard you as a fool or a knave.

In the present case the right thing was to snub him. Es-pecially as there was no disagreement on general matters, but only on Russo-Polish problems. Where Switzerland was concerned, Radek had no choice. Since he opposed Grimm, he was forced into alliance with Lenin—and what an ally he was!

Zinoviev, too, had acted like a scoundrel in this business of the 'Japanese', and urged him to give in. They were all un-stable. You couldn't rely on the closest of them.

To put a stop to Bukharin's capers it was necessary to carry the argument to Russia too, and finish off the 'Japanese' on Russian soil. Shlyapnikov had been ordered to do so. But Shlyapnikov was another muddlehead, and his girl-friend Kollontai was worse. (Incidentally, he mustn't forget that it would be a good idea to sneak her into the Scandinavian Conference of Neutrals, perhaps as interpreter to one of the delegates, and sniff out their plans!)

There were so many of them, these pseudo-Socialist muddlers, everywhere, in the warring countries, among the neutrals, in Russia. Was Trotsky any better, though, with his pious fatuities—'neither victors nor vanquished'? What rubbish. No, of course he was seeking cheap popularity— but let's see to it that Tsarism is nevertheless vanquished, don't let it struggle out of the present free-for-all! You can't be 'against all wars' and remain a Socialist.

Where Shlyapnikov was at present he didn't know. Still in Stockholm? Or had he already gone to Russia? Letters reached Sweden through Kesküla and his people as occasion offered—but did they get any further? There was nobody with any sense there, no system. There was no end to Shlyapnikov's delays; he went to Russia only rarely, and once there always stayed too long, the sluggard. If you said anything to him he took offence. And if he didn't go, there was nobody else. So to make him look important they had had to co-opt him to the Central Committee.

At this point the librarian came up to Lenin's desk and with a whispered apology and an apologetic bow laid the pile of material on Persia before him.

Many thanks! Half an hour or so to the lunch break, and along comes Persia! Should he make a start, or not?

Of course, Shlyapnikov was not yet ripe for membership of the Central Committee, he lacked Malinovsky's maturity. But he had taken Malinovsky's place, and the titles 'member of the CC', 'Chairman of the Russia Bureau' had turned his head, given him a taste for power. First he was shouldering Litvinov aside to get in on talks with foreign Socialists, then he was giving idiotic advice in practically every letter he wrote: 'Why don't you move to Sweden?' He was sickeningly sure of himself, but he couldn't be cut adrift, he was doing a serious job, and he had to be answered, formally at least, or with respect.

Somehow he couldn't settle down to his work. His brain was in too much of a whirl. He couldn't concentrate, couldn't adjust to the leisurely movement of Persia's feudal economy.

Malinovsky, Malinovsky! The Russian Bebel *manqué*. How he could work! How well he had handled the masses! What a remarkable type, what a personality! A natural leader of working men, a collective symbol of the Russian proletariat. Lenin had long felt the lack of such a working-class leader in the Party at his right hand, to complement him, to convert his ideas into mass action. What Lenin had particularly liked in him was that he moulded himself to his allotted place, carried out orders with alacrity and without demur—but brilliantly and effectively. He had what is called in bourgeois terms a criminal record—a few thefts—but this only threw into relief his proletarian intolerance of private property and the colourfulness of his character. So that, when excessively suspicious comrades began casting aspersions, Lenin's confidence in him grew stronger all the time. Imagine him as a provocateur? Impossible! (And it was still impossible.) After his incendiary speeches in the Duma, and his skilful management of the split between Bolsheviks and Mensheviks in the Duma group, Lenin had not only been glad to introduce Malinovsky himself on to the Central Committee, but had brought in others solely on the strength of Malinovsky's recommendation—Stalin, for instance. When they were living in Poronin, no guest from Russia was more welcome than Malinovsky. Except for that last, dreadful night in May, when he had appeared unexpectedly after his sudden and unauthorised withdrawal from the Duma. But still, he had put in an appearance and not run away. Would he have dared to do so if his hands were not clean? ... Their discussion had gone on all night. It was in any case impossible to *prove* anything against Malinovsky. (And what good could it do?) Who could believe the stupid tale that the secret police themselves had found it 'embarrassing' that one of their informers was amongst the best orators in the Duma and had ordered him to withdraw? What rot! Were the secret police stupid enough to work against themselves? He, Kuba and Grishka had constituted themselves a sort of Party tribunal, found Roman Malinovsky not guilty, and vouched for his innocence before the International Socialist Bureau.

None the less, they had quietly parted company for the time being. For personal reasons.

Lenin would never have another such helper! ... Shlyapnikov? No, no.

Now the lunch break was upon him. How on earth did these Swiss manage to work up an appetite for lunch by twelve o'clock?

However, Lenin had noticed that the librarian on duty today did not always go to lunch. He went over and enquired. No, he wasn't going. Was it at all possible to stay through the lunch break? It was.

Here was a bit of luck. Lunch wasn't worth the disturbance it would involve. It was easier to work on an empty stomach. And he would gain time.

He needn't hurry now. The best thing in fact, though, would be to stock up with newspapers right away. To save money, Lenin never bought them, never took out subscriptions, though he needed to read thirty or forty of them—all the various *Arbeiter*s and *Stimme*s.

He collected all there were and carried them over to his desk.

Reading the papers was one of his most important daily tasks, his entrée to the world outside. Reading the papers heightened his sense of responsibility, his firmness of purpose, his militancy, helped him to feel that his enemies were alive and real. Socialists, social patriots and centrists from every spot on the face of the earth, not to mention all the bourgeois donkeys, seemed to crowd round you in the reading room, gesturing, babbling, all speaking loudly at once, and you seized your opportunity to strike back, to note their weak points and hit out at them. Reading the papers meant making abstracts at the same time. By analogy, by association, by contradiction, sparks of thought were continually struck off, flying at a tangent to left or right, on to loose scraps of paper, on to the lined pages of exercise books, into blank margins, and every thought must be stitched to paper with a fiery thread before it could fade, to smoulder there until it was wanted, in a draft summary or else in a letter begun there and then so that he could forge his sentences red-hot. Some of these thoughts were intended to clear his own mind, others for use in argument, to sting or to stun, others as a more effective rehash of things which the stupid found difficult, others again to keep distant comrades, perhaps as far away as Russia, theoretically attuned to him.

Vandervelde and Branting, Huysmans and Jouhaux, Plekhanov and Potresov, Ledebour and Haase, Bauer and Bernstein, the two Adlers, even Pannekoek and Roland Holst—Lenin felt as though all these exasperating opponents were close enough to touch. No matter where their nests were, in Holland, England, France, Scandinavia, Austria or Petersburg, he felt them to be within sight, within hearing, he was connected with all of them in a single complex of throbbing nerves—asleep or awake, at his books, at table, or out walking.

There were no readers left. Evidently the lunch break had begun. The librarian went through a glass door into the depths of the book stacks. All the desk lamps were extinguished and the reading room was lost in the soaring dimness, the tomb-like silence of the church it once was. Taking advantage of this rare opportunity to discharge his excess nervous tension, Lenin began briskly pacing the longest straight walk in the building, the central aisle from the entrance under the wooden gallery to the two long transverse steps before what had been the altar. A distance of fifty paces unobstructed by book-shelves or desks.

He was used to walking in city streets or in the mountains, and he had always lived in poky little places with no room to move around. Now, pacing faster and faster with his hunter's stride, brushing aside the Hilferdings, Martovs, Greulichs, Longuets, Pressmanes and Chkheidzes, abruptly choking them off in mid-sentence, pulling them up short, routing them—in this frenzied pendulum-like oscillation he beat off wave after wave of enemies.

He was liberating himself from his enemies.

And he felt more and more ready for methodical work.

At a certain moment, half-way along the aisle, he suddenly felt that it was enough.

And sat down to work.

He had been wrong to think like that about Inessa. He had nothing at all to go on.

No! He had been sitting at the wrong desk. Now he would have to move the lot—books, newspaper, notebooks—into the gallery, to his usual desk. He had to make two journeys of it.

[86]

The steps creaked slightly in the grey Gothic hush.

And suddenly he felt very weary. He almost collapsed on to his chair.

His head was ...

Although he had missed lunch he did not feel at all hungry. He could make do with very little food: he generated energy almost without eating.

Right by the window, without lamplight for the time being. But it was a gloomy day.

He started reading the newspapers. He read about the general military situation. There was nothing there to cheer him.

Not so bad, of course, as in August, at that terrible moment when a still fresh Roumania had suddenly joined in, enormously reinforcing her allies, and it had seemed that Russia would extricate herself after all. But Germany had proved strong enough to smash Roumania almost effortlessly. It was astonishing—no one could have prophesied it two months earlier. Nevertheless, and also contrary to all predictions, Germany was not winning the war in Europe as a whole. On the Western Front there was an unbreakable and hopeless impasse. On the Eastern Front, too—and this was the greatest shock—1916 had brought no victory. A year ago Tsarism had already been close to collapse, was *already* shaken to its foundations, yet now it was on its feet again and holding its own. The greatest hope, the greatest victory, had ebbed, seeped away, vanished.

In one corner of his head, just in that one little spot, near his left temple, it was as though a vacuum had formed. That was bad. He had let himself get too excited.

In no country did it appear that even the third year of this bloody war had awakened the people to reality. The Russians as always were the most hopeless of all. It was they who were bearing the most extravagant losses, they whose stacked bodies barred the way to German efficiency and German technology. Reporting on the Eastern Front was generally vague and inaccurate, there were no war correspondents there, people knew and cared little about it, and of course the press in the Entente countries tried not to say much about an ally of which it was ashamed. But it often gave figures of Russian casualties.

[87]

Lenin always looked for these figures and made a nail-mark by them—with surprise and satisfaction. The bigger the figures, the happier they made him: all those soldiers killed, wounded or taken prisoner were stakes falling out of absolutism's fence and leaving the monarchy weaker. But at the same time the figures drove him to despair: no people on earth was so long-suffering and so devoid of sense as the Russians. Their patience knew no bounds. Any abomination, any filth dished out to them they would lap up with nothing but reverent gratitude for their beloved benefactor.

Should he put the lights on after all? The words seemed to swim before his eyes.

This damp Russian firewood refused to catch fire! The best blazes were all ancient history—the salt riots, the cholera riots, the copper coin riots, the Razin rebellion, the Pugachev rebellion. Except perhaps to seize the estate of a neighbouring landowner, which was there before their eyes, neither proletariat nor professional revolutionaries would ever set the dark peasant mass in motion. Corrupted and emasculated by Orthodoxy, the peasants seemed to have lost their passion for the axe and the torch. If a people could endure such a war without rebelling, what could be done with it?

The game was lost. There would be no revolution in Russia.

He covered his eyes with his hands and sat still.

Whether from tiredness or from depression something seemed to have sagged inside him.

The readers were reassembling. Chairs were moved. A book fell. Lamps were turned on.

There might be worse to come. Was Tsarism already wriggling out of the trap? By making a *separate peace??* (Treble underlining.) And what else could Germany do, if she couldn't win a war on two fronts?

That was really frightening. The worst thing possible. All would be lost. The world revolution. Revolution in Russia. Lenin's whole life, two decades of ceaseless effort.

A report that a separate peace was in the making, that secret negotiations between Germany and Russia had already *officially* begun, and that the two powers were already agreed on the main points, had recently been published by Grimm in the *Berner Tagwacht*. It was signed K.R. Without asking

[88]

the rascally Radek you could safely guess that it was he. (But how had he managed to persuade Grimm?!) And if you knew his gift for sparkling improvisation you could safely assume that he had not eavesdropped on diplomats, sneaked a look at secret documents, or even picked up a stray rumour, but that as he idled the morning away in bed, with newspapers over and under the blankets and books on the floor, he occasionally composed such items 'From our own correspondent' in Norway or Argentina.

What mattered was not where this particular report had originated. Nor that the Russian Ambassador in Bern had denied it—what else could he do? What did matter was that it had the piercing ring of truth: for the Tsar this really was *the right way out!* Just what he ought to do! Just what Lenin would do in his place!

So they must strike and strike again at this weak point! Raise the alarm! Put a stop to it! Forestall him! Not let him pull his feet out of the trap unharmed!

Of course, you could expect only utter stupidity from Nicholas II and his government. You wouldn't have expected them to start this war if they had had any sense at all. But they did start it—and what a wonderful present they've given us!

So perhaps it was still possible to frighten them with publicity and avert the danger?

A separate peace! It would of course be a remarkably neat way out. But still, they weren't clever enough for it.

In any case, there was nothing to be done in Russia for the present. Nobody there read the *Social Democrat*. All eyes were on the Milyukovs and Shingarevs. All anyone ever talked of was the Cadets. And just look how their delegation had been received in the West. The Tsar might take it into his head to move over a little, let Guchkov and the Cadets have ministries—and then you'd never get them, never break through.

How could you knead sad Russian dough into any sort of shape! Why was he born in that uncouth country? Just because a quarter of his blood was Russian, fate had hitched him to the ramshackle Russian rattletrap. A quarter of his blood, but nothing in his character, his will, his inclinations made him kin to that slovenly, slapdash, eternally drunken country. Lenin knew of nothing more revolting than back-slapping Russian hearties, tearful tavern penitents, self-styled geniuses bewailing their ruined lives. Lenin was a bowstring, or an arrow from the bow. Lenin could size up a situation, and the best or only means to an end, at half a glance. What then tied him to that country? With a little more work he could have mastered three European languages, as he had mastered that semi-Tartar tongue. He was tied, you say, to Russia by twenty years as a practising revolutionary? Yes, but by nothing else. Now, after the creation of the Zimmerwald Left, he was sufficiently well known in international socialist circles to step over. Socialism made no distinctions of nationality. Trotsky, for instance, had left for America. He had made the right choice. Bukharin was on his way there. Perhaps that was the place to go.

No, there was something wrong with him today. The day had started wrong, and had never got going properly. It was as though the working of his mind was too fast for his body, his physical frame, his breast. And there was that little pocket of emptiness near his left temple. He felt hollow with fatigue, and the tissues of his body seemed to sag around the cavity within him.

Too much had happened at once, and he suddenly felt that he would not get through a good day's work, but would roll on downhill, enervated, ineffectual, dejected.

A true politician is not at the mercy of his years, his feelings, circumstances, but brings at all seasons and times of day an unvarying mechanical efficiency to bear in his actions, his speeches, his battles. Lenin, too, was a remarkably smooth-functioning machine, with inexhaustible drive, but even he experienced one or two days in a year when his drive slackened, leaving him despondent, exhausted, prostrate. On such a day there was nothing for it but to go to bed early and sleep soundly.

Lenin might seem completely in control of his mind and his will, but even he was helpless against these attacks of despair. His certainties, his firm perspective, his proven tactics would suddenly become blurred, indistinct, elusive. The world would turn its stupid grey backside on him.

[90]

And the disease which sat inside him, ever watchful, would suddenly make its sharp corners felt, like a stone in a sack.

He felt it in his temple.

Yes, he had always followed the path of refusal to compromise, to smooth over differences, and by doing so had created a conquering force. He had a prophetic certainty that it would conquer. That it was important to preserve a strictly centralised group, no matter how small, no matter who its members were. The conciliation and unification movements had long ago shown that they spelt ruin for a workers' party. Reconciliation with disarmers? Reconciliation with the *Nashe Slovo* gang? Reconciliation with the Russian Kautskyites? With the swine on the Menshevik Organising Committee? Become a flunkey to social chauvinists? Embrace the village idiots of socialism? No, to hell with that! Give him a tiny minority which was firm, sure, his own!

However, he had gradually found himself almost isolated—betrayed and deserted, while all manner of unifiers and disarmers, Liquidators, and defensists, chauvinists and anti-statists, trashy scribblers and mangy time-serving petit-bourgeois riff-raff had gathered elsewhere in a tight bunch. Sometimes he was reduced to such a small minority that nobody at all remained at his side, as in 1908, the year of loneliness and misery after all his defeats, the most dreadful, the hardest year of his life—also spent in Switzerland. The intellectuals had abandoned the Bolshevik ranks in a panic: so much the better, at least the Party was rid of that petit-bourgeois filth. Amongst those foul caricature-intellectuals Lenin had felt particularly humiliated, insignificant, lost. It filled him with despair to feel himself sinking into their mire. It would have been idiotic to become like them. In every gesture, every word, every oath even, he was determined not to resemble them! ... But it looked as though soon there would be no one at all left. It reached the point when he was desperately clinging to his last ten or fifteen supporters! And simply in order to capture fifteen Bolsheviks, and to deny them to the Machists, he had dashed off to London for material and written a philosophical work three hundred pages long, which no one had ever read; but he had discredited Bogdanov and dislodged him from the leadership! Then throughout the damp autumn those endless chilly walks by Lake Geneva, endlessly assuring themselves that they were not downhearted, and were on the road to victory.

Even with the cleverest of them, like Trotsky or Bukharin, he could find no common language. Of the few who stayed near he could never be sure for more than a month ahead—Zinoviev, for instance, with his weak nerves and his precarious beliefs. (Grishka really had no beliefs at all.)

So that after all no 'victorious force' had been created. His whole career, twenty-three years of uninterrupted militant campaigning against political stupidity, vulgarity, opportunism, his whole grim life under a constant hail of hatred had brought him—what? Only isolation. The force of inertia carried him on along the same line—splitting with one, branding another, dissociating himself from a third—but he wearily realised that he was in a rut, that he could no longer look forward to real success.

The loneliness.

If only there were someone to tell, someone to share it with, so that he would hear his own voice.

What a day ... Everything had come to pieces in his hands. He had sat away the hours to no purpose.

Piles of books. Piles of newspapers ... In his years as an émigré he must have read, scanned, written, stacks, reams, pillars of paper.

When he was young, the scent of imminent revolution was fresh in the air. The path towards it seemed simple and short. He told everyone, again and again, that 'The universal belief in revolution is in itself the beginning of revolution!' A time of happy expectancy.

But these last ten years, since his second emigration, had been filled, stuffed, packed tight with—what? Nothing but paper—envelopes, packets, newspaper wrappers, routine letters, express letters—so much time went on correspondence alone (not to mention the cost of postage, but that came from Party funds). Almost his whole life, half of every day, went into those endless letters. Nobody lived near him, his sympathisers were scattered to the four corners of the earth, and from a distance he had to keep their loyalty, rally, direct, advise, interrogate, beg, and thank them, coordinate resol-

utions (all this with his friends, at the same time never interrupting for a moment the fierce struggle with his enemies),
and nothing was ever more urgent and important than the
letter of the moment (though tomorrow it might seem trivial
and too late, and anyway wrong). You exchanged articles in
outline, proofs, criticisms, corrections, reviews, summaries,
points for discussion, excerpts from the press, newspapers by
the cartload, sometimes issues of your own journals, which
never got beyond the first few numbers—and all the time you
felt that none of it was serious, you couldn't believe, couldn't
imagine, that a social movement could force its way up through
the heaps of paper and newspaper wrappings littering the
earth to the cherished goal of state power—where you would
need qualities quite different from those required during
your dozen years in reading rooms.

He was nearing the end of his forty-seventh year, in an
anxious, monotonous life of nothing but ink on paper, en-
mities and alliances, quarrels and agreements that sprang up
and faded in a day or a week, all enormously important, all
requiring enormous tact and skill, and always with politicians
so much inferior to himself, all of it water into a bottomless
bucket, instantly lost and forgotten, labour in vain. In a life
of constant agitation, twisting and turning, his whole achievement was to fight his way into an impassable rubbish heap.

His arms dangled limply, his back would not straighten, he
looked utterly played out.

Meanwhile his disease grew heavier, fitfully stirring and
nagging inside him. It made not a sound, entered into no
disputes, but no opponent was more powerful.

An evil which now would never leave him.

His vocation—he knew no other—was to change the course
of history, and fulfilment had been denied him.

All his incomparable abilities—appreciated now by everyone in the Party, but he set a truer and still higher value on
them—all his quick-wittedness, his penetration, his grasp, his
uselessly clear understanding of world events, had failed to
bring him not only political victory, but even the position of
a Member of Parliament in toyland, like Grimm. Or that of a
successful lawyer (though he would hate to be a lawyer—he
had lost every case in Samara). Or even that of a journalist.

Just because he had been born in accursed Russia.

It was his habit to carry out even the most laborious and thankless tasks conscientiously, and he was still trying to draft his detailed theses for the education of the Swiss left Zimmerwaldists on the cost of living, on the intolerable economic position of the masses. What should be the maximum salary for office workers and bureaucrats? What to watch for in the Party press? How to rid the Party of Grütlian reformists ...

It was no good. His work would not take shape. The heart had gone out of his routine and left a hollow. His head was beginning to ache. Breathing was difficult. The very sight of his papers sickened him. By tomorrow the attack should be over, but at present he felt such a loathing for everything that he could have lain down and died.

Guiltily deciding not to sit through the working day (not that there was much of it left), he bundled the notebooks and manuscripts into his shopping bag as best he could, slammed the books shut and stacked them, made a neat bundle of the newspapers, put some things on their shelves, and took the rest back to the librarian, treading carefully on the steps so as not to come crashing down with that great pile.

At the door he pulled on his heavy overcoat, carelessly crammed on his bowler hat and shuffled off.

Walking the same way, day in and day out, gave neither legs nor eyes enough to do: it had become automatic.

It was beginning to get dark, and there was some mist, too. Electric lights were already lit in the windows of shops and restaurants.

A huge barrel was being rolled along the narrow side street, and behind it came a wheelbarrow. There was no way round them.

He might easily, very easily, never escape from this cramped, apathetic, petit-bourgeois Switzerland, and end his days here with the Skittle Club.

Through the window of a food shop he could see a nickel-plated machine rhythmically cutting an appetising ham into even slices. The grocer, looking as smug as all Swiss, came out on to the threshold of his establishment, and—whether he knew them or not—presented a *grötzi* free of charge to one passer-by after another. In the third year of war the shops still

[94]

importunately flaunted their plenty, though prices had risen by leaps and bounds because of the submarines. The bourgeoisie could still pick and choose.

Luckily it was too cold to put café tables out on the pavement, or they would be sitting, lounging, sprawling there, goggling at the passers-by, making you step round them with a curse. Through all his years as an émigré Lenin had hated cafés, those smoke-filled dens of logorrhoea, where nine-tenths of the compulsive revolutionary windbags were in permanent session. During the war Zürich had drawn in another dubious crowd from the belligerent neighbours. It was because of them that rents had gone up—this mob of adventurers, shady businessmen, profiteers, draft-dodging students and blethering intellectuals, with their philosophical manifestos and artistic demonstrations, in revolt against they knew not what. And they were all there—in the cafés.

America was no doubt just as well off. The upper stratum of the working class everywhere would sooner get rich than make a revolution. No one, either here or there, needed his dynamite, the sweep of his axe.

He, who was capable of taking the world apart, or blowing it up and then rebuilding it, he had been born too soon, born merely to be a torment to himself.

At its mid-point the Spiegelgasse rose in a hump, riding over a little hill of its own. Leaving home, wherever bound, he half ran downwards. Coming back, wherever he had been, he faced a steep hill. If he had got into his stride, or was in a good humour, he thought nothing of it. But now he could scarcely drag himself along. He seemed not to be walking but scraping the ground with his feet.

The steep, narrow staircase of the old house held the smells of many years. It was dark now, but the lamps had not been lit, and he had to tread cautiously.

Third floor. A polyglot babble. The oppressive smells of the apartment.

His room was like a prison cell for two. Two beds, a table, chairs. An iron stove, with its pipe running through the wall, no fire in it (although it was getting cold enough). An upturned crate that had once held books served as a dresser. (Because they were for ever on the move they bought no furniture.)

[95]

In the last rays of daylight Nadya was still writing at the table. She looked round. She was surprised.

But her eyes were used to the poor light, and when she saw him looking sixty, saw his yellow-grey face, his fixed dead gaze, she did not ask why he was so early.

She had some experience of these attacks, which could prostrate him for days at a time or sometimes for several weeks, when he was burnt out with excitement, or the strain of battle was too much even for his iron body. He had suffered nervous attacks of this sort after 1903, again after *One Step Forward, Two Steps Back*, and more than once after the Fifth Congress.

The bowler hat weighed heavily on his head, the overcoat on his shoulders. It was a struggle to rid himself of them ... Nadya helped him ... He dragged his feet and the shopping bag with books across the room.

He found strength to look at what Nadya had been writing and raised it to his eyes. Their accounts.

A depressingly long column of figures.

Though 1908 had been gloomy and lonely, they had been rolling in money after the Tiflis expropriation. They had an account with the Crédit Lyonnais. To escape from their misery they went to concerts in the evenings, had a holiday in Nice, travelled, lived in hotels, took cabs, rented a Paris apartment for a thousand francs, with a mirror over the fireplace.

He sat down on the bed.

Sat, slumped, shrank. His body sank into the mattress, his head sank on to his shoulders, his neck disappeared: his chin rested on his chest, the back of his head on his spine.

With one hand he held on to the edge of the table in front of him.

One eye was half closed. His mouth was half open. A tough, untidy stubble bristled on his upper lip. His flat-tipped nose was pushed outwards.

He sat like that for one minute, two, three.

'Do you want to lie down? Get undressed?' Nadya asked in her soft, toneless voice.

He was silent.

'Why didn't you come to dinner? Were you working too hard?'

[96]

He nodded with an effort.

'Will you eat now?' But her voice held no promise of carnivorous delights. She just couldn't learn to cook.

How different from Shushenskoye! Then there was always a fire in the stove, pots on it, a roast in the oven (a whole sheep was meat for a week), tubs of pickles, snipe, blackcock, you could bathe in milk if you felt like it. And everything was washed sparkling clean by a little servant girl.

His dome was completely bald now. He had kept only his back hair, and that was thinning. (They themselves had made things worse in 1902: they had grudged the money for a good doctor, and a half-trained Russian medical student prescribed iodine for a rash on his head, which caused his hair to fall out.)

Nadya came closer, gently, timidly stroked his head.

Several long, deep lines furrowed his brow from temple to temple. He sighed loudly, jerkily—more like a man pulling a heavy load than a desk-bound intellectual. Without raising his submerged head, looking not at his wife but straight ahead, over the table, he said wearily, oh so wearily: 'When the war ends we'll go to America.'

She couldn't believe her ears.

'But what about the Zimmerwald Left? The new International?' She stood there, forlorn and frumpish.

Her husband sighed, and answered in a hoarse, flat, weak voice.

'It's obvious which way things are going in Russia. The Tsar will make a deal with the Cadets, and they will form a government. Then we shall have twenty or thirty years of boring, vulgar, bourgeois evolution. With no hope at all for revolutionaries. We shan't live to see the day.'

Very well, then. They would go. She stroked the thin hair on the back of his head.

Suddenly the landlady knocked at the door. Someone had come to see them.

This was all they needed. Whoever it was had chosen a fine time! Without even asking, Nadya went to send the visitor away.

She came back looking bewildered: 'Volodya! It's Sklarz! From Berlin ...'

47

To establish regular secret contact with anyone you please, without ever meeting face to face, you need only set up a chain of regular intermediaries—at least two, but preferably three. Your immediate contact habitually meets twenty people besides yourself, only one of whom is the next link in the chain, and each of these meets twenty others. This gives four hundred possible combinations, and no secret police, no Burtsev, can ever investigate all of them.

The ultra-cautious Lenin had several such lines of communication.

Last summer, after meeting Parvus in Bern, Lenin had released Hanecki to join him in Scandinavia, as director of his agency for trade and revolution. However, the line between Copenhagen and Zürich was down, so they had chosen a new intermediary—Sklarz, a Berlin businessman, who also had shares in Parvus's agency and could travel freely both to Denmark and to Switzerland. They had, however, agreed that when he came to Zürich he should follow the rules about intermediate links and not meet Lenin personally, but use Bronski's lady-friend, Dora Dolina, as his go-between. The fact that he had come to Lenin's lodgings in person meant either a breach of conspiratorial discipline or that something extraordinarily important had happened.

How untimely it was, though! Lenin was exhausted, he could not think clearly, his heartbeat was irregular. But since Sklarz had come, since he had been seen in the street, on the stairs, at the door, it was too late to turn him away.

To greet Sklarz he had not merely to rise from the bed, but with his enfeebled legs to project his hollow body upwards from the bottom of a well. And only then, with his head thrust forward, could he see the energetic little Jew from the south-west.

Very conscious of his own importance he was, too, more expensively dressed than ever, that overcoat, that hat (he had placed it on the one and only desk-cum-dining-table, but still, there was nowhere else), and he was holding a light commercial traveller's case of crocodile skin, or maybe hippopotamus hide.

At least he refrained from the ritual German '*Wie gehts?*' and the forced how-nice-to-see-you smile. He gave a business-like bow, and extended his little hand with dignity. He looked round to see that it was safe, that there were no witnesses. Nadya had gone out, and they were alone.

Why, though, had he come straight there and in person?

Here it came. From a deep inner pocket he produced an envelope.

Expensive pale green paper, with an embossed crest. A fat envelope, a positively obese one.

How shamelessly Parvus displayed his wealth even in little things! This envelope for instance. And on his visits to Zürich he stayed in the most expensive hotel, *Au Bord du Lac*. In Bern he had ambled about a cheap student canteen (dinner 65 rappen) in search of Lenin, puffing the most expensive of cigars.

To think that this was the man with whom in Munich long ago he had started *Iskra*.

All right, he had a letter. But why couldn't he have sent Dora with it? These fleeting visits had to be explained to *comrades*.

Sklarz was surprised to find Herr Ulyanov so ill-educated. That was no way to do *business*. He had been told to destroy the letter before leaving.

His finger went through the motions of striking a match and holding it to the envelope.

Tell me something I don't know! What d'you *think* we do? The letters we've burnt in our time! ...

Right, let's read it. A familiar situation for anyone in the underground. Lenin too would have to ensure that his reply,

[99]

once read, was not preserved. One such scrap of paper could destroy a whole political career.

Neither knife nor scissors were handy. The table was bare. And Nadya was in the kitchen. Tearing off one corner, Lenin inserted his thick index finger and used it as a paper-knife. It left jagged edges like dog's teeth on both sides of the tear. So much for you and your blasted money! How much pleasanter to handle the cheapest of envelopes, to write on the cheapest paper.

He took out the letter. That's why it was so fat, because the paper was even thicker and more opulent than the envelope. And the letter was written in bold capitals, with wide spaces between the lines, and on one side only. Now here was the way not to do *business*. Parvus had forgotten how they used to send *Iskra* into Russia on super-thin paper.

Careful. He must pull himself together, clear his mind. (He had eaten nothing since breakfast time.) Must examine it thoroughly.

Sklarz made himself unobtrusive. He was not troublesomely familiar. Without superfluous talk, without even removing his coat, he went over to the other chair, by the window, leaving, however, his soft grey hat with its elegantly dented crown on the table.

His case too he did not carry over to the window but put down on the floor in the middle of the room.

Polite of him, of course, but on a dull day the best place for reading was over by the window. Sklarz, however, had already occupied the other chair, taken a crumpled illustrated magazine out of his pocket and solemnly unfolded it.

Should he light the lamp? No matches in sight. And Nadya was in the kitchen.

Hallo—the lamp was already lit! It was half hidden by the hat, and its wick was turned right down. Had Nadya lit it? He didn't remember her doing so. Perhaps Sklarz really had struck a match? Could he have ...? Strange.

Thick vellum, crested. Three pages of writing altogether. And a fourth, empty except for one line.

There was nothing special about Parvus's handwriting—it was not noticeably hostile, or imperious, or impertinent, and his signature, 'Dr Helphand', was unrevealing.

[100]

But Parvus's hippopotamus blood spurted from the letter into Lenin's feverish hands, poured into his veins, swirled threateningly in his bloodstream. To prevent it rising above his elbows Lenin dropped the letter on the table as though it were heavy. And flopped down helplessly on his chair.

In twenty years of life and struggle Lenin had experienced every kind of opponent—the haughtily ironical, the sarcastic, the sly, the base, the obstinate, the stalwart, not to mention the spluttering-rhetorical, the quixotic, the effete, the slow-witted, the lachrymose, and other miscellaneous shits. With some of them he had been engaged for many years on end, and not all of them had he sent flying, laid out at a blow, but he had always been aware of the immeasurable superiority given to him by his clear view of the situation, his firm grip, his ability to floor any of them sooner or later.

With this man alone he felt unsure of himself. He did not know whether he could stand up to Parvus as an enemy.

But there had hardly been a day of enmity between them. He was Lenin's natural ally, had offered an alliance many times in his life, insistently, importunately, last year in particular, and now of course was doing it again.

But alliance with Parvus was something which Lenin had hardly ever been able to accept.

He read. His eyes moved along the lines, but somehow his head would not take in the meaning. He was too unwell.

Lenin knew the key to open every Social Democrat in the world, knew the shelf to put him on. But Parvus would not open, would not be put anywhere, and he stood across Lenin's path. Parvus did not fit into any classification. He had never joined either Bolsheviks or Mensheviks (and had even naively attempted to reconcile them). He was a Russian revolutionary, but at nineteen he had come here to Switzerland from Odessa, and immediately chosen the Western path, decided to become a purely Western Socialist and never return to Russia. He had said jokingly: 'I'm looking for a homeland which doesn't cost too much.' All the same, he hadn't found himself a cheap one, but had knocked about Europe for twenty-five years like the Wandering Jew, never acquiring citizenship. It was only this year that he had finally become a German subject—but at too high a price.

His eyes happened to fall on Sklarz's case. It was so heavy, so tightly packed. How did he lug it about? He was so small himself. Why did he need it?

Ah, that was why he didn't seem to be able to read—there wasn't enough light.

Two points at the end were clear enough. Both complaints. One against Bukharin and Pyatakov for their overzealous investigation of the German network in Sweden: these silly little boys must not be allowed to get out of hand. The other against Shlyapnikov: he is very self-willed, refuses to collaborate, goes his own way, although unity is essential to our forces in Petersburg. Write and tell him not to rebuff our representatives.

He called himself Parvus—'little'—but was indisputably big. He had become one of the outstanding publicists in the German Social Democratic Party. His capacity for work was no less than that of Lenin. He had written brilliant Marxist articles, which had delighted Bebel, Kautsky, Liebknecht, Rosa and Lenin himself (how he had lambasted Bernstein!), and had brought the young Trotsky under his sway. Then he had suddenly abandoned his newspapers and the position he had won for himself in the journalistic world, and fled, first to peddle Gorky's plays (and of course rob him), then to sink out of sight altogether. His vision was keen and far-reaching. He had been the first, back in the nineteenth century, to start the fight for the eight-hour day, the first to hail the general strike as the main method of struggle for the proletariat. But it could hardly be said that any proposal of his had started a movement, won him followers: instead of organising them he would detach himself and drop out after a while. He had to be first, and alone, on the road he followed.

Lenin had now read the letter right through, without even noticing whether it was written in Russian or in German. It alternated between the two from sentence to sentence. There were spelling mistakes in the Russian.

Parvus was full of contradictions. A desperate revolutionary, whose hand would not tremble to overthrow an empire; and a passionate trader, whose hand trembled as it counted out money. At one time he went around in broken shoes and shiny trousers, but back in Munich in 1901 he was for ever dinning into Lenin the need to get rich, the immense power of money. Earlier still, back in Odessa, while Alexander III was still on the throne, he had come to the conclusion that the liberation of the Jews in Russia was impossible until Tsardom was overthrown—and immediately lost all interest in Russian affairs, left for the West, returning clandestinely only once, as the companion of a doctor specialising in the study of famine, after which he had published *Starving Russia—A Traveller's Impression*. Then he seemed to have immersed himself completely in German Social Democracy. But at the very beginning of the Japanese war, which was almost ignored in Geneva émigré circles, Parvus had been the first to declare it 'the bloody dawn of great events'.

There was not enough light. He kept screwing up the wick, but it only smouldered and smoked. Of course, it was empty, she'd forgotten to put paraffin in it.

There and then, in 1904, Parvus had prophesied that the industrial states would arrive at a world war. Parvus invariably leapt—or rather with his unwieldy bulk stepped—forward to prophesy earlier, and farther into the future, than anyone else. Sometimes his predictions were very accurate, as, for instance, that industry would destroy national boundaries, or that in future revolution would be the inseparable companion of war, and world revolution of world war. He had, in essence, said before Lenin all that there was to be said about imperialism. Sometimes, though, he talked the wildest nonsense: about Europe as a whole declining and being caught in a vice between America and Russia; about Russia needing only schools and freedom to become a second America. Another time, showing scant respect for the central tenets of Marxism, he had suggested that private industry should not be nationalised, because it might prove unprofitable. Then there was his grotesque fantasy about the possibility of a socialist party winning power and then turning it against the majority of the people, suppressing the trade unions. But, right or wrong, his massive, elephantine figure always moved to a position so distinctive that he half blocked the Social Democratic horizon: though he had never wholly blocked the true path, he had always been so much in Lenin's way that there was no passing him without collision. Never an opponent, always an ally, but one who, if you were not careful, might crush your ribs. He was, uniquely, incomparably, Lenin's rival—and more often than not successful, always ahead. In no way his enemy, always extending the hand of an ally—which it was quite impossible to take.

What did Sklarz want with that case? It looked as big as a pig.

Things might have gone very differently between them, but for 1905. Lenin had taken no part at all in the 1905 revolution, done absolutely nothing—entirely because of Parvus: Parvus with his heavy and unerring tread, never straying for a moment, had filled the road ahead, and robbed Lenin of the will to go forward, of all initiative. At the first thunderclap of Bloody Sunday Parvus had made his proclamation: *Set up a workers' government!* His quick-sightedness, his impetuosity had taken even Lenin's breath away: surely decisions could not be taken so swiftly and simply! And he had retorted in *Vperyod* that Parvus's slogan was premature and dangerous, that they must act in alliance with the petit bourgeoisie, with the revolutionary democrats, because the proletariat was too weak! But Parvus and Trotsky had scrawled a hasty pamphlet and flung it at the Geneva émigrés, Bolsheviks and Mensheviks alike, as a challenge: Russia had no experience of parliaments, the bourgeoisie was feeble, the bureaucratic hierarchy was insignificant, the peasantry was ignorant and unorganised, so that the proletariat had no alternative but to take command of the revolution. Those Social Democrats who recoiled from the initiative of the proletariat would become an insignificant sect.

The whole Geneva emigration, however, had stayed lethargically where it was, as though to make this prophecy come true—all except Trotsky, who rushed to Kiev, then to Finland, drawing closer to make his jump, and Parvus, who charged in at the first signal of the October General Strike, which, once again, he had been prophesying back in the last century. Neither Bolsheviks nor Mensheviks, these two were free from all discipline, and fellows in audacity.

Yes, it was the size of a large pig. Its swelling bulk blocked the whole room. While Sklarz, by the window, seemed surely to have grown smaller?

It's not something I could put on paper, or say at the most restricted conference—but yes, I did make a mistake. Belief in yourself, political maturity, skill in assessing situations, all come to you gradually, with age and experience. (Though Parvus was only three years older.) Yes, I made a mistake, I was shortsighted, and I wasn't bold enough. (But you must not talk like that even to your closest supporter, or you may rob him of his faith in his leader.) Yet how could he help making this mistake? The months had dragged by in that year of turmoil and confusion, everything was in ferment, there was thunder in the air, but real revolution never looked like breaking out. There in Geneva, still unable to travel, he was filled with indignation: couldn't those dolts back home get a move on, couldn't they start a proper revolution? He wrote letter after letter to Russia: energy is what is needed, frantic energy! You've been babbling about bombs for half a year now and haven't made a single one! Let everyone arm himself at once as best he can—with a revolver, a knife, a petrol-soaked rag for starting fires, anything! The combat groups should not wait, there would be no special military training. Let each group begin training itself—if only by beating up policemen! Or by killing a plainclothes man! Or blowing up a police station! Or attacking a bank! These attacks, of course, might degenerate into reckless extremism, but never mind! A few dozen casualties would be handsomely repaid if the Party gained hundreds of experienced fighters!

No, his tired mind would not take in this untimely letter. He read on, understanding nothing.

... It had all seemed so obvious. Knuckledusters! Clubs! Paraffin rags! Spades! Gun-cotton! Barbed wire! Nails (for use against mounted police)! These were all weapons, and good ones! If one Cossack is accidentally cut off from the rest, attack and take his sword from him! Climb to the upper storeys of buildings and rain stones on the troops! Pour boiling water on them! Keep acid up there to pour on the police!

Parvus and Trotsky had done none of these things, but merely arrived in Petersburg, issued a proclamation and convened a new organ of government: the Soviet of Workers' Deputies. They asked no one's permission, and nobody hindered them. A pure workers' government! Already in session! Although they had arrived a mere two weeks before the others, they had taken control of everything. The Chairman of the Soviet was their man of straw, Nosar; its outstanding orator and general favourite, Trotsky; while its inventor, Parvus, directed it from behind the scenes. They had taken over the struggling *Russian Gazette*, which sold at one copeck and was popular in style and tone, and suddenly its sales rose to half a million and the ideas of the two friends flowed out to the masses.

Over by the window, Sklarz had slid lower in his chair, shrunk till he looked like a little bird with its beak buried in a picture paper.

During those last days in Geneva, Lenin's pen had raced to spell out the whole theory and practice of revolution, as he had learnt it in libraries from the best French authorities. He had kept up a rapid fire of letters to Russia. They needed to know how large a combat group should be (from three to thirty people), how to maintain communication with Party military committees, how to choose the best places for street fighting, where to store bombs and stones. They must find out where the arsenals were, and the working routine in government offices and banks, get to know people who could help them to infiltrate and take over ... To begin an attack under favourable conditions was not just the right but the direct duty of any revolutionary. Fighting the Black Hundreds would be a splendid baptism of fire: beat them up, kill them, blow up their headquarters!

He had gone to Russia on the heels of his last letter, and found things there very different. No combat groups were being formed, no one was laying in acid, bombs or stones. He found instead that even the bourgeois came to listen to the Soviet, with Trotsky on the platform spinning and whirling and coruscating like a Catherine wheel. He and Parvus, as though born for a life in the public eye, dazzled all Petersburg—the editorial offices, the political salons—they were invited everywhere and received with applause. There was even a group of people calling themselves 'Parvusites'. Instead of sneaking round corners with paraffin-soaked rags, Parvus was preparing a collected edition of his works, Parvus was buying up tickets for satirical shows and distributing them to friends. A fine revolution, if in the evening there was no measured tread of patrols on deserted pavements, and theatre doors were open wide ...

He couldn't run over to the window—the swollen black case stood big as a trunk in the way. And there was no strength in his legs.

In that revolution Lenin had been bruised by Parvus, as though he had stood too near an elephant. He had sat at meetings of the Soviet, listening to the heroes of the day with his head in his hands. Parvus's slogans, repeated and read out over and over again, were perfectly correct: after the victory of the revolution the proletariat *must not let go of its weapons, but prepare for civil war! It must regard its liberal allies as enemies!* Excellent slogans, and he himself was left with nothing to say from the platform of the Soviet. Everything was going almost as it should, indeed so well that there was no room for the Bolshevik leader. His whole life had been adjusted to the demands of the underground, and his legs would not carry him up into the broad daylight. Lenin had not gone to Moscow when the rising began there, no longer caring whether the insurgents were following his instructions from Geneva or someone else's. His self-confidence had failed him, and he had skulked through the revolution in a daze, sitting it out in Kuokkala, forty miles from Petersburg—and over the Finnish border where he was safe from arrest—while Krupskaya travelled to the capital every day to gather news. He couldn't understand it himself: all his life he had done nothing but prepare for revolution, and when it came his strength had ebbed and deserted him.

Next, from the shadows—he always tried to operate behind the scenes, not to get in front of cameras, not to feed biographers—Parvus had fathered an anonymous resolution on the Soviet, its Financial Manifesto. What looked like a set of uncouth and primitive demands from the illiterate masses was really the programme of a clever and experienced financier striking at the foundations of the hated Russian state, to bring it down in ruins at a single blow. Give Parvus his due—it was a superb, a most instructive revolutionary document. (But the government, too, had seen its significance and arrested the whole Petersburg Soviet on the following day. As it happened, Parvus was not present, and had survived to set up a second Soviet at once, with a different membership. They came to arrest this new body, and again Parvus escaped.)

There was no paraffin in the lamp, yet it had been burning for an hour, giving no less light than before.

It took years for the ribs dented by Parvus to straighten out again, for Lenin to regain his assurance that he, too, was of some use in the world. What had helped most was seeing Parvus's mistakes and his failures, seeing this hippopotamus, this elephant, crashing blindly through the thickets, his hide punctured by broken branches, seeing him stumble into holes in his headlong charge. He had been expelled from the Party for misappropriation of funds, become a ruthless profiteer, boozed with his bosomy blondes in public—and ended by openly supporting German imperialism: he had expressed his views frankly in print and in speeches, and defiantly left for Berlin.

The hat behind the lamp shifted and revealed its satin lining.

No, it was lying quietly, just as Sklarz had left it.

Rumours had already reached Lenin, through Christo Rakovsky in Roumania and David Ryazanov in Vienna, that Parvus was coming to him with *interesting proposals*—so careless was he about covering his tracks. But Parvus's reputation as an undisguised ally of the Kaiser had preceded him, while he was boozing in Zürich on the way. They were all used to poverty, year in and year out, and suddenly their former comrade turned up in the role of an Oriental pasha, something of a shock to the émigré mind, but also a source of largesse. When he had found Lenin in the canteen at Bern, wedged his enormous belly behind the table, and loudly declared in the presence of a dozen comrades that they must have a talk, Lenin, without hesitation, without even thinking about it, had replied with a curt rebuff. He had come from warring Germany to chat like a peacetime tourist, had he? (Lenin was no less eager for a talk!) Well then, Lenin must request him to *take himself away again*! (It was the only possible thing to do!)

The handle of the big case flopped to one side.

But they had to see each other, of course! They couldn't keep putting things on paper, in case one of their letters fell into the hands of enemies. So Lenin whispered to Siefeldt, who ran after the fat man and gave him the address. (Lenin told Siefeldt afterwards that he had sent the shark away unfed.) And in the Ulyanovs' spartan room the broad-beamed Parvus, with diamond studs in his dazzlingly displayed cuffs, had with some difficulty seated himself on the bed next to Lenin, lolling against him and pushing him towards the pillow and the iron bed-rail.

Snap! The suitcase had finally burst open ... and freeing his elbows, straightening his back, he unfolded, rose to his full height and girth, in his dark-blue three-piece suit, with his diamond cuff-links, and, stretching his cramped legs, he came one step, two steps closer.

There he stood, life-size, in the flesh, with his ungovernable belly, the elongated dome of his head, the fleshy bulldog features, the little imperial—looking at Lenin with pale watchful eyes. Amicably, as ever.

True, true—they should have had a talk long ago. They had always talked in hasty snatches, been out of touch or at logger-heads, and it was so difficult for them to meet: with enemies, and friends too, on the watch. The utmost secrecy was necessary! But now that he had found his way here, this was better than writing letters. The critical moment for an eye-to-eye talk had arrived.

'Izrail Lazarevich! You surprise me! Whatever has become of your remarkable intelligence? Why are you so indiscreet? Why have you put yourself in such a vulnerable position? You yourself are making it quite impossible for us to collaborate.'

No 'hallo', no proffered hand (and it was just as well, because Lenin lacked the strength to rise and greet him, his hand seemed paralysed, and a 'hallo' would have stuck in his throat), Parvus simply slumped, not of course on the chair, but on the bed again, his unwieldy bulk sprawling against Lenin and squeezing him into the corner.

Training his protuberant, colourless eyes directly on his companion's face, he spoke with casual irony, teasing a friend, not addressing an audience.

'I'm surprised, too, Vladimir Ilyich. Have you still nothing to occupy you but agitation and protests? What's the use of all this childish noise-making? All these so-called conferences —thirty silly women in the Volkshaus one day, a dozen deserters the next?'

He unceremoniously pushed Lenin farther along the bed, and his unhealthily enlarged head loomed close.

'Since when have you sided with those who want to change the world with a broad-nibbed pen? What children all these Socialists are, with their eternal indignation! But you mustn't be like them! If you want serious *action* should you really be hiding in holes and corners, not letting it be seen where your sympathies lie in this war?'

Although speech was still difficult his head was clearer, as though he had drunk strong tea. Even without words they understood each other perfectly.

Well, of course, this was no pathetic Kautsky, demonstrating 'for peace' and refusing to meddle with the war.

'Neither of us looks at war like a sister of mercy. Casualties, bloodshed, suffering are inevitable. What matters is the outcome.'

Well, of course, Parvus was utterly right. If Russia was to be shattered, Germany must be victorious, and they must seek German support. So far, so good. But Parvus overstepped the mark. Not for the first time.

'Izrail Lazarevich, if a Socialist has one real asset, it is his honour. If we lose our honour, we lose everything. Between ourselves, the closeness of our positions naturally makes us allies. And of course we shall need each other and help each other very much. But nowadays you are politically in such bad odour ... It would take just one Burtsev to ruin everything. So we shall have to make a show of disagreement, attack each other in the press. Not a full-time controversy of course ... just occasionally ... so if I should call you ...' (Even face to face Lenin never moderated his language: the more harshly you speak, the better you understand each other.) 'If I should call you, for instance ... Hindenburg's morally degenerate toady ... that renegade, that filthy lackey ... you can see for yourself that you leave me no alternative ...'

'By all means, it doesn't matter a bit.' A bitter smile

creased Parvus's puffy face. 'In Berlin last spring I was given a million marks, some of which I sent at once to Rakovsky, to Trotsky and Martov, and to you here in Switzerland—did you get it? What? You weren't aware of it? Do please check with your treasurer, maybe he's pocketed it ... Trotsky took the money ... although he'd already publicly disowned me. "Falstaff in politics" he called me ... He's written my obituary before I'm dead[1]. I say nothing. It's all right, of course, I understand.'

A fixed, glassy stare from under the faint raised brows.

Parvus and Trotsky had parted company earlier over the theory of permanent revolution. He had loved Trotsky like a younger brother.

But now he had high hopes of Lenin, and leaned on him with all his podgy immensity, forcing him farther and farther along the bed, until he was sitting on the pillow and could feel the bedhead against his elbow.

'Aren't you afraid that mere slogans will be a dead letter without money? With money in your hands, power will be yours! How else will you seize power? That's the unpleasant question. And, if you don't mind me saying so, I seem to remember you in 1904 taking what looked very much like Japanese money for the Third Congress and for Vperyod. That was all right, wasn't it? And now I'm Hindenburg's lackey, am I?' He did his best to laugh.

It was just like last time. Perhaps it *was* last time? ... In Bern, in the room he had rented from a housewife? Or was he in his room in the Zürich cobbler's house? Or not in a room at all? He seemed to be hearing it all for the second time. No table, no Sklarz. Just a massive Swiss iron bed, with the two of them upon it, great men both, floating above a world pregnant with revolution, a world which looked up to them expectantly, as they sat with their legs dangling, and the bed sped again round its dark orbit. There was just enough light from some invisible source for him to see his companion, just enough sound for him to hear.

'Never mind ... It's all right ... I understand.'

Parvus despised the world. That world, far below, under the bed.

'As I see it, if you want to *convert the war into a civil war,* one ally is as good as another. At present you have—*how much*?' He was being funny. 'I won't ask you, it isn't done. But I have—not for myself, but for the *Cause*—well, I got a million last spring, and I shall get another five million this summer. And there's plenty more to come. What do you say to that?'

He and Parvus alike had always despised the emigration for its unreality, its ineffectualness, its drivelling intellectualism—it was all talk, nothing but talk. But money was something more serious. Oh, yes.

Lenin was sickened by his self-assurance, but fascinated by the reality of his power.

Parvus opened his pale eyes wide, and smacked his lips under the straggly moustache.

'The Plan! I've produced a master plan. I've submitted it to the German government. And, let me tell you, I can get as much as twenty million to carry it out. Only I have reserved the most important place in my plan for *you*. What are you ...'

A gust of marsh breath, right in his face.

'... going to do? ... Go on waiting? ... Well, I ...'

His dome was no smaller than Lenin's, half his face was bare brow, half his head a thinly covered backward slope. Ruthless, inhuman intelligence in his eyes, as he spoke.

'I AM SETTING THE DATE OF THE RUSSIAN REVOLUTION FOR THE NINTH OF JANUARY[2] NEXT YEAR!'

48

How are great yet simple plans born? Ideas are conceived and grow in the subconscious before you have any definite purpose for them. Then suddenly elements long familiar perhaps to others as well as yourself spontaneously converge, and it is in your head that they fuse to form a single plan, a plan so clear and simple that you wonder why no one has arrived at it before.

Why had it not taken shape earlier in the minds of the German General Staff, who should have been the first to think of it?

True, they did not understand Russia very well. Since the autumn of 1914 and the battle on the Marne, they had realised that their plans for a quick victory had failed, but until the autumn of 1915 they had gone on hoping for a separate peace with Russia, busily putting out feelers, never imagining that the Romanovs would rebuff them. This was what had distracted them.

Parvus, insulated from the main events, stranded in bronze and blue Constantinople, in possession of the riches he had so desired, and with them every imaginable carnal delight—the East knows how to sate the male soul and slake male desire—remote from the great battle ('in the socialist army of reserve', as Trotsky had advised), and in no danger of experiencing its consequences—had never, even at his most jaded and dissipated, abandoned the quest which had begun in his distant youth on the diagonally opposite shore of the Black Sea.

He had not abandoned it when, earlier, he went to the

Balkans, where he was more widely read than Marx and Engels. He had not forgotten it when he was earning his bread in the low dives of Constantinople and rallying the dockside beggars for a May Day demonstration. He had been still more mindful of it when he rose in the world under the Young Turks and converted his financial genius from an axe hacking at the Russian trunk to a gardener's spade mulching the Turkish sapling. The millions which so mysteriously flooded in on him and carried him along on their tide had not dazed him or made him forgetful. He did not forget while he was founding banks and trading with mother Odessa or stepmother Germany. The shot at Sarajevo had stung him like the lash of a whip. Parvus had a seismographic sense of movement in the depths, he knew at once that the rock-bed was slipping! That the stupid old bear would be trapped! At last it had come, the Great War, the World War! He had long foretold it, described it, evoked it—the most powerful locomotive of history! The first chariot of socialism! While socialist parties all over Europe were in an uproar over war credits Parvus made not a single speech or published a single line. He wasted no time, there was not a minute to lose, but scurried about his secret passages, trying to persuade Turkey's rulers that only by siding with Germany could their country break loose from the endless chain of 'capitulations'. He hurried up the delivery of equipment and spare parts for Turkish railways and flour mills, to supply the towns with grain and put Turkey in a position not only to declare war in the autumn but to begin serious military operations in the Caucasus as soon as possible. (He was working just as busily on Bulgaria, which he also succeeded in preparing for war.) Only after these essential feats could Parvus allow himself to settle back comfortably into his favourite and long neglected occupation—propaganda: this time in the Balkan press, with the slogan 'FOR DEMOCRACY! AGAINST TSARISM!'

This needed explanation, careful argument, to convince as many as possible—and the sparks rained merrily from his unblunted pen. Why ask who bears the 'war guilt', 'who attacked first', when world imperialism has been preparing for this fight for decades—somebody had to attack first, and it might have been anyone. Don't look for meaningless

[114]

'causes' but think like Socialists: how are we, the world proletariat, to make use of the war, or in other words, on which side should we fight? Germany has the most powerful Social Democratic party in the world, Germany is the strong-hold of socialism, and so for Germany this is a war of self-defence. If socialism is smashed in Germany it will be defeated everywhere. The road to the victory of world social-ism lies through the reinforcement of German military power, while the fact that Tsarism is on the same side as the Entente reveals even more clearly where the true enemies of socialism are: thus, the victory of the Entente would bring a new age of oppression to the whole world. So workers' parties through-out the world must fight *against Russian Tsarism*. Advising the proletariat to adopt neutrality (as Trotsky does) means opting out from history, it is revolutionary cretinism. So the object of world socialism is the crushing defeat of Russia and a revolution in that country! Unless Russia is decentral-ised and democratised the whole world is in danger. And since Germany bears the main burden of the struggle against Muscovite imperialism, the revolutionary movement there must be suspended for the time being. At a later stage victory in war will bring class victories for the proletariat. THE VICTORY OF GERMANY IS THE VICTORY OF SOCIALISM!

The first to come and consult Parvus in response to this publication were the 'League for the Liberation of the Ukraine', based in Vienna (there were old acquaintances from *Iskra* days among them), then the Armenian and Georgian nationalists. His door in Constantinople was open to all en-gaged in fighting Russia.

Thus Parvus's dynamism magnetically attracted people of different experience, and from this explosive combination of socialist and nationalist interests the Plan was born. Until then socialist programmes had always babbled about auton-omy. But no! Only the disruption and dismemberment of Russia could bring down absolutism, and give the nations freedom and socialism simultaneously.

While the first Ukrainian and Caucasian expeditionary groups were collapsing (in their haste they had recruited all sorts of braggarts and adventurers, the conspiratorial scheme was suddenly made public in the émigré press, and Enver

Pasha stopped the expeditions), the magnetic combination of iron components into a single plan was gradually perfected in Parvus's grotesquely capacious head. Just as engineers like triangular supports because of their resistance to deformation, so Parvus found that the nationalist and socialist components lacked a third partner—the German government. The aims of all three very closely coincided!

Parvus's past life might have been deliberately designed for the faultless creation of this Plan. It now only remained for him—happy amalgam of theorist, operator and politician that he was—to formulate the Plan point by point in December 1914, give the German Ambassador an inkling of it in January, receive a hospitable summons to Berlin, and stagger the high-ups at a personal interview in the ministry. In nineteen years that country had not even tossed him a set of naturalisation papers, it had closed down all his journals, hounded him from city to city, contemplated handing him over to the Russian secret police, and now the highest in the government gazed deferentially into his prophetic eyes. In March 1915, on presentation of a definitive and detailed memorandum, he received his first advance of a million marks.

The Plan was to concentrate all their potential, all their forces, all their resources under a single command, to control from a single headquarters the activities of the Central Powers, the Russian revolutionaries, and the border peoples. (He knew the strength of this bull, and had chosen his axe to match it.)

No uncoordinated, private improvisations. The Plan was insistent that German victory could never be final without a revolution in Russia: until it was carved up Russia would remain an unabated menace. The Russian fortress, however, could not be destroyed by any one of these forces in isolation, but only by a single-minded alliance of all three. There must be a simultaneous explosion of social revolution and national revolution, with German financial and material support. Experience of the 1905 revolution—and the author should know! What induced the Imperial government to treat their adviser seriously was that he was no mere footloose businessman but the father of the first revolution—made it clear that all the symptoms were recurring, that all the conditions for revolution were still in being, and that it would indeed proceed more quickly in conditions of world war, but only if it were given a skilful push, only if the catastrophe were speeded up by action from outside. The Putilov, Obukhov and Baltic works in Petersburg and the shipyards at Nikolaev would be made ready to serve as centres of *social* revolution (the author had particularly strong links with Southern Russia). The date was set—one which already had a painful significance in Russia, the anniversary of Bloody Sunday—in the first place for a one-day strike in memory of the victims, and a single street demonstration in favour of the eight-hour day and a democratic republic. But when the police began to disperse the demonstrators they would resist, and if there was the slightest bloodshed—the flame would race along all the fuses! The one-day strikes would merge into a general strike 'for freedom and peace'. Leaflets would be distributed in the biggest factories—and weapons would be ready for use in Petersburg and Moscow. Within twenty-four hours a hundred thousand men would be set in motion. The railwaymen (also primed in advance) would join them, and all traffic would be halted on the Petersburg–Moscow, Petersburg–Warsaw, Moscow–Warsaw, and South-Western lines. To ensure a total and simultaneous stoppage, several bridges would be blown up, as in 1905. Bridges should also be blown up at several points along the Trans-Siberian trunk line, and a team of skilled agents should be dispatched for this purpose. Siberia was dealt with in a separate section of the Plan. The forces stationed there were extremely weak, and the towns, under the influence of political exiles, were in a revolutionary mood. This made it easier to organise sabotage, and once the disorders began the exiles should be transferred *en masse* to Petersburg, so as to inject into the capital thousands of practised agitators, and bring millions of conscripts within range of propaganda. Propaganda would be carried on by the whole Russian left-wing press, and reinforced by a flood of defeatist émigré leaflets. (It would be easy enough to get them printed in bulk in Switzerland, for instance.) Any publication which sapped the Russian will to resist and pointed to social revolution as the way out of the war would be useful. The main target for propaganda would be the army in the field. (Parvus also envisaged a mutiny in the Black Sea fleet. He had established links with the Odessa sailors on his way through Bulgaria long ago. He had always strongly suspected that the Japanese were responsible for the *Potemkin* mutiny.) Experienced agents would also be sent to fire the Baku oil-wells, which presented no difficulty since they were so inadequately guarded. The pace of social revolution must be further accelerated by financial means: counterfeit roubles would be showered on the Russian population from German planes, while bank notes with identical serial numbers would be put into simultaneous circulation abroad, in Petersburg and in Moscow, to undermine the exchange rate of the rouble and create panic in the capitals.

For all their Clausewitzes, Elder Moltkes and Younger Moltkes, for all their self-confident strategy, for all the haughty precision of their staff work, limited Prussian brains had never risen to a concept of such grandeur!

Germany had never had such an adviser on Russia and its weaknesses. (So much so that even now she did not fully appreciate him.)

And that is by no means all! The *national* revolutions will begin simultaneously. Our most important lever is the Ukrainian movement. Without the Ukraine to buttress it the Russian edifice will soon topple over. The Ukrainian movement will spread to the Kuban Cossacks, and the Don Cossacks too may prove shaky. There will naturally be collaboration with the Finns, who are the most mature of the Empire's peoples and almost free already. It will be easy to send weapons to them, and through them to Russia. Poland is always just five minutes away from rebellion against Russia and only awaits the signal. With Poland and Finland in revolt the Baltic lands in between them will be stirred to action. (In another version of the Plan Parvus provided for the voluntary union of the Baltic provinces with Germany.) The Georgian and Armenian nationalists are already actively collaborating with the governments of the Central Powers and in their pay. The Caucasus is fragmented and will be more difficult to rouse, but with Turkey's help, by means of Moslem agitation, we'll stir them up to a Gazavat, a holy war. And with that all around them the Terek Cossacks will scarcely want

[118]

to lay down their lives for the Tsar rather than break away themselves.

So the highly centralised Russian Empire will collapse never to rise again! Internal struggles will shake Russia to its foundations! Peasants will start taking the land from its owners. Soldiers will desert the trenches in droves to make sure of their share when the land is divided up. (They would mutiny against their officers, shoot all the generals! But this part of the prospect must be tactfully concealed—it might stir unpleasant forebodings in Prussian breasts.)

Wait a bit, though (catching his breath), that's not all! That's not the end of it! Shaken by destructive propaganda within, Russia must simultaneously be besieged by a hostile world press. An anti-Tsarist campaign will be mounted by socialist newspapers in various countries, and the excitement of Tsar-baiting will spread to their neighbours on the right, the liberals—that is to say, to the dominant section of the press throughout the world. A newspaper crusade against the Tsar! In this connection it is particularly important to capture public opinion in the United States. And by exposing Tsarism we shall simultaneously unmask and undermine the whole Entente!

This then was Parvus's proposal to Germany: instead of the desperate butchery of infantry and artillery warfare—a single injection of German money, and, with no German losses, the most populous member of the Entente would be torn away in the space of a few months! Not surprisingly, the German government jumped at the programme!

Parvus, indeed, had never doubted that they would. He was, however, anxious about the reaction of others in Berlin: the Socialists. How would his project be received by his step-mother party? His ideas had always been too deep for use in their mass agitation, and too far in advance of his time to seem practical even to the leaders of the party in which he had been knocking his head against the wall and wasting his ideas for nineteen years now, without ever holding office or voting rights at a single congress. He had, for a short time, been one of its heroes—when he had just returned from Siberia and everyone was devouring his memoirs, *In the Russian Bastille*. Then he had dirtied his hands in the unfortunate Gorky affair, a secret party commission had condemned him to expulsion, and five years of excommunication had still not wiped out the stain. Worst of all, though, was his legendary and inexplicable rise to riches in a single year—something people in general, and democratic Socialists in particular, are too narrow-minded to forgive. (It was a psychological puzzle: had his wealth been inherited no one would ever have reproached him with it.) His wealth alone was bound to make them hate and reject him, but they had also found nobler grounds for indignation: he had become a henchman of imperialism! Klara and Liebknecht he could understand, but Rosa! Rosa, with whom he had once been on intimate terms (though even then she had been ashamed of him—because of his appearance perhaps—and always concealed their relationship), Rosa too had shown him the door. In the meantime, Bebel had died, Kautsky and Bernstein had split up and impaired their authority, and a complacent new leadership was looking for weaknesses in the position of this Socialist drifter. How, they asked, would the Prussian government behave after victory? Why should revolution in Russia make Prussia look more tolerantly and kindly on socialism? Would it not see its chance to put the lid on English and French democracy?

Of course, there was some truth in their objections, there were grounds for doubt—but there was nothing here of that bold and perfect vision that can shake and remake a world! No one, or hardly anyone, in Europe could lift himself far enough out of his rut to see that *the destruction of Russia now held the key to the future history of the world*! All else was secondary.

Meanwhile the Socialists of the Entente were mounting a campaign to expose Parvus.

The bitterness of their reproaches poisoned the pleasure that his success should have given him, although the majority of European Socialists were neither well versed in theory nor effective in practice. They could not rise to a general view of the terrain, they lacked the skill to match each turn of events with a tactical twist. They were merely bureaucrats of socialism, stuck fast, confined in the corridors of dogma: they no longer moved, no longer crawled along these corridors, but lay down in them, not even daring to imagine a turning ahead. When Parvus first openly called on them to help Germany he had filled them with maidenly horror. How nice it would be for them to sit the war out as innocent neutrals, salving their consciences with moral indignation, both against war and against those who dared to interfere with it.

But the decisive role belonged to the Russian Socialists, and they were the subject of careful analysis in the Plan as submitted to the German government. They were broken up into scattered groups, and thus impotent—but not one of these groups must be neglected, each must be turned to use. It was therefore necessary to lead them along the road to unity—arrange a unification congress, for which Geneva would be a suitable venue. Some groups, such as the Bund, the Spilka, the Poles, the Finns, would certainly support the Plan. But unity could not be achieved without reconciling Bolsheviks and Mensheviks. And that would depend entirely on the Bolshevik leader, who was at present in Switzerland.

Various difficulties might arise, and it might even turn out that some Russian Socialists were patriots and did not want to see the Russian Empire dismembered. But there were grounds for confidence: these beggarly émigrés had been short of money for decades, both for everyday needs—they had never known where their next meal was coming from, and they were quite incapable of earning a living—and for their incessant journeys and congresses, and their endless scribbling of pamphlets and articles. They would not be able to resist if a fat purse were held out to them. Why, even the strong, legal Western parties and trade unions rose readily to offers of financial help, for their workers, of course, but still— who in this world does not want to eat well, be better dressed, live in a warmer and more spacious house? (Discreet help for leaders who live modestly also greatly reinforces our friendship with them.) How then can the émigrés refuse?

On his way to Switzerland Parvus had anticipated with particular relish a successful meeting with Lenin. Their collaboration in Munich was a thing of the past, they had not seen each other in years, but Parvus's keen eye had never lost sight of this unique Socialist, who had no equal in all Europe: uninhibited, free from prejudice and squeamishness, ready in

[121]

any new situation to adopt whatever methods promised success. The only hard-faced realist, never carried away by illusions, the greatest realist in the socialist movement except for Parvus himself. All that Lenin lacked was breadth. The savage, intolerant narrowness of the born schismatic harnessed his tremendous energy to futilities—fragmenting this group, dissociating himself from that, yapping at intruders, petty bickering, dogfights, needling newspaper articles— wasted his strength in meaningless struggles, with nothing to show except mounds of scribbled paper. This schismatic narrowness doomed him to sterility in Europe, left him no future except in Russia—but also made him indispensable for any activity there. Indispensable now!

Now that Parvus's younger comrade-in-arms, Trotsky, whom he had so dearly loved, had abdicated once and for all, now that Trotsky's vitality and clarity of vision had deserted him—the cold gleam of Lenin's star summoned him irresistibly to Switzerland. Quite spontaneously, Lenin had been saying the same things; that it did not matter who was the aggressor, that Tsarism was the stronghold of reaction, and must be shattered first, that ... Nuances in parenthetic remarks, buried in subsidiary clauses and noticed by hardly anyone else, told Parvus that Lenin had not changed, that he was still as demanding in some matters and as undemanding in others as he had always been, that he would not jib at an alliance with the Kaiser or the devil himself if it helped to crush the Tsar. Parvus had therefore warned him in advance to expect interesting proposals: there was no reason to doubt that an alliance would be concluded. The only trouble was those miserable artificial disagreements with the Mensheviks, about which Lenin was particularly stupid and stubborn. Still, a million marks in subsidies should carry some weight. In his memorandum to the German government Parvus had specifically mentioned Lenin, with his underground organisation throughout Russia, as his main support. With Lenin at his right hand, as Trotsky had been in the other revolution, success was assured.

Sure of success, Parvus had travelled to Bern, paced the student canteen, cigar in mouth, and been surprised at first by Lenin's resounding refusal, but quickly appreciated the other's prudence and tact. Sitting on the cramped bed, he had used his bulk to squeeze the lightweight Lenin into a corner.

'But you must have capital! What will you use to seize power? That's the unpleasant question.'

Tha-a-a-at was something Lenin understood very well! That bare ideas will get you no further forward, that you cannot make a revolution without power, that in our time the primary source of power is money, and that all other forms of power—organisation, weapons, people capable of using those weapons to kill—are begotten of money. All very true, nobody would deny it!

With his incomparable mental agility which made reflection unnecessary, his expression changing from one moment to the next—Parvus even glimpsed a smiling hint of complicity—Lenin coolly shifted his ground and answered in his burring voice.

'Why unpleasant? When people take the right Party attitude to money the Party is pleased. It is displeased when money is turned into a weapon *against* the Party.'

'That's all very well, but you can't help giving yourself away.' Parvus spoke with friendly irony. 'The *Social Democrat* costs something to publish. Or maybe—' his Falstaffian belly shook with laughter—'maybe you tell the Swiss tax inspectors that on the contrary you live on your fees from the *Social Democrat*?'

Lenin often wore a mocking look, but very rarely smiled: instead he screwed up his naturally deep-set eyes, hiding them completely. He chose his words carefully.

'Philanthropic donations keep coming from somewhere. It is perfectly correct from the Party's point of view to accept charity—why shouldn't it be?'

(Money in fact was not so short as all that, they could all have lived more easily if they were as shameless as some of those through whose hands it flowed. Bagotsky threw money about in a scandalous fashion, and nobody would think of checking the Austrian money held by Weiss. It was no good putting pressure on them, that might spoil everything. But it ran through their hands like water.)

Parvus's eye found no comfort anywhere—not in Lenin's frayed jacket, nor in his patched collar, nor in the worn-out table-cloth, nor in the bare room, where two boxes, one on top of the other, did duty as a bookcase. But Parvus felt not in the least apologetic about his diamonds, his cheviot coat, his English shoes: this parade of poverty on Lenin's part was all a game, the Party line, intended to set the tone and serve as an example of a 'leader beyond reproach'. In this adopted role, faithfully performed for years on end, could be seen the narrowness and drabness of his mind. But this could be corrected, and even Lenin could be taught to cut a figure.

(But no! No! A deep antipathy, an instinctive protest made Lenin *spontaneously* always shut himself off from any luxury, however easily available. To have sufficient was a different matter, that was reasonable. But luxury was the beginning of degeneracy, and Parvus had been caught that way. Let the money pour in by the million, but for the revolution, while he himself kept within the limits of the necessary, counting every rappen and proud of it. It was not at all a pose, and only partly by way of example to those whom he could not coerce.)

Glancing swiftly sideways and upwards, Lenin spoke without hostility or resentment.

'Izrail Lazarevich! Your undying faith in the omnipotence of money is what has let you down. You know what I mean.'

(If your expenses are small it is like being in a locked room, your secrets are safe: nothing leaks, you feel secure, you will never recklessly let yourself go, all is firm and fast. But riches are like uncontrolled chatter. No! There must be discipline in this as in everything. Only self-limitation makes it possible to build up a powerful drive. Thus, although he could afford to put down the 1,200 francs security for permission to reside in Switzerland—which was essential to his safety and his work—he just wouldn't pay, but chose instead to make a fuss, write letters, declare himself destitute, beg for a discretionary reduction to one tenth, waste precious time calling on the chief of police, sometimes accompanied by Karl Moor, who had a well-stuffed wallet in his pocket, so that he need only hold his hand out and extract a banknote from him. When he was finally granted a reduction to three hundred, he still paid only a hundred, and went on haggling. Then when he moved to Zürich he wouldn't pay at all, but wrote begging to be excused, and corresponded with Bern, requesting the transfer of his hundred francs to his present canton. Lenin was good at this: good at lacing himself tight: only tight-laced did he breathe freely.)

The purpose of any conversation is to understand your partner fully without unnecessarily exposing yourself.

With a sharp, probing look and a sceptical grin, he asked: 'Why do you need wealth of your own? Come on, tell me! Explain yourself.'

A child's question. One of those 'whys' which it is ridiculous to answer. So that every wish can become reality, of course. The feeling it gives you is probably like that which a physical giant gets from the play of his muscles. Affirmation of his rights on earth. The meaning of life. Parvus sighed.

'It's only human to like being rich. Surely you understand, Vladimir Ilyich?'

But looking at that bald brow, at the ageing skin of his temples, at the too sharp, too tense vee of his eyebrows, Parvus suddenly suspected that Lenin really didn't understand, that he wasn't pretending. His all-penetrating gaze only saw what was in front of him.

Parvus spoke again, more gently.

'How shall I put it?... It's pleasant to have perfect sight or perfect hearing, and it's just the same with wealth ...'

But was his decision to get rich really the result of conscious thought, of a theoretical belief? No, it was an innate necessity, and his commercial impulses, his flair for *Geschäft*, his reluctance to let slip any profit which loomed in his field of vision, were not a matter of plans and programmes, but almost a biological function which proceeded almost unconsciously yet unerringly. It was a matter of instinct with him always to feel the movement of economic life around him, the emergence of disproportions, imbalances, gaps which begged him, cried out to him to insert his hand and extract a profit. This was so much part of his innermost nature that he conducted his multifarious business transactions, which by now were scattered over ten European countries, without a single ledger, keeping all the figures in his head.

(Lenin of course accepted that in the final analysis personal wealth was a *Privatsache*, a private matter. But his eyes bored into Parvus, probing for an answer: was he or was he not a Socialist? That was the problem. Twenty-five years of socialist journalism—but was he a Socialist? ...)

Parvus hurriedly returned to the point.

'Let me tell you—wealth means *power*. Power is what the proletariat aspires to, isn't it? I was a big name for twenty-five years, better known than you, and it did nothing for me. But all roads are open to the wealthy. Take these negotiations, for instance. What government would believe a beggar and give him millions for a project? Whereas a rich man obviously won't take it for himself, he has his own millions.'

The inordinately large, asymmetrical head tilted trustfully, and the colourless, philosophical eyes gazed amicably and peaceably at Lenin.

'Don't miss your chance, Vladimir Ilyich. Life offers you opportunities like this only once.'

Yes, this he understood. At the beginning of the war he had enjoyed an unaccustomed luxury; a friendly eagle (Austrian in this case) had taken him on its wing and carried him in a twinkling where it was bidden. (There was no passenger transport to Switzerland, and the Ulyanovs had travelled in a troop train.) Lenin had discovered with a thrill that it might be better not to hover helplessly, to drift on a sea of words and ideas, but to abandon once and for all his helpless and uneasy émigré existence, and cling instead to real material forces, move in unison with them. As always, and in everything, Parvus had been ahead of him.

'To make a revolution takes a lot of money,' Parvus insisted, his friendly shoulder pressing against Lenin. 'But to hold on to power when you get there will take even more.'

An odd way of putting it, but strikingly true.

The innermost nucleus of Parvus's thought was undoubtedly correct.

But the innermost nucleus of Lenin's thought was also undoubtedly correct.

'Just think, if only we combined your capacities with mine. And with such powerful support! With your incomparable talent for revolution. How much longer do you want to go on kicking your heels in these émigré holes? How much longer can you go on waiting for a revolution somewhere ahead—

and refusing to recognise it when it arrives and grabs you by the shoulder? ...'

Oh dear, no! Nothing, neither shared joy, nor fervent hope, and still less flattery, could dim Lenin's vigilant gaze. He had a quicker and keener eye for the narrowest chink of disagreement than for the broad expanse of converging platforms. He might be an outcast and a failure, but he had invariably known that Parvus in all his successes, all his prophecies, was wrong, or at least not altogether right! Although he himself had achieved nothing—right was on his side!

Now Parvus was amused. Laughter was shaking that unwieldy body which so loved its bottle of champagne before breakfast, its leisurely bath, its little suppers with the ladies, when it was not chained to its couch by rheumatism.

'Do you intend to go on in the same way, raising money by bank raids? What are you going to do next—rob the Crédit Lyonnais? You'll be deported to New Caledonia, comrades! To the galleys!'

He was overcome with laughter.

Lenin's brows twitched slightly in disagreement. But his searching gaze considered the problem dispassionately.

There was no theoretical objection to raiding a bank before general expropriation was legalised—it was, so to speak, borrowing against your future. But in practice it might or might not be worth while. If there was one thing the Bolsheviks had undoubtedly been good at in the revolutionary years it was the 'exes'. They had begun with raids on ticket offices and trains. The first 200,000 from Georgia had simply transformed the life of the Party. And if only they had succeeded in taking that fifteen million from Mendelssohn's Bank in Berlin in 1907 ...! (Kamo was arrested en route, and it fell through.) It was a risky method, but very effective, and in any case it dirtied the Party's hands less than dealings with the general staffs of foreign countries.

'Don't like dirtying your hands? Afraid of getting caught out?' Parvus too narrowed his eyes to slits, deliberately, contemptuously, shaming and reproving him. 'You can rely on my experience: in *big* enterprises you'll never be found out. It's those who balk at little ones who get caught.'

What a pachyderm! He didn't give a damn what people

said, just clumped about the world on his great flat feet, crushing everything in his path.

Lenin's right eye darted an angry glance at him.

Parvus became sympathetic. He took both of Lenin's hands in his own jelly-like paws (an unpleasant habit of his) and spoke like the closest of friends. (At one time they had almost been on first-name terms.)

'Vladimir Ilyich, you must not neglect to analyse the reasons for your failure in one revolution already. Perhaps the fault lies in you? It is important to recognise that for the future. Mind you don't lose next time.'

Where did he get his brazen self-assurance? What the hell did he mean by setting himself up as a teacher? Was this another attempt to impose his leadership? Self-infatuation must have blinded him.

Lenin wrenched his hands free and spoke with a savage grin, one of those grins of spontaneous mockery that forced up his eyebrows and brought a flush of joy to his face as he savoured his triumphant retort.

'Izrail Lazarevich! It's you who should rather be analysing *your own* failings! I didn't lose last time, because I wasn't running the revolution! You were the one who lost! How did *you* come to grief?'

So far he had said nothing irreparable. Just a businesslike argument. He could still stop in time. But all those years of gasping for breath with that great hulk crushing his ribs, and the spontaneous urge to tease, made him go further than he need. (And was there anything to the man except ambition? Except the thirst for power? Except wealth?)

'Why did you lose heart so quickly in the Peter and Paul Fortress—was it the solitary confinement, the damp? Why such tender concern for your miserable carcass? How do you explain that diary full of cheap pathos for German philistines? All that balderdash about amnesties? How you came as near as dammit to petitioning the Tsar? Is that the behaviour of a revolutionary leader? A fine revolutionary leader you are!'

And he himself? A baldheaded, spiky-browed, flinty-eyed little man with fussy, fidgety movements?

Yet, except for the two of them, there was no one left for the job.

[128]

Parvus never blushed, as though the fluid coursing in his veins were not the usual red, but watery green, like the colour of his skin. There was no reason at all for him to lose his temper, but when Lenin thrust that sarcastic grin in his face, and shook with mocking laughter, and went on shaking, Parvus suddenly forgot his great qualities and foolishly retorted, 'Anybody would think you had fought on the barricades! Or that you had marched just once in a street demonstration with Cossack whips waiting for you! At least I escaped from a transit prison on the way to Siberia! But why should you get away, when you had a false medical certificate and got yourself sent to the Siberian Riviera instead of the north?'

(There were plenty of other things on the tip of his tongue. All very well for you, he thought, to give the call to arms from neutral Switzerland, especially when you've never been called up in your life!)

If anyone insults you like that in public you would have to commit political murder, fatally blacken his reputation, but when it happens in private you have a choice. You can even suppose that this criticism is not wholly unsympathetic. Or admit that you have been unnecessarily rough yourself, as you often are in discussions.

No, thought Parvus, it was stupid of me to speak like that! I didn't come to Switzerland just to quarrel.

Parvus, thought Lenin, may be very useful. He is in a unique position. Why quarrel with him?

Lenin is the pillar on which the whole Plan rests. If he deserts me who will make the revolution?

Another smile from Lenin, but a different one, not at all caustic, but infinitely knowing, a smile to be shared between the cleverest people in the world. His hand fell on Parvus's shoulder, and he spoke in a half whisper.

'I tell you what. Do you know what your main mistake was in 1905? Why the revolution was a failure?'

Parvus responded with selfless objectivity, like a scientist ready to admit error however painful it might be.

'The Financial Manifesto? Was I in too much of a hurry?'

Lenin wagged his finger in the little space left between their heads, and smiled like a Kalmyk extolling a melon in an Astrakhan bazaar.

'No, no, no. The Financial Manifesto was a stroke of genius. But those Soviets of yours ...'

'My Soviets united the whole working class instead of splitting it up like the Social Democrats do. My Soviets were gradually becoming the centre of power. If only we'd succeeded in getting the eight-hour day—that and nothing else—there would have been risings in imitation of us throughout Europe, and there you would have had your *permanent revolution*!'

Slyly, slit-eyed, Lenin watched Parvus erecting defences for his vanity, and was in no hurry to interrupt. This damned muddle over permanent revolution was another reason why he, Parvus and Trotsky had quarrelled. As though they were riding behind each other on a merry-go-round, they had all at different times moved to this position, and as each of them emerged from its shadow he had insisted that the other two were wrong. The other two were always somewhere ahead or still far behind.

Lenin parried in a confidential whisper, with the same slyly good-natured Asiatic smile.

'Not a bit of it. As you yourself so rightly said at the time, there must be uninterrupted civil war! The proletariat must not lay down its weapons! Where *were* your weapons, though?'

Parvus frowned. Nobody likes remembering his blunders.

Lenin had thought so much about it, never thought so much about anything, and now, still gripping his companion by the shoulder, bending towards him, narrowing his eyes to a piercing squint, he was in the mood to share his thoughts.

'You shouldn't have waited for a National Assembly in addition to the Soviets. Once you'd convened the Petersburg Soviet you had your proletarian National Assembly. What you should have done ...'

He leaned forward as though sharpening the focus of his gaze, his mind, his words, and spoke still more confidentially.

'What you should have done was to set up the very next day an armed punitive organisation under the Soviet. That would have been your *weapon*!'

Then he sat silent, with Parvus fixed in his searchlight beam. Nothing seemed so important to him.

A typical armchair philosopher, a dreamer. After years of thought he had made his discovery, and although it was a decade late he thought it incomparably important. The crippling frustrations of émigré existence, remote from the scene of action, from the real forces—what a miserable fate! All his energy for years and years had gone into quarrels and wrangles, and schisms and squabbles, and now Parvus had flung wide the gates into the world arena! But all he did was sit curled up on his bed like a gopher and grin.

The second most powerful mind in European socialism was going to waste in an émigré bolt-hole. He must be saved —for his own sake.

But also for the Cause.

For the Plan.

'Well, then, do you understand my plan? Do you accept it?'

How to break through that frozen fixity? Had he dozed off? Was he in a trance? He wasn't taking anything in.

Parvus moved still nearer, and spoke right into his ear, so that he could not help hearing. 'Vladimir Ilyich! Will you join our alliance?'

Like a man deaf and dumb. His eyes were unreadable. His tongue did not answer.

Holding on to his shoulder, Parvus tried again.

'Vladimir Ilyich! Your hour has struck! The time has come for your underground to work and conquer! In the past you had no strength, I mean no money, but now I'll pump in as much as you like. Just open the pipes for it to flow in. Tell us which towns we should give money, and to whom. Give us names. Who is to receive leaflets and literature? Transporting weapons is more difficult, but we'll take weapons in too. And how are we going to coordinate our actions? I can't imagine how you manage from here, from Switzerland. Shall I arrange a move to Stockholm? It's very simple ...'

On and on. Pushing. Pumping in his hippopotamus blood! Lenin wriggled his shoulders and shook off Parvus's hand.

49

He had heard and understood it all perfectly. But a candid answer would not have passed the barrier of distrust and distaste in his breast.

His frankness about 1905 was quite enough to be going on with.

Of course he saw the merits of Parvus's Plan. If he couldn't, who could? A splendid programme—a *sound* programme! The offensive tactics were practicable, the means chosen reliable, the forces enlisted adequate.

Now he would admit it: there was no third thinker of such power, such penetrating vision in the International. Just the two of them.

And that was why he must be immensely circumspect. In political negotiations always suspect a trap where the ground looks smoothest.

Had Parvus then stolen a march once again? No. Theoretically and in a general way Lenin had formulated the same ideas when war first broke out. But what was impressive in Parvus was his businesslike attention to concrete detail. Parvus the financier.

Faced with this grandiose programme Lenin could question neither its soundness nor its desirability.

It was all quite right. On the simple calculation that my worst enemy's worst enemy is my friend, the Kaiser's government was the best ally in the world. That such an alliance was permissible he agreed without a moment's hesitation: only an utter fool disdains serious assistance in a serious struggle.

An alliance—yes. But the dictates of caution must come before the alliance. Caution not as a merely negative measure, but as the condition of any effective action. Without super-super-caution, to hell with your alliance and to hell with your Plan! We don't want the chorus of Social-Democratic grannies all over Europe tutting and spluttering! Lenin too admitted to himself—cautiously—that he had no qualms about France—the *rentiers'* republic. But he always knew where to stop, what to leave unsaid, where to keep an emergency exit open. Whereas Parvus had paraded his wild views, and irredeemably compromised his political reputation.

This was when Lenin had realised the other man's weakness and his own superiority. Parvus had always been first to discover new ground, and tramped on ahead, blocking the way. But he lacked the stamina for a long race. He hadn't been able to lead the Soviets more than two months. Twenty years and more of trying to re-educate the German Socialists was too much for him—he had come unstuck, fallen by the wayside. Whereas Lenin felt that he had the stamina to run for ever, without ever losing his breath, to run as long as he was conscious—if need be, he would collapse into the grave with his race unfinished. But he would never drop out.

An alliance—certainly, with pleasure. But in this alliance he would be the coy bride, not the eager bridegroom. Let them run after *you*. Behave in such a way that even when you are weak you keep the upper hand and your independence. In fact, Lenin had already done something of the sort in Bern. He had of course not gone knocking on Romberg's, the German Ambassador's, door, like Parvus in Constantinople. But when he had made his theses public he knew very well whose ears they would please—and the theses had reached the right ears. Romberg himself had sent the Estonian revolutionary Kesküla to discuss things with him and discover his intentions. And, of course, while remaining within the limits of his actual programme—the overthrow of Tsarism, a separate peace with Germany, secession of the non-Russian peoples, renunciation of the Turkish straits—he felt entitled to offer a slightly juicier bribe: without being untrue to himself, or distorting the line, he could and did promise Romberg the invasion of India by a Russian revolutionary army. In this there was no betrayal of *principles*: an assault on British imperialism was necessary, and who if not Russia could mount it? One of these days we shall invade. Of course, it was a concession, a sop, a swerve, a skid, but there was no danger in it. True, Kesküla had a wolfish look and wolfish ways, and he was stronger-minded and more effective than any wishy-washy Russian Social Democrat, but here too Lenin sensed no danger. Since Estonia must in any case be released, like all the subject peoples, from the Russian prison-house, there was no distortion of the line: each of them used the other without fear of stumbling. They introduced Artur Siefeldt and Moisei Kharitonov into the chain, and Kesküla went off to Scandinavia, where he was most helpful, especially with publications. He found money for pamphlets and helped organise contacts with Shlyapnikov, and so with Russia.

All this lacked the grandeur of Parvus's Plan, but in its quiet little way was politically sound. And Lenin had kept his nose clean.

Parvus had now begun to show impatience. (Another of his faults.) Seeing that the conversation was not going as he wished, that he was not making a sale, he said bitterly and contemptuously (which could do no good at all): 'So you are like all the rest? Afraid of getting a smudge on your nose? Waiting for something?'

He had set such hopes on Lenin! He at least, he had thought, is with me! If I can't get together with him, who else is there?

In some agitation, losing his millionaire's complacency altogether, he haltingly produced his last arguments.

'Vladimir Ilyich, you must not fall behind the times. With other people it doesn't matter, but in you it would be unforgivable. Surely you must see that the age of revolutionaries with parcels of illegal literature and home-made bombs has gone never to return. The new type of revolutionary is a giant, like you and me. He counts everything in millions—people and money alike—and he must be able to get his hands on the levers by which states are overthrown or established. Getting at those levers is not easy, and at times it is even necessary to join the chauvinists.'

Also true. True enough. But . . .

(Should he ask what price the Russian revolution would pay for German help? He refrained from doing so, but kept the question in mind for the future. It would be naive to expect such help for nothing.)

When you enter into an alliance the first rule is not to trust your ally. On the treacherous ground of diplomacy always see every ally as above all a potential cheat.

Lenin had not been dozing at all. He had been weighing things up. If anyone had been dozing, it was probably Parvus in his Berlin negotiations. He finally opened his eyes and radiated anxious enquiry, rattling off his questions like a drum roll.

'Will Wilhelm's government really want to overthrow the Russian monarchy? Why should they? All they need is peace with Russia. They would happily go on living in friendship with the Russian monarchy. They only need our strikes to scare the Tsar and force him to make peace, that's all.'

As though Pa-arvus needed to be told! No one should be deceived by the way he looked—rich, well-fed, with a carefully groomed imperial on his pendulous double chin. To speak frankly (and sometimes, with some people, he would go so far) the shadow of separate peace had troubled all his negotiations with the German government. Peace between Russia and Germany would be the graveyard of the Great Idea. All the time there was a suspicion that, although the Germans were giving money for revolution, in their hearts they thought only of separate peace with the Tsar, and were surreptitiously sending people to make contact.

These muffled secret tunnellings must be detected, and frustrated by timely ridicule: the Tsar is *no longer* in a position to make peace! If he suddenly decides to make peace with you, power in Russia may pass to a strong right-wing nationalist government, which will not respect the Tsar's undertakings—and you will only have reinforced their position! . . . It must be drilled into Prussian skulls that only a government having the people's confidence could sign a *real* peace with Germany. Let 'Peace' be the revolution's first slogan, the first concern of the new government! That government would find it easier to make concessions because it would bear no guilt for the war. From such a government Germany could expect *much more* ...

He could already see the treaty, and was ready to sign it himself in advance.

And he caught a gleam in Lenin's eyes which meant that he could see it too.

You couldn't go into every detail (nor should you): there were various schools of thought among the Germans. The majority were inclined to view England as the main enemy, and were prepared to make peace with Russia. And unfortunately Secretary of State von Jagow, the most Prussian of Prussians, although he considered the onslaught of Slavdom a greater danger than England, did not, you know, much like the plan to break up Russia by revolution. (It was impossible to understand him fully: with his aristocratic mannerisms and his effete scepticism, he did not conceal his distaste for the diplomacy of secret agents, *hommes de confiance*, dubious middlemen. It was of course a great hindrance that such a man should be the head of the German Foreign Office.)

Parvus, however, in spite of his exquisite ugliness, could be captivating. The German Ambassador in Copenhagen, Count von Brockdorff-Rantzau, enchanted by Parvus's incomparable intelligence, was his already.

All arguments must be used to prevent the catastrophe of a separate peace. They must strenuously try to convince the Germans that revolution in Russia was inevitable, that the whole country, and the army with it, was in ferment, that educated society was seething with discontent, not to mention the workers, including those in arms production—a single match would be enough to blow the lot up! Why, it was even possible to set an exact date—and keep to it!

But the sharp little man with the big head, the bald brow and the grin which hardly ever left his lips seemed even less convinced than von Jagow, and showed no mercy. 'So you have in fact no agreement with them? Just the semblance of one? Still just talking?'

The eternal privilege of those who never act themselves: to interrogate, be dissatisfied, find fault.

Paddling with both hands to prevent his body collapsing backwards like an overstuffed sack, Parvus straightened up.

'Not on crested paper, of course! It's all very fluid. And you have to keep its contours in view at every moment and determine its direction.'

Try even to determine the direction of strategic offensives. Explaining, urging, insistently advising that whatever happens they should not advance on Petersburg! That would cause an upsurge of patriotism, Russia would unite, and the revolution would peter out. At the same time, the Tsar must be denied any success in the field, and in particular must not be allowed to reach the Dardanelles, which would irreversibly reinforce his prestige. The best place to strike was on the southern flank: make the Ukraine your ally, detach the Donets coalfields, and Russia is finished.

Then again, they were afraid that the earthquake might set up tremors in Berlin. So that he also had to persuade them that revolution in Russia would not spread to Germany.

The little man jumped. 'What's that? What did you say?' Steadily pushing his obese companion away, and winning more room for himself on the bed. 'What do you mean? Have you reconciled yourself to the idea that the revolution will not go beyond Russia? Do you really think that?' His eyes were hard and inquisitorial. Suddenly—he would never mince his words when a principle was threatened—he burst out indignantly: 'Why, that's treason!'

(No, Parvus was simply not a Socialist. He was something quite different.) He, who never ventured outside Switzerland, never set his hand to anything *practical*, had been proved right again, must attack, must denounce.

'How short-sighted! What poverty of vision! How could the revolution survive in a single country?'

It was the same old *permanent revolution* all over again, the enchanted roundabout on which they were doomed to circle for ever, eternally following and fleeing, hurling yesterday's or tomorrow's reproaches at each other, neither of them ever in the right.

Did he not want revolution in Germany? Was it really not his aim? Was it true what they wrote about him, that he had become a German patriot?

Parvus, though, was no longer a child, to go on riding that roundabout. A revolutionary of the new type, a millionaire revolutionary, a financier and industrialist, can afford to express himself more frankly.

'World revolution is not at present feasible, but a socialist revolution in Russia is. Tsarism is the enemy against which *all* workers' parties everywhere must unite!'

More frankly does not mean frankly. It was a ticklish problem, one which you could not put into so many words in public discussions among Socialists. Even *tête à tête* you wouldn't mention it to every fellow Socialist.

You never knew where you had him—this mercurial creature with the bullet head and the sharp tongue. You could hardly ever tell what his next slogan would be—he always surprised everybody. You could never discover at all what he was thinking. Did he not understand that Russian socialism had special tasks to perform? Did he not accept them? Had his specific interest in Russia declined?

It was easier to discuss this problem with Brockdorff, even. (Indeed Parvus had noticed that you could discuss anything more straightforwardly and simply with diplomats than with Socialists.)

All he could do now was emphasise the elementary.

'It is Tsarism which must be destroyed here and now, by any means possible, and that's all we must think of!'

And so to the main question—how do you destroy it? The whole point of his visit and of this conversation was to find out what underground organisations in the capitals and in the provinces Lenin was willing to assign immediately to the preparation of a rising. Who and where were these people, with their iron unity and their invincible battle-readiness? Parvus knew what he was doing when he recommended this man to the German government as the most fanatical of Russian revolutionaries! He knew why he had come now to enlist him as an ally! For decades Lenin had seemed merely a mad sectarian. He had cast off all allies, fragmented all his forces, refused to hear of a 'party of professors', would have nothing to do with 'smooth economic development', cared for nothing but the underground, always the underground, and his party of professional revolutionaries! In peacetime Parvus and everyone else had thought this absurd, but now that there was a war on they began at last to see clearly how provident, how far-sighted and how clever he was! The time had finally come to use his powerful, well-trained secret army! Now at last it would prove its worth. Parvus was counting on this army in his negotiations in Berlin, he was counting on it when he had drawn up his Plan.

But Lenin was not to be diverted, not to be thrown out of his stride like that. He had his own end in view and stubbornly pursued it.

'And how can you equate the revolutionary situation of 1905 with the present situation in such a primitive fashion?'

Well, obviously this war was more destructive and more protracted, the masses incomparably more exhausted and embittered, the revolutionary organisation stronger, the liberals also stronger, while Tsarism had utterly failed to reinforce itself.

Lenin, however, persisted. His eyes seemed never to look directly at the other man, but to zig-zag around him.

'Very well. But how can you so confidently set a starting date from outside?'

'Well, Vladimir Ilyich, we must have some date to aim at, if we are to concert our actions. Suggest a different one, if you like. But January 9th is best, because it is symbolic, everybody remembers it, and many will begin without any signal from us. It will be easier to bring them out into the streets. And once the first few are out there'll be no stopping it!'

Lenin was being very difficult. Understandable, though: to uncover his beloved underground would be like handing it over to someone else. Of course he didn't like the idea.

If Parvus was so ardently persistent, it meant that he was trying to take advantage of you.

'So what do you say, Vladimir Ilyich? The time has come to act!'

(Oh yes, I understand your Plan! You will emerge as the unifier of all the Party groups. Add to that your financial power and your theoretical talent, and there you are—leader of a united party and of the Second Revolution? Not again?!)

From the inscrutable eyes, from the set lips, through the impenetrable bald dome, Parvus, himself extraordinarily percipient, seized Lenin's thoughts, opened them out, read them and answered at a tangent.

[139]

'My reason for suggesting that you go to Stockholm is so that you can be in charge from beginning to end. You need give me no names, tell me no secrets—just take the money, the leaflets, the weapons, and send them on! I'm not, you know,'—Parvus sighed weakly; so exhausting, these political discussions—'I'm not the man I was ten years ago. I shall not go to Russia. I consider myself German these days.'

(All the more suspicious. Why in that case did he think of nothing but Russia?)

'I only want to see the Plan carried out.'

... But perhaps we see the Plan, too, in different ways? He was quicksilver: no argument could hold him.

'You mean that I too should be seen dirtying my hands, like you, on the German General Staff? A revolutionary internationalist can't afford that.'

Two more pulls at his invisible oars brought Parvus alongside his armour-plated companion.

'You needn't get dirty! Why should you? I'll take all the dirty work on myself—I already have. The millions I give you will be clean. Just show me how to pipe them in. Once we've tied in your subterranean, submarine, secret connections with mine we'll touch off the Second Russian Revolution! Well??'

The eyes, which at the expense of colour in the iris, lashes and brows were pellucid concentrations of pure intelligence, tried to understand. Why this refusal?

But Lenin's eyes themselves were piercing gimlets. There was no way into them.

With his gimlet eyes and his crooked little grin—suspicious, shrewd, derisory—Lenin resisted these enticements.

'And for this purpose, you say, we need a conciliation conference in Geneva?' His voice was silky and venomous. 'We must make peace? With the Mensheviks?' And he recoiled, as though from a shock, as far as the bedstead would permit. 'What are you thinking of? What does *making peace* mean? *Giving in to the Mensheviks???*' He tossed his head violently, as though he were butting someone. 'Ne-ver! Not for the world! Peace with the Mensheviks? I would sooner see Tsarism survive another thousand years than give a millimetre to the Mensheviks!'

[140]

And anyway—was he or wasn't he a Socialist?!

Lenin went on butting the air after he had stopped speaking as though he were finishing someone off. As though he were finishing what he had to say soundlessly, with frenzied dumb-show.

No-ot a thing did Parvus understand. This, after all, was not what he had come for. The greatest, most indefatigable and most extreme of revolutionaries in the most favourable of situations, with assistance lavished upon him—would not make a revolution?

Parvus, losing hope by now, asked point blank: 'So why have you spent thirty years on theoretical battles and border disputes? Where is your logic? You built up an underground, didn't you? Here is the best possible occasion for using it, there'll never be another like it as long as you live! Surely you weren't just playing a part?'

Lenin was never stuck for an answer.

'If we're going to accuse each other of inconsistency ... You used to say that a handful of people cannot revolutionise the masses. Do you still say so?'

Parvus's chin was suddenly too heavy for his head, his head for his neck, and his neck for his body, his hands drooped between his knees.

'We-e-ell ...'

With Lenin's refusal the Great Plan was almost in ruins.

'All right then ... Good ... Or not so good ... there's so little time ... I shall have to create my own organisation.'

Lenin has miscalculated! He'll be sorry some day.

'You might at least let me have one of your men, our mutual friend perhaps?'

(No good burning bridges, no good quarrelling, Parvus might come in very useful.)

'Whom do you mean?'

'Hanecki.'

'He's yours.'

'I've already got Chudnovsky and Uritsky. What about Bukharin?'

'No, that's not for him.'

'All right. But you yourself, will you go to Scandinavia? I can get you there quickly.'

Lenin's eyes were gimlets.

'No, no, no!'

Parvus was helpless under the burden of his own weight. He heaved a deep sigh.

'Ah, well ... There's one other thing I've dreamt of all my life and can now afford: to bring out a socialist journal of my own.' He tried to throw back his swollen head proudly, in imitation of the bold and ardent spirit who had first thought of it. 'The *Bell* I'll call it.'

Four feet felt a jarring bump as the bed landed on the shoe-maker's floor.

50

The revolutionary who succeeds underground is not the one who hides like a mouse under the floor-boards, shunning the light of day and social involvement. The successful and resourceful underground worker takes a most active part in the everyday life of those around him, he shares their weaknesses and passions, he is in the public eye, in the hurly-burly, with an occupation which everyone understands, and he may spend much of his time and strength on his daily routine—but his main, his secret activity goes on side by side with his overt, daily round, and all the more successfully if they are organically connected. The wisest way is also the simplest: to combine your secret and your overt activity easily and naturally.

This was how Parvus saw it. (His experience of underground work was short—the few months in 1905, between the suppression of the Soviet and his arrest, then between his return from banishment and his departure abroad.) He understood still better that a man's natural occupation is one for which he has a vocation and talent. So, in May 1915, as he prepared to carry on alone after Lenin's disastrous refusal to join him in making a revolution, he decided, with as little conscious thought as he gave to breathing, that he and his collaborators would make commerce their first and chief occupation, and that revolution would run in tandem with business.

That same summer he set up in neutral Denmark—which retained the main prerogative of all free Western countries, to trade without impediment—an import–export agency, which in present circumstances would naturally be ready to deal with firms in any country at all—Germany, Russia, England, Sweden, the Netherlands—buying and selling where prices were most favourable. With Lenin's agreement, Hanecki at once became business manager of Parvus's new concern. The combination of two such ardent commercial spirits does not merely double their power, but increases it many times over. Then they were joined by a third, who was very nearly their equal—Georg Sklarz. (Not, it must be said, blown along by a whim of fate, but obligingly sent to co-operate with them by the Intelligence branch of the German General Staff.) This Sklarz (who achieved notoriety in post-war Germany, amongst other things in a succession of court cases in which he showed himself to be a remarkable actor) proved an indispensable member of the trio—a business genius like his partners, resourceful, quick-thinking, reacting silently and quickly to any assignment or any twist of events, and always emerging successful. (He had brought with him two other Sklarz brothers: Waldemar, who went to work in the trade-and-revolution agency itself, and Henryk, who, under the pseudonym of Pundik, and in partnership with Romanovich and Dolgopolsky, already ran a secret office in Copenhagen, investigating illicit exports from Germany on behalf of the German General Staff.) The idea of combining business with political activity soon proved its value: *Geschäft* served politics, and politics smoothed the path of *Geschäft*. Support from the General Staff made the agency's transactions easier and its profits greater.

Within a few months of its foundation the import–export agency was a flourishing business, buying, selling and shipping, with no thought of narrow specialisation, copper, chrome, nickel and rubber, transferring from Russia to Germany mainly grain and foodstuffs, from Germany to Russia mainly technical equipment, chemicals, medicines, but the range of goods supplied included also stockings, contraceptives, salvarsan, caviare, cognac, and used motor vehicles —in Russia, they were able to stipulate that these should not be commandeered for military purposes. In trade with Western countries this was one of many such agencies uncomfortably jostling each other, but in trade with Russia, which for him mattered most, Parvus's agency had a monopoly. Some goods were shipped openly, with legal export licences, others were shipped under false bills of lading, or even smuggled. This required ingenuity in packing and loading, and there had to be someone to take responsibility if caught, but it was Hanecki and Sklarz who involved themselves in all this, letting Parvus remain quietly in the shade, his favourite place, to deal with matters of high policy.

What made the combination of commercial and revolutionary activity an idea of genius was that revolutionary agents posing as business representatives, with the Petersburg lawyer Kozlovsky playing the main part, could travel quite legally to Russia, inside Russia, and back again to Parvus. But Parvus's brilliance was seen still more clearly in his arrangements for sending money. To pass money from the German government quickly and without hindrance into the hands of Russian revolutionaries might seem an impossible task, but the import–export agency performed it with ease. It sent to Russia goods and nothing but goods, and always in excess of what it bought there. The earnings of collaborating firms, such as Fabian Klingsland, were banked in the normal way (in the Petersburg branch of the Bank of Siberia), and it was then entirely a matter for the agency to decide whether or not to withdraw the money from Russia—in fact it was to Russia's advantage that it should stay there. Hanecki's intermediary in Petersburg, Evgenia Sumenson, could withdraw any sum at any time and hand it over to revolutionaries.

This was where Parvus showed his genius: the import of goods which Russia badly needed to wage war provided funds for knocking Russia out of the war.

Parvus's method of selecting the agency's revolutionary staff showed the same insistence on combining the overt and the covert. He set up for this purpose yet another subsidiary organisation in Copenhagen—the Institute for Research into the Consequences of War. To recruit its personnel he frequently and openly sought the acquaintance of Socialists and met them for discussions. Whenever a candidate was eager, and qualified, to plunge into the depths, he did so and became a secret agent. Those who proved unsuitable or intractable were kept in the dark, the conversation followed its natural course, and they might be kept on as overt members of a legal Institute. The Institute itself was not fictitious, but gratified Parvus's besetting passion for economic research, just as the heavily subsidised *Bell*, published in Germany, gratified his passion for socialism. (One who longed to join the Institute was Bukharin—and there could have been no better place for him, nor could the Institute have found a more useful member—but the fastidious and puritanical Lenin forbade his young comrade to associate with the shady Parvus, just as he forbade Shlyapnikov to go near the dubious Hanecki.)

All this Parvus managed brilliantly, because here he was in his element. But what came next was more difficult. To *whom* should this money be given in Russia? And how could you bring about a revolution in that huge country with a dozen business representatives and a few Western Socialists like Kruze? It was easiest in Petersburg, where he had many contacts, where the lawyer Kozlovsky could receive clients without arousing suspicion and recruit the necessary people in the factories, and where the fanatical Inter-District group was active—following what had always been Parvus's own line, recognising neither Bolsheviks nor Mensheviks, and readily accessible to him through one of their members, Uritsky. Although the socialist forces in Petersburg were split, Parvus had knocked together a strong group of activists, especially in the Putilov works. But although it has been truly said that revolution in any state succeeds or fails in the capital, there was no assurance that the initial shock would be effective in such a large country without disturbances in the provinces. Parvus, however, had live connections of his own only in Odessa, and through Odessa with Nikolaev. There was no one to stir up this inert, mute country as a whole. A few agents, however freely they spent, could not create a network in the few remaining months. Whereas Lenin had a ready-made network—and had treacherously concealed it.

But Parvus, from his memories of 1905, understood very well how disturbances begin. To start a strike, or a riot, to bring the people out on the streets, you do not need the unanimous consent of the majority, or even one in four; indeed, it is wasted effort to try and prepare even a tenth of them for

[146]

action. A single shrill cry from the thick of the crowd, a single orator at the factory gates, two or three toughs brandishing fists or sticks are often enough to keep a whole shift from their benches or bring them into the streets. Then there are neighbourly conversations condemning the government, the transmission of alarming rumours (which with no further effort can be left to strike at a distance like a charge of electricity), the scattering of leaflets in factory lavatories and smoking rooms, under work-benches—for each and any of these preliminary blows you need no more than five men to a factory, and if you cannot find five who will do it out of conviction you can buy help in the nearest tavern—what tavern scrounger refuses money?

In any other circumstances sporadic troublemaking in factories would not have been enough, but now, in the second year of a war which had already devoured so many, with hunger suddenly threatening, with the army losing battle after battle, with the whole country in ferment, with revolution still fresh in the minds of the present generation, a few such jolts—Parvus was convinced of it—could set off a landslide. That was his strategy—to start an avalanche with a few light snowfalls. Without Lenin's help in the remaining months he could do no more. But the date itself was fraught with menace for Tsarism: even if there were no agents at work, if Evgenia Sumenson spent not a single rouble, January 9th could still not pass quietly. All the same, it would be as well to give a helping hand.

So Parvus, who had Count von Brockdorff-Rantzau completely under his spell, and practically dictated his dispatches from Copenhagen to the German Foreign Ministry, confidently promised revolution in Russia on January 9th 1916.

He hoped, at least, that it would be so. Over-generously endowed with the gift of far-reaching and penetrating prophecy, he was none the less a creature of earth, and could not always distinguish a flash of prophetic insight from the uprush of desire. He longed so violently for a devastating revolution in Russia that he could be forgiven for misinterpreting his emotion.

This was not, however, something which the German government, and especially Secretary of State Gottlieb von

Jagow, would readily forgive. Always the ironist, always contemptuous of this grubby Socialist millionaire, von Jagow now concluded that Parvus had been deceiving the German Reich all along, that he had never seriously tried to bring about a revolution, that he had most probably simply pocketed the millions given to him. Intelligence services have a rule that such expenditure is not subject to audit. But for the rest of 1916 the Ministry of Foreign Affairs paid Parvus not a pfennig more.

This didn't mean total defeat, and outwardly it was not a defeat at all. The wheels of the import–export agency went on turning and making money. The General Staff compassionately filled the gap left by the Foreign Ministry. The Research Institute continued collecting information and studying it. Parvus took an active hand in supplying Denmark with cheap coal, won over the Danish trade unions, was treated as their friend and equal by the Danish and later by the German Socialist leaders. He finally obtained German citizenship, which he had been begging for since 1891, and there seemed to be no doubt that at the first post-war elections he would take his place among the leaders of the Socialist group in the Reichstag. His *Bell* continued to appear, exhorting Germany to patriotic socialism. His exorbitant personal wealth grew and grew, and he had holdings in almost all neutral countries, as well of course as in Turkey and Bulgaria, where he had founded his fortunes. His house in the aristocratic quarter of Copenhagen was furnished with the flamboyance of the *nouveau riche*, guarded by savage dogs, and an elegant Adler carried him from his door. He even managed to preserve intact his influence on Count von Brockdorff-Rantzau, and to impress on this constant partner-in-conversation the full complexity of the revolutionary's task, the intricate mechanics of his difficulties. Through Brockdorff, too, as far as tact allowed, he tried to obstruct the renewed German quest for a separate peace with Russia.

You might suppose that the long procession of successes which came to meet him would have more than satisfied him. Not so! His uneasy consciousness of a mission unfulfilled— although he no longer had any intention of returning to *that* country—secretly teased and tormented him. In his leisurely suppers with the Prussian aristocrat he expounded a variant, adapted to the German outlook, of what was now not so much a programme as his political testament, a hazy outline of the future. How the revolution, once begun, must quickly broaden its scope, like the Great French Revolution, by trying and executing the Tsar: only such an inaugural sacrifice could show the revolution that it need recognise no boundaries for itself. How the peasants must feel free to take the redistribution of land into their own hands—which alone would open the floodgates of anarchy. And when anarchy was at its height, in full flood, that was the very moment when Germany, by military intervention, with minimal losses and enormous advantages, could rid itself for ever of the threat from the East: sink Russia's fleet, take away her arms, raze her fortifications, forbid her ever again to form an army or establish war industries, or better still any industry at all, cripple her by amputating all that could be amputated— leave her in short a *tabula rasa*, so that she could forget her ten centuries of nastiness and begin her history all over again.

Parvus never forgot an injury.

But he could not see at present what more he could do.

Meanwhile the government of the German Empire was disgracing itself by seeking a separate peace with this still undestroyed power.

But Secretary of State von Jagow's health was steadily declining, and in the late autumn of 1916 he was happy to retire, giving up his post to the more active Zimmerman, who did not take over with it his predecessor's old-world distaste for secret agents and political hucksters.

New plans of action soared into view! And Parvus's old grudge against Lenin raised its head. *Why* had he done it? What did he mean by it?

The bed hit the shoemaker's floor with all four feet and Parvus was catapulted upright on his pillar-box legs. Painfully stretching, he shuffled across the room, carrying his pampered body like a heavy sack. He went round the table and sat on the other side, taking no care not to soil his snow-white cuffs on the Ulyanovs' dirty oilcloth.

His smile now was not for a man of power and an equal, but for a pathetic little animal in a hole.

'That's it, then, is it? Zimmerwald?... Kienthal?... Getting the leftists to vote correctly?... And what has the great Party done at home in Russia these past two years?... Why isn't there a single bubble to be seen on the surface?'

Lenin just sat there, sinking into the bed, and bent his heavy head without answering.

'Didn't you say you had no need of money?'

Lenin was embarrassed and almost inaudible.

'We never said that, Izrail Lazarevich. We need money very, very badly. Desperately.'

'But I offered you money! And you refused!'

Lenin's voice was parched and strained.

'What do you mean, refused? A sensible offer of help, without strings, we never refuse. We're only too glad ...'

'You're just playing children's games here in Switzerland.' The great hulk would have liked to gloat, but there was nothing to gloat over. Russia was not losing the war, Germany was not winning it, Germany's main ally, and his own, was giving up the fight.

Lenin's words seemed to stick in his throat.

'For serious games you have to pay a serious price.'

He looked sick. His eyes, less secretive than usual, were full of pain, and his next words were spoken without vehemence, with no other motive, it seemed, than to distract himself from his pain.

'After all, Izrail Lazarevich, your revolution too was a will o' the wisp, a soap bubble. It was naive to expect anything else.'

Parvus heaved indignantly, and the lamp flame flickered, leapt and smoked as his breath played on it.

'We had forty-five thousand on strike in Petersburg! Do you think you, sitting here, could bring forty-five thousand out?'

He forestalled Lenin's retort that the forty-five thousand included some of his people.

'... The Putilov workers got the date wrong—but they were marvellous! What a rumpus they kicked up! But the Nevskaya Zastava let me down—why didn't you bring them out?

[150]

I staged a splendid strike in Nikolaev—ten thousand came out! With impossible demands, so that a rising was certain! But they, too, were four days late. It's not so easy from this distance to tie them all to the same day. But how is it that Moscow never stirred? What was your Moscow committee doing?'

(Lenin only wished that he knew!)

Parvus warmed to his theme, crooking a finger for each of his successes, as though he were boasting about his wealth.

'I brought out the Yekaterinoslav Iron Works! And the Tula Copper Works! And the Tula Cartridge Factory! ...'

All these strikes had indeed broken out in January though not on the 9th—but who had started them, who had led them, there on the spot? It was not clear at this distance, and everybody claimed credit, including the Mensheviks.

'We came very close—but where were *your* people? The Inter-District group gave me wholehearted support, they've got fire in their bellies, but they're a mere handful. While you and the Mensheviks are still tossing balls to each other! Russia is flooded with leaflets—are you going to tell me they're yours? It was I who blew up the *Empress Maria*—or didn't you notice it?' Parvus thundered on, his eyes staring wildly. 'The Black Sea battleship—didn't you notice it????!'

He threw up his manicured white hands—look at the hands that blew up a battleship!

'Why wouldn't you join us, Vladimir Ilyich? Where are *your* strikes? Where are your riots? Which factories can you bring to a standstill at a predetermined date? Which of the nationalist organisations are you working with?'

Does he really not understand? ... For all his cleverness? My façade is a success, then! I must keep it up!

Why hadn't he joined in! ... Of course, he could have got round the Mensheviks somehow. Made some arrangement to share the leadership (although this, yes, this, was the most painful and difficult thing of all). Only ...

Only—everyone's abilities are limited. Lenin was—a writer of articles. And pamphlets. He gave lectures. He made speeches. He carried on agitation amongst young leftists. He trounced opportunists everywhere in Europe. He believed that he had acquired a thorough knowledge of problems

[151]

connected with industry, agriculture, the strike movement, trade unions. And now, after reading Clausewitz, of military matters too. He understood now what war was, and how an armed uprising should be carried out. And he could explain it all, with tireless clarity, to any audience.

There was only one thing of which he was incapable— action. The one thing he could not do was—blow up a battle-ship.

'But all is not yet lost, Vladimir Ilyich,' said Parvus, con-soling, encouraging, from across the table. He took his gold watch from his waistcoat pocket, and nodded at it approving-ly. 'We'll postpone the revolution until January 9th 1917! But let's do it together! Shall we be together this time?'

Why on earth shouldn't they? The perspicacious Parvus simply couldn't see it.

Lenin could not keep his end up in this conversation. He was lost for an answer. How could he talk about entering or not entering into an alliance, when his position was so ridicu-lously weak? Dignified concealment of his impotence was what he must aim at: hiding the fact that he had no function-ing organisation, no underground in Russia. If it existed at all it was a law unto itself, and he had no control over its motions or their timing. He simply did not know what *was* there—he was not in uninterrupted communication with Russia, had no means of sending instructions or receiving a reply. He was only too glad if Shlyapnikov, who was all by himself, managed to pitch a bundle of *Social Democrat*s over the frontier. He had corresponded with his sister Anya in invisible ink, but even this link had snapped. How could *he* stir up rebellion among the national minorities? It would be something if he could preserve a fragment of his own party ...

Parvus, flabbily draped over his creaking chair, had not exhausted his generosity.

'How do your collaborators cross the Russian frontier? Surely not on their own feet, or in rowing boats? That's all out of date, nineteenth-century stuff. It's time you forgot all that! If you like we'll provide them with splendid documents and they can travel first class, like my people ...'

Parvus, no doubt, was ugly—as seen by women, or a public meeting. But his colourless, watery eyes were irresistibly clever—and cleverness was something Lenin appreciated.

If only he could get away from them. Parvus must not guess the truth.

Must not guess that *action* was just what Lenin could not manage. All the rest he knew how to do. But one thing he could not do: bring the great moment nearer, make it happen.

Parvus with his millions, with his weapons probably already in the ports, with his conspiratorial skill, with the Putilov works already securely in his grip—Parvus clapped his hands, the hands of a man of action, white and pudgy though they were, and continued his interrogation.

'What *are* you waiting for, Vladimir Ilyich? Why don't you give the signal? How long do you intend to wait?'

Lenin was waiting for—for *something* to happen. For some favourable tide of affairs to carry his little boat home—to a *fait accompli*.

Ludicrously, all the ideas on which Lenin had based his life could neither change the course of the war, nor transform it into a civil war, nor force Russia to lose.

The little boat lay like a toy on the sand, and there was no tide to float it ...

All this time the letter on expensive greenish paper lay there asking him: what do you say then, Vladimir Ilyich? Will *your* people cooperate or won't they? Where are your meeting points? Who takes delivery of weapons? Tell me what you have there of any real use.

Just the question which Lenin could not answer, since he had nothing. Switzerland was on one planet, Russia on another. What he had was ... a tiny group, calling itself a party, and he could not account for all its members—some might have split off. What he had was ... *What Is To Be Done?*, *Two Tactics*, *Empirio-criticism*, *Imperialism*. What he had was—a head, capable at any moment of providing a centralised organisation with decisions, each individual revolutionary with detailed instructions, and the masses with thrilling slogans. And nothing more, no more today than he had had eighteen months ago. So that tactical caution and simple pride alike forbade him to reveal his weak spot to Parvus, any more than he had eighteen months ago.

But Parvus hung over the table, his fishy eyes full of

mockery, his brow no less steeply terraced than Lenin's, and awaited, demanded an answer.

He had very cleverly seized the initiative, asking question after question so that he need do no explaining himself. But he must have his own reasons for this approach at this particular time, after eighteen months of silence.

Avoiding the puzzled hovering gaze from under Parvus's upturned hairless eyebrows, rolling his head as he perused the letter, Lenin tried to think how he could refuse help without giving offence, without losing an ally, how to conceal his own secret while divining that of his companion. Skipping what was in the letter and looking for what was not there.

Lenin was always eager above all to seize on weaknesses which offset his own. If there was no chink in Parvus's armour —why was he making this second approach, and so insistently? Had his strength failed him? Or his funds perhaps? Had his network broken down? Or perhaps the German government was no longer paying so well? They made you work for your money, once they had you hooked.

How good it was to be independent! Oh no, we're not so weak as you think! Not nearly as weak as some!

His right hand as usual made pencil marks in preparation for his reply—straight lines, wavy lines, squiggles, question marks, exclamation marks ... While his left hand restlessly rubbed his forehead, and his forehead gathered in the points he would make.

Trotsky's complaints against his former mentor—that he was frivolous, lacked stamina, and abandoned his friends in time of trouble—were so much sentimental rubbish. These were all pardonable faults, and need not stand in the way of an alliance. If only Parvus had not committed gross political errors. He should not have exposed himself publicly by rushing at a mirage of revolution. He should not have made *The Bell* a cesspool of German chauvinism. The hippo had wallowed in the mire with Hindenburg—and destroyed his reputation. Destroyed himself as a Socialist once and for all.

It was sad. There were not many Socialists like him!

(But although he had destroyed himself, there was no sense in quarrelling. Parvus might still be enormously helpful.)

[154]

Regaining his confidence, Lenin raised his eyes from the letter, from the edge of the table, and looked at his indefatigable rival. The contours of his head, shapeless enough at the best of times, and of his pudgy shoulders blurred and trembled.

Trembled as though they were shaking with grief. Grief that even with Lenin he could not make himself fully understood.

His features faded, till he was no more than a lengthening streak of bluish mist. He bowed, drifted across the room and seeped through the window.

But while there was still just time Lenin shouted after him, not crowing over him, but just so that the truth should not go untold: 'Let myself be tied to someone else's policy? Not for anything in the world! That's where you made your mistake, Izrail Lazarevich! I'll take what I need from others—of course! But tie my *own* hands? No!!! It would be absurd to speak of an alliance which meant tying my own hands!'

The whole scene vanished like smoke, leaving no trace of Sklarz or of his case. His hat, too, belatedly whisked off the table and flung itself after them.

Lenin had proved the more far-sighted of the two! Though he had made no revolution, though he was helpless and ineffectual, he knew that he was right, he had not let himself be misled: ideas are more durable than all your millions, I can soldier on without them. Never fear, even the conferences for women and deserters will prove to have been worthwhile. Under the crimson flag of the International I can wait another thirty years if need be.

He had preserved his greatest treasure—his honour as a Socialist.

No, it's too soon to think of surrender! Too soon to leave Switzerland. A few more months of purposeful work, and the Swiss Party will be split.

Soon after that—we shall start the revolution here!

And from Switzerland the flame of revolution will be kindled throughout Europe.

March 1917

L-1

That past winter had seen an unbroken series of dramatic struggles, which might have culminated in a proletarian revolution spreading from Switzerland throughout Europe, but for the base betrayal of a gang of leaders who had defiled, polluted, debauched the whole Swiss Party, foremost and vilest amongst them the scoundrelly intriguer and political prostitute Grimm. And that old ruin Greulich. And other filthy blackguards.

The superficial, philistine eye—that of most people, and even most revolutionaries—cannot discern the tiny cracks in a huge mountain mass, cannot understand that if you know how to widen them you can bring the whole mass crashing down. The terrified man in the street, observing all Europe at war, armies numbering millions, millions of shellbursts, could not believe that it was in the power of a tiny group of extremely resolute men to stop this iron hurricane (and change its direction). True, an enormous event must first take place—a revolution, like the war, involving all Europe. But revolution in Switzerland, which though small and neutral was trilingual and at the heart of Europe, might suffice to set it off. To this end, it was necessary to gain control of the Swiss Social Democratic Party or, if that proved impossible, to split it and detach its battleworthy section. And all that was needed to split such a party—though opportunists and armchair theorists would hardly believe it—was some five resolute members together with three foreigners capable of providing the local comrades with a programme, drafting texts or theses for their speeches, and writing pamphlets for them.

Thus, fewer than a dozen skilful and steadfast Socialists were enough to turn Europe upside down! The Skittle Club!

They had thought it all out in the autumn, and now they set to work. At first, merely to repair the psychological damage caused by their failure at the Party Congress in November, Lenin drafted outline instructions for the young leftists, summarising their practical tasks in the struggle. Many months of absorption in the subject, and even the reading of insignificant Swiss newspapers, now came in useful. Next he started holding meetings to explain his theses in detail. The theses were allowed to leak to the country at large. The idea was that if even one tiny local Party organisation *adopted* the theses, it would be legitimate to demand their publication in the socialist press and broaden the discussion. They explored the possibility of publishing the theses in leaflet form and distributing several thousand copies. (Nobody was any good at distribution: they were all talk and no action, depressives or malingerers.)

Perhaps they should start publishing leaflets independently? Münzenberg, leader of the young and Lenin's main support, grumbled that there was plenty of *literature* already. (As though they had ever had literature *like this*.) They were weak, the Swiss leftists, infernally weak.

The impatient gaze of the revolutionary noticed another welcome crack, which promised more, and sooner: another Party Congress was due to be held soon, at the end of January, and the leadership had been forced to promise that it would be specially devoted to the Party's *attitude to war*. This provided a marvellous opportunity to badger and batter the whole opportunist leadership, to bombard them in full view of the Swiss masses with vitally important questions which they could not evade. Was it right that Switzerland should be brought to the brink of war? Was it right that descendants of William Tell should die for the international banks? Was this right, was that right ... you could go on like that for ever. Another reason why such a congress was particularly danger-ous for the opportunists was that parliamentary elections were due in September 1917—next year—and whether the Congress now decided *for* or *against* the fatherland, the Party would undoubtedly split during the elections, or even cease to exist. (And that is exactly what we want!)

The opportunists took the point and began manoeuvring: could they perhaps postpone the rashly promised Congress altogether, avoid taking any decision at all on the war question, as long as Switzerland itself was not at war, or leave the decision until all wars came to an end?

They still did not know how the blow would be struck, how the question would be put: not in terms of 'Support for the fatherland' or 'Opposition to militarism', but with relentless straightforwardness: the struggle against war is impossible without socialist revolution! The vote, in effect, would be not about war but for or against the immediate expropriation of the banks and industry! The Skittle Club busily prepared a resolution for the Congress: Platten wrote a feeble version, and Lenin re-drafted it in his name. (No easy work, but worth while. The Swiss left must be given all possible help by their foreign comrades.) They must attack heavily on all fronts. Demobilise the Swiss army immediately! Defence of Switzerland is a hypocritical phrase! *Switzerland's* peace policy is criminal! The result could be a colossal success: a resolution of this sort adopted by the Swiss Congress would win the enthusiastic support of the working class in all civilised countries!

But the opportunists bestirred themselves. It was learnt confidentially that the people at the top were preparing to postpone the Congress—shameless wretches! In cases like this you must get your blow in first! Rob them of the initiative! So they instructed Bronski to put forward a resolution at a meeting of the Zürich organisation against 'agitation behind the scenes for the adjournment of the Congress', and 'condemning symptoms of a lapse into social chauvinism'. It had been possible to demand a recount, and they managed to get the resolution carried! This was hitting the centrists where it hurt—they dreaded being thought of as chauvinists.

But the opportunist gang were by now so shameless that even this did not deter them! They called a meeting of the presidium for the following day, and threw off their masks. (Platten, Nobs and Münzenberg were all present, so that all this was reliably reported.) Old Greulich stooped to defamation of the whole Zürich Party organisation: it includes many deserters, he said, people vouched for by us, and it is only to be expected that their views on the question of national self-defence ... Somebody else shouted out that if the Party was going to be insulted as it had been by Bronski's resolution, 'We, from St Gall, shall be forced to withdraw from it!' 'These comrades,' he said, 'have a poor opinion of the Swiss workers,' (hinting that it was *foreigners* who were muddying the waters) ... Another of them had an attack of chauvinist hysteria: go, and take the formulas of your international congresses with you! Discussing the war question in wartime is madness! At such moments any nation is united by recognition of its common destiny. (United with its capitalists ...) How can we demobilise the army, when it is defending our frontiers? Why, if Switzerland is in danger, the working class will rise to its defence! (Hear, hear!) But Grimm behaved even more shamelessly than the others. What a political crook he was, the chairman of the Zimmerwald and Kienthal conferences: think of it, he said, if war begins we are supposed to raise a rebellion! ...He made vile innuendoes against *foreigners* and the young. He, the centrist, sided with the chauvinists, and his vote decided the issue: by an insignificant majority—seven to five—they agreed to postpone the Congress *indefinitely* (*scilicet*—till the end of the war) ... A uniquely disgraceful decision! Grimm was an out and out traitor.

The scoundrel, the treacherous swine! Enough to drive you insane! It was all the more necessary now to intensify the war within the Party as never before. The only thing left to them was to cut the ground from under Grimm's feet! He blocked their way completely: it was urgently necessary to ruin his reputation, expose him, strip off his mask. Just as in a fight the hand feels for the most suitable object to grip and to strike with, so the brain of an embattled politician chooses amongst possible moves as deviously swift as lightning. His first thought was—Naine! Naine was not very far to the left, and it was unusual for him to vote for them. So that it would be particularly advantageous to overthrow Grimm with Naine's help! How exactly? By writing an open letter to Naine's newspaper publicly calling Grimm a scoundrel and saying that it was henceforward impossible to remain in the Zimmerwald organisation with him! ... Better still, let's get everyone we can find to write to Naine's paper—and bury Grimm for ever under an avalanche of open letters and votes of protest! Every minute is precious. We must rally the left everywhere, and set them on Grimm!

A dramatic moment. At La Chaux-de-Fonds the faithful Abramovich supported the move. In Geneva Brilliant and Guilbeaux were undecided.

While in Zürich the leftists and the young met night after night to work out their plan of attack. It became clear that open letters were not enough. They must commit *political murder*, make sure that Grimm would never get on his feet again.

The way of it was this. All supporters in Zürich at the time were quickly called in, and Lenin, Krupskaya, Zinoviev, Radek and Levi walked over to Münzenberg's lodgings, several streets away. Then, when all the militants were assembled, Willi summoned Platten by telephone, giving no reasons, but saying that it was urgent. They had to set a trap for him. For some time he had obviously been afraid—of Grimm and of a split—and had been reluctant to learn from international experience, shown himself too Swiss, too parochial—and so, for that matter, had Nobs. (Where, when you came to think of it, had they sprung from? They had merely *enrolled* with the left at Zimmerwald ...) So Platten had to be taken unawares, and by the throat.

In he came—and when he saw not just Münzenberg as he had expected, but six of them in a tight huddle in the little room, three squashed together on the bed, and all of them looking sombre, his big-browed, candid face, which was not equipped to dissemble, expressed bewilderment and alarm. If there had been just one to whom he could turn for support or encouragement! There was no one. They shoved him into a corner seat away from the door, behind a chest of drawers, and all six of them bore down on him, shifting their chairs closer or leaning forward on the bed. Then Münzenberg (cast for the part) announced in his insolent, ringing voice that 'We, our whole group I mean, have decided to break immediately and finally with Grimm, and to discredit him in the eyes of the whole world!' Platten must choose: 'Either you're with us, or you're with Grimm.' Platten didn't know where to put himself, he gazed round that ring of faces in agitation, looking for a hint of kindness, but even Nadya wore the frozen stare of a witch. Platten mopped his brow, kneaded his weak chin, pleaded for time to think, but while he talked the six remained motionless, grimly silent, looking at him as though he were their enemy—all this was the joker Radek's idea—and nothing could have frightened him more. Platten lost his head and began to give way, but suggested that perhaps it needn't be done so abruptly! They could warn Grimm, call him to order ... No!!! It was all over! All decided! All Platten could do was to choose: you're either with us, in an honourable international alliance, or with your Swiss traitor, and we shall disgrace the pair of you! And we want your answer now!

Platten seized his head with both hands. Sat still for a while. Surrendered.

Writing a pamphlet to discredit Grimm was to be Radek's task. He could easily have done it, puffing away at his pipe, before the night was out. But the lazy creature wrote nothing. Lenin had to spend hour after hour walking round Zürich with him, coaxing and scolding, urging him to write and to make it really scathing, as he alone could. Whatever else, he was an incomparable journalist!

The next step was to attack Grimm at a session of the International Socialist Commission. Lenin himself stayed away, not wishing to make himself conspicuous, and Zinoviev, Radek, Münzenberg and Levi were the accusers; Grimm's activities in Switzerland were criminal, outrageous, depraved—and he should therefore be expelled from the Zimmerwald leadership. (Dethroned.) A simultaneous attack was mounted in Münzenberg's Youth International. Their next idea was to press for a referendum in the Party, to decide whether a congress should be organised immediately, in March. The argument for the referendum—Lenin had to write it himself—was the best thing in the whole campaign: the postponement of the congress was called a *defeat for socialism*!

What an uproar there was! What a dust-storm! It was m-m-marvellous!!! The Party leaders howled with indignation, rushed off to refute the charges! No Socialist can stand up to a bold, harsh indictment from the left! One accusing voice can lay low a thousand opportunists!

M-m-marvellous! It had come off! Just what was wanted!

At the cantonal congress they managed to collect a sixth of the votes for the left's resolution. This was a major victory!

It was also the high point of the campaign. After that it began to peter out.

Grimm attacked the referendum furiously—and frightened the youngsters. Nobs, foxily cautious, publicly dissociated himself from the referendum.

While Platten, the weakling, said nothing ... Some good planning a battle round him! He was hopeless. He didn't want to learn how to organise a revolutionary party.

Nor was anyone willing to publish Radek's pamphlet: 'If we do we shall be hounded out of the Party.' There are your leftists for you! There are your fire-eaters!

Sensing their weakness, Grimm called an ultra-private conference and invited the leftists. Münzenberg and Bronski of course did not go. But Nobs and Platten came to heel.

No, they were already three-quarters of the way down the slope to social patriotism. The Swiss left were a thoroughly worthless lot, people without backbone.

Instead of sharpening disagreements they blurred them, glossed over them. Mean, sneaking creatures!

Next came the scandalous Bronski affair. At a general meeting of the city Party organisation some of those elected to the executive refused to serve.

Substitutes were taken from among the runners-up, and luckily Bronski was high enough on the list to be included. Suddenly Bronski was in! Whereupon the rightists, by now utterly without shame, declared that they would not be able to work with him and would stand down. Unfortunately Nobs was in the chair—and agreed to annul the election!

As for Platten, he meekly accepted this slap in the face.

Lenin was at the meeting, saying nothing, but beside himself with rage.

He had not a minute's sleep that night.

[165]

These daily meetings always had the same effect: they played hell with his nerves, gave him headaches, ruined his sleep.

The whole Swiss Party was opportunist through and through, an almshouse for petit bourgeois. It consisted of bureaucrats, future bureaucrats, and a handful of people terrorised by bureaucrats.

The leftists fled from his offers of help, both in Zürich and in Bern. Only Abramovich was doing well, but he was too far away. Guilbeaux and Brilliant still wavered.

The leaders of the young, even bold, tough, inflexible Münzenberg, were inclined to compromise. Even Münzenberg turned Radek's pamphlet down! (And Radek went off to Davos for his health—he too was worn out with it all.)

It would be funny, if it were not so disgusting. Evidently his labours with the Zürich left were at an end ...

But he had nothing to regret, though he had lost. He had always known how rotten European Socialist parties were. Now he had personal experience of it.

He had nothing to regret. What had been done would not vanish without trace. Others will take over from us, and create a party of the left in Switzerland!

A meeting of the left was called for March 8th—and never took place. They simply didn't come, no one wanted it. Lenin had intended to deliver a report, but went down there for nothing and came back in a rage. Rage kept him awake all night.

He envied Inessa and Grishka Zinoviev who were travelling around addressing meetings—in places where you saw in front of you not socialist petit bourgeois, but unspoilt people, workers, the crowd, and could directly influence the masses.

There were many other things to disturb him. He and Radek—who was unbearable when he put on his professorial airs—were friends one day and quarrelling the next, and Inessa and Grishka were distressed by the discord between them. Then there was his quarrel with Usievich. (With Bukharin he had never stopped quarrelling—the one good thing was that they had not made it public.) Then Shklovsky had misappropriated Party funds. Then Inessa had taken it into her head to 'reconsider' the question of national self-defence, and he had wasted far too much time on superfluous argument.

In letters. She had never once come to Zürich.

It would soon be a year ...

Then there was a spine-chilling rumour that Switzerland would shortly be drawn into the war, and he had quickly calculated that it would be best for Nadya and himself to remain in the German occupation zone, while Inessa went to Geneva, where the French would seize her—in this way they could improve communications with Russia. To his relief it turned out that there would be no war. Then Nadya was ill with bronchitis and a high temperature, he had to run for the doctor several times and his life was completely disorganised.

All the same, he could not sit with folded arms. What if they left the Swiss Socialists out of it, and themselves provoked a mutiny in the Swiss army? The scheme that grew out of this was to write a leaflet ('Let us spread the flames of revolutionary propaganda in the army! Let us turn the stale civil peace into revolutionary class action!'), keep its origin absolutely secret (you could suffer severely for this sort of thing and even be expelled from Switzerland), sign it 'The Swiss section of the Zimmerwald Left' (let the authorities suspect one of the group, Platten for instance), and distribute it by a roundabout route to conceal their connection with it. Inessa would quickly translate it into French. But the rough drafts must be burned to ensure absolute secrecy. (They had satisfied themselves that the Post Office did not check letters.)

They set to work. But this scheme gave rise to another. Perhaps they should write, and sign with someone else's name, a leaflet to bring *the whole European proletariat* out on strike on May Day? Why not? Could there be any doubt that the proletariat would respond? What a show of strength that would be at the height of the war! Mass revolutionary actions might easily spring spontaneously from the strike! One good leaflet and all Europe would rise in revolt! What about that?! Only they must hurry, May Day was not far away—the leaflet must be quickly translated into French, printed, distributed. (And all this in absolute secrecy.)

But before the European general strike could be properly thought out, before the translations of the leaflet were finished,

[167]

a letter suddenly arrived from the Kollontai woman, now back from America and in Scandinavia. Another fuse was lit under the powder barrel! The Congress of the Swedish Party, as it turned out, had ended in a split.

What an unexpected piece of good luck! Yet how could he have forgotten his loyal Zimmerwald comrades-in-arms? What chaos, what infernal confusion there must now be in those Swedish heads.

How could he influence them? How could he help them? Sudden illumination: *this* was what he had been waiting for, the greatest and noblest of tasks—to bring about revolution not in Switzerland but in Sweden! To begin it all from *there*!

Kollontai wrote further that the younger Swedes had decided to hold a congress on May 12th and to found a new party 'on Zimmerwald principles'. Innocent fledglings, so sincere and so inexperienced—who will explain to you that the principles of Zimmerwald and Kienthal have been betrayed! Betrayed and trampled in the mire by nearly every Socialist party in Europe! Zimmerwald is bankrupt, Zimmerwald is dead! But you are sincere and unsullied, and at all costs someone must help you to understand the shoddiness of Kautskyism, the vileness of the Zimmerwald majority. (Oh, why am I not there with you?!) The time has come to trim Branting's claws! I must help you by sending my theses! We all have a moral and political responsibility towards you. This is the crucial moment for the Scandinavian workers' movement!

The momentary pessimism and helplessness which had taken possession of him after his setbacks with the useless, spineless, hopeless Swiss leftists were swept away by an upsurge of joyous impatience to *set Europe ablaze from the North*!!! But there was little time left, and masses to be done, and sending correspondence through Germany was beset with difficulties. No matter—life had begun all over again! A life of vigorous, active, purposeful struggle! The gloomy vaults of the reading rooms in the old Zürich churches, the stacked newspapers and well-thumbed pamphlets in the Centre for Socialist Literature were suffused with a new light. By May Day there must be a leaflet! By May 12th, a set of theses and an agreed plan! All forces must be concentrated on the European general strike and on the Swedish split! Only the young were worth working on! *We* shall never do anything, never see anything. But the crimson sun of revolution will yet rise on *them*!

On March 15th[1] he was at home and just finishing lunch when there was a sudden knock. Bronski. A somewhat untimely visit. (He had banked heavily on Bronski in his unsatisfactory dealings with the leftists, and then there was the electoral fiasco, so that seeing him was no pleasure just now. And he was not yet fitted into the latest plans.) In he came, and without sitting down, in his usual languid, somewhat melancholy manner, asked: 'Haven't you heard?'

'Heard what?'

'About Russia ... been a revolution ... so they say ... it's in the papers.'

As was his way, he spoke without emphasis, in a hesitant drawl. Ilyich raised his eyes from the boiled beef on his plate—he had finished the broth—and looked at the soft-spoken Bronski as calmly as though he had announced that the price of meat had gone down five rappen a kilo. A revolution in Russia?

'What rot. Who says so?'

He went on eating, cutting crosswise, to get lean and fat together. It made no sense. The nonsense people talked! He dipped the bits of meat in the mustard on the rim of his plate. It annoyed him when people interrupted his meals and wouldn't let him eat in peace.

But Bronski stood there without taking his overcoat off, crumpling the damp felt hat he always took such care of. For him this was a sign of great excitement.

Nadya ran her hands down her chequered grey frock as though she were wiping them, and asked:

'What do you mean, Moisei? In which papers? Where did you see it?'

'Agency reports. In the German papers.'

'Is that all! German newspapers writing about Russia! It's all lies.'

He calmly continued his meal.

News about Russia in the European press was scanty and always garbled. With no reliable information of your own it was hard work sifting the true from the false. And letters from Russia hardly ever came. Two new Russians, escaped prisoners of war from Germany, had flashed across his field of vision— he had rushed to look at them and talk to them, out of interest. He occasionally mentioned Russia in talks, but no more often than the Paris Commune, long vanished.

'What exactly do they say then?'

Bronski tried to repeat it. Like most other people—though a revolutionary should be ashamed of it!—he was incapable of reproducing the exact sense, let alone the exact words, of what he had read.

'Disturbances in Petersburg ... crowds in the streets ... police ... The revolution ... is victorious ...'

'And what exactly does its victory amount to?'

'The ministers ... have resigned or something, I can't remember ...'

'I thought you'd read it for yourself? What about the Tsar?'

'There's nothing about the Tsar.'

'Nothing about the Tsar? So where's the victory?'

Such rot. Perhaps it wasn't Bronski's fault, perhaps the news item itself had been just as vague.

Nadya's hands hovered at her breast, puckering her dress, which looked shabbier than ever in the dimness of their room— a steady drizzle had been falling since early morning.

'Maybe there is something in it, though, Volodya? Where would such a report come from?'

Where from! It was an ordinary bourgeois journalist's *canard*, another petty contretemps in the enemy camp blown up out of all proportion, like so many they had seen in the course of the war.

'If there were a revolution is this how we should hear of it? Remember Geneva and the Lunacharskys!'

Walking along the street one January evening he and Nadya had met the Lunacharskys, radiantly happy. 'Yesterday, the 9th of January, troops fired on the crowd in Petersburg! Many people were killed!!' How could he forget that evening of triumphant celebration among the Russian émigrés! They had rushed to a Russian restaurant, where the whole colony assembled and sat talking excitedly, singing songs ... Everyone was suddenly young, vigorous, alive again ... Trotsky, his outstretched arms making him look taller than ever, busily proposed toasts, congratulated everybody, kept saying that he was going home at once. (And he had gone.)

'All right. Give me some tea.'

Or should he not bother?

It would probably be no good going back to the reading room and carrying on with his routine work: in spite of himself, he was caught, disturbed. He must see what it was all about. There might be some hindrance here to all his plans.

Only the newspapers with today's dispatches would not be in the reading rooms until tomorrow.

Yes, but late news flashes were pinned up in the *Neue Zürcher Zeitung*'s window at Bellevue.

Right, let's get down there.

Nadya was still not going out very much after her bronchitis in February, and wanted to stay at home. So Ilyich pulled on his heavy, well-worn, much-mended overcoat, planted his old bowler on his head as though it were a hatblock, and set off with Bronski.

'Here lived the poet Georg Büchner,' said a plaque on the house next door. Along the damp, narrow alley, where loose slushy snow still lay unmelted under the walls, they walked quickly, almost rolled, down the hill. They took short cuts along back streets to reach Bellevue as quickly as possible.

As usual the Swiss were all carrying umbrellas, passing each other with difficulty in the narrow streets, and in danger of poking each other's eyes out. But Lenin didn't like dragging an umbrella around: sometimes it was useful, sometimes not. Anyway, his clothes were all old, no need to worry about them. Bronski, too, did without.

In the newspaper office's windows they found things more or less as Bronski had said. Except that the ministers were supposed to have been arrested. Arrested? ... And further, that power had passed to—members of the Duma. But what of the Tsar? There was not a word about the Tsar. So obviously the Tsar was at liberty, with his army, and would soon settle their hash.

If of course the whole thing wasn't a pack of lies.

No, no, *that sort of thing* couldn't happen in Russia today.

[171]

Nor was there any crowd around the windows, no one in fact except the two of them.

A fine drizzle was falling on the square and on the lake. The sky over the lake was monotonously overcast, and Uetliberg on the other shore was swathed in milky grey mist. Hansom cabs with dark roofs went by, and there was a monotonous procession of dark umbrellas. No, no, there was no revolution! ...

All the same, he must get to the bottom of it.

They went to the newspaper kiosk at the Heimplatz, hoping to find something there. Lenin never bought newspapers, but on such an occasion he could allow himself to do so, out of Party funds.

The artless newsvendor, however, admitted that there was nothing of the kind in any of his papers, so they bought nothing.

He must cut this nonsense out and go to the reading room to work. But Bronski, shaken and confused, seemed determined to keep it up, to trail around the streets or wait in the rain by the windows for the next dispatches—drifting with the current, like all rudderless people. Lenin reproved him, and went his own way. Once again, once again, along streets he had walked a thousand times, with eyes neither for houses, nor shop windows, nor people, he set out for the cantonal reading room.

Then, with its pointed windows before him, he hesitated.

Something would not let him enter. It was as though he was meant to get stuck in the doorway. As though something had swelled up inside him in the last half-hour, something which would not let him through.

In the meantime it had stopped raining.

He stood there, angry with himself. He could of course force himself, and sit there till evening, but ... A clear and immediate task summoned him—his work for the Swedes—but ... This distraction could not have come at a worse time. Then there were his notes for *Marxism and the State* ... But still he could not go in.

Instead, an uncharacteristic, alien, even criminal thought surfaced in his mind: he would go to the Russian reading room. That nest of Social Revolutionaries, anarchists, Mensheviks, and nondescript Russian riff-raff. Like a nest of snakes—he always tried to avoid it, not to walk along Culmannstrasse, not to breathe the same air, not to meet or even see any of them. But now he thought: that's where they'll probably all gather, if they haven't already ... They may know nothing, but they can be relied on to talk. Might hear something. Tell them none of my business, but try to get something out of them.

He broke all his rules and let himself be drawn to that ordinarily repugnant place.

Culmannstrasse was not at all near, and he would have quite a way to go uphill. He went.

As he had expected, he found that about twenty people had come in from the cold and damp to pack the overheated little room in their damp clothes, some of them sitting, some with no thought of sitting—but not one of them silent, all talking at once, babbling and bawling, so that the general din swept across the room in waves. Nothing surprising in that! Your Russian loves to pour out his heart.

He had been mistaken in one respect only: he had thought that they would go for him, be surprised to see him, show hostility. But no. Some did not even notice his arrival, but those who did took it as natural, as though he were a regular visitor.

Lenin answered questions—without answering. He asked no direct questions himself. He sat on the edge of a bench in a corner of the room and took off his bowler. Sat and listened, as only he could: picking up the nuances which others did not even hear.

No one, as it turned out, knew more than was in the same old dispatches, except for this one thing: victory had come 'after three days of struggle'—'after three days' was a bit of fresh news brought by someone. This 'three days' gave it the stamp of authenticity, did it not, they gasped, and no longer doubted. Lenin found it unnecessary to voice his objection: why, in that case, had there been no report during those three days? All in all, no one knew more than was in the dispatches, but they stopped every last gap in their information with a multitude of words.

One man—he had never seen him before—with his tie

tugged awry, kept rushing at person after person, waving his arms like a cock flapping his wings, leaving his incoherent sentences unfinished and moving on. A woman, a tall woman, sniff-sniffed at a little nosegay of snowdrops: whatever anyone said to her set her rocking in amazement and sniffing.

Contempt was all that Lenin felt for the mouthings of these quasi-revolutionaries eloquently discoursing on *freedom* and revolution, with no understanding at all that events might fall into patterns as varied as the combinations on a chess-board, knowing nothing of the enemy or of his skill in inter-cepting a movement under way or even forestalling it. They might have been talking about a day of general rejoicing, as though it were all decided, had already happened. (But *what* had happened, and what was needed to make it happen—which of them understood that?) What was the Tsar doing? What counter-revolutionary armies were advancing on Petersburg? Would not the Duma most probably panic and hurriedly do a deal with the reactionaries? Were not the proletarian forces still weak and unorganised? These were things they did not think about, questions which they did not attempt to answer. Suddenly, it seemed, reconciled to each other, forgetful of party differences, these animated ladies with ribbons round their hats filled each other's ears with jubilant twaddle, and lo and behold, after an hour or two they felt themselves no longer involuntary inhabitants of Switzer-land, but 'simply Russians', and indulged in simply Russian and typically groundless speculation as to how all of them could most quickly make their way home together.

I ask you!

Lenin too was buttonholed by effusive bores with chim-erical projects. People came and sat next to him—some of them knew him, and some did not, for not all of those present were politically minded. He looked through screwed-up eyes at these arm-wavers, drunk without wine, these twittering ladies, and gave no one a sharp answer, or indeed any answer at all.

The plan they were working on was this: all émigrés must now unite, irrespective of party (petit-bourgeois heads, chock-full of rubbish!), and form a General Committee for the Repatriation of Russian Émigrés in Switzerland. And

[174]

then ... and then ... and then they would somehow return, just how nobody knew, though all sorts of suggestions were made. And they were convening a preparatory commission that very evening!

Return, without knowing what was going on there? Perhaps revolutionaries were already being shot against every wall?

There was an influx of fresh people—but not of fresh ideas. Once again, everybody compared his news with everybody else's, and once again no one had a single word to add. Lenin left these vacuous chatterers as he had come, almost unnoticed.

Outside not only had the rain stopped but the clouds had thinned and it was lighter. The damp was lifting, but it was as cold as ever.

His legs wanted to take him downhill, first to the library, then home.

The right thing was to go straight home.

He no longer knew where he should go.

He stood still.

Only two hours ago, at lunchtime, everything had been so clear: he had known that he must split the Swedish Party, known what he must read, write and do for this purpose. Then an unauthenticated, improbable and unwanted event had crept up on him, seemed at first not to have impinged on him, not to have pushed him off course—but it was doing so now. Diverting his energies and wrecking his routine.

Suddenly it was impossible to go back to the library.

Nor did he want to go home. In the past year talking everything over with Nadya had somehow begun to bore him: her replies, delivered with longwinded solemnity, were so obvious as to be superfluous. Never a fresh and original response, no help from her in testing his ideas.

His legs were impatient for motion.

Yes, but not through the streets, he was sick of them, couldn't stand the sight of them. Why not go up the Zürichberg which was close by?

A wind was blowing, cold but not too strong. There would be no rain, and indeed the sky was growing lighter, the sun might break through any minute.

In his overcoat, which had almost dried in the reading room,

Lenin turned sharply uphill. Your legs are less tense in the mountains and your thoughts more settled; you begin to understand things.

The steeper and shorter the street, the more quickly he would be there, on top. His legs were as strong as a young man's. Boys with satchels on their backs were hurrying from afternoon school in the same direction, and Ilyich kept up with them. He wasn't even out of breath, and his heartbeat was healthy.

So far, so good. But—his head ... His head Lenin carried like some precious and stricken thing. This apparatus for instantly taking unerring decisions, for discovering un-answerable arguments, was, through nature's mean vin-dictiveness, afflicted, and the disease, so it seemed, had ramified, making itself felt in new places all the time. It was probably like mould germinating in a massive lump of living matter—bread, meat, fungus—a thin greenish film with fibres penetrating deep inside: the whole was at once appar-ently sound and yet ineradicably infected, and when his head ached he felt the pain not all over but in patches and filaments. You could tell yourself that it was just an ordinary headache, the sort everyone has, and that if you took a powder it would go. But when at other times you found yourself thinking that it ached in a special way, irremediably, and that the powder would give only illusory relief for a few hours, you were gripped by a dread like the dread you had felt in the cell at Nowy Targ: you would never break free of it! There was no escaping that head. The whole world awaits your judgement and your decisions! The whole world can be steered by your will! But you yourself are gripped fast, and cannot break loose!

Heart, lungs, liver, stomach, arms, legs, teeth, eyes, ears, all healthy—an inventory to be proud of. But with nature watch-ing like a sharp-eyed and pitiless examiner you had omitted something from the list—you couldn't include everything— and the disease had immediately noticed your omission and crept and crept through the secret passages of destruction. Just one wormhole was enough to bring the whole statue of health down in ruins.

This weakened his regret for their disagreements and

misunderstandings. It makes things so much worse when you try too hard to be friends again. In a year you can learn to do without someone. He needed her. Needed her. But did she need him as much?

Such a short way away, and she hadn't come to see him in a year?

Yes, of course. She was with somebody else …

But a protective cover of half-dead resignation settled around him.

From the cantonal hospital he wound his way up the slopes where the richer Swiss burghers had clambered above the city, closer to forest and sky, with a view far over the lake, and built their houses, the miniature palaces of the bourgeoisie. Every one of them had thought of ways to beautify his home—whether with patterned brickwork, ornamental trees, a spire, big gates, a veranda, a coachhouse, a fountain, or by calling the house 'Mountain Rose', 'Gordevia', 'Nisetta'. Wisps of smoke were rising from the chimneys—the fires of course were lit for comfort.

This carefully contrived combination of beauty and comfort, shut off from the world by fences, railings, title deeds and convenient Swiss laws, remote from the herd down below, filled him with seething irritation. Oh, how splendid it would be to swarm up here and destroy those garden gates, windows, doors, flowerbeds, with stones, sticks, heels, rifle-butts— what could be finer, what could be jollier? Were the deprived masses so demoralised, had they sunk so deep into the mire that they never would rise in rebellion? Never remember Marat's burning words: *Man has a right to wrest from his fellow man not only his surplus but even his necessities. So as not to perish himself he has a right to cut his neighbour's throat and devour his still quivering body!*

This splendid Jacobin attitude to life would never awaken in the proletariat of the lackeys' republic because it was fattened on scraps which fell from its masters' tables. And opportunists like Grimm entangled it in their spider webs.

But in Sweden perhaps …?

And what was going on in Russia now?

A great deal could happen in Russia, but there was no one to give it direction. Probably all was lost by now and drowned in blood—but they would learn about it from newspaper reports two days late.

It was getting lighter all the time, not because he was climbing higher but because the sky was clearing. On foot-paths and carriageways the smooth, close-packed cobbles never sullied by dust or mud were dry now underfoot. Should a passing carriage splash you from a puddle the water would be clean. There were many trees along the hilly streets, thicker woodland higher up, and higher still the forest.

Here you met people simply taking a stroll, not going about their business. First one, then another slow, sedate bourgeois couple went by, with furled umbrellas and dogs on leads. Next came two old ladies, conversing in loud complacent Swiss voices. Then somebody else. All enjoying the luxury of living in such a district. Then passers-by, and signs of life generally, became fewer and farther between.

On the very edge of the forest a level street ran across the mountainside, neither rising nor falling. It led to a railed-in observation platform, where you were supposed, as far as the foliage of trees lower down allowed, to admire the distant view of an inlet and the whole city under the blue-grey haze in the hollow—the spires, the chimneys, the dark blue double trams as they crossed the bridges. Here, too, the cold, mechanical, metallic clangour of bells floated up once again from the monotonously grey churches.

There was also a little avenue of tall trees, gravelled, with benches, only a dozen paces in length, leading to one solitary grave, and made for no other purpose. When Nadya and he had been on the great oval face of the Zürichberg they had always ascended by other streets and to different places, and had never wandered this way. Now he went up to this grave on its high vantage point.

Breast-high from the ground stood a rough, rugged grey gravestone, and on a smooth metal plate set in the stone these words were engraved: 'Georg Büchner. Died in Zürich leaving his poem *The Death of Danton* unfinished ...'

He didn't at first understand why this name, Georg Büchner, seemed familiar ... The names he knew best were all those of Social Democrats, politicians. But a poet? ...

Suddenly he realised. It was his neighbour, who used to

live at No. 12 Spiegelgasse, right alongside, their walls adjoined, their doors three steps apart. An émigré. Lived in the neighbourhood. And died there. Leaving *The Death of Danton* unfinished.

Idiotic nonsense. Danton was an opportunist, Danton was no Marat, who cared about Danton? But never mind him, here lay a neighbour. He too, no doubt, had yearned to go home from this accursed, stifling, narrow little country. But had died in Zürich. In the cantonal hospital, or perhaps at 12 Spiegelgasse. The inscription did not say what he had died of. Perhaps his head had ached like this, ached and ached ...

What was he to do about his head? His sleeplessness? His nerves?

And what in general was going to happen? One man was not strong enough to fight all the rest, to correct and direct them all.

Not somehow an enjoyable encounter.

All Zürich, probably a quarter of a million people, locals or from all over Europe, thronged there below, working, doing deals, changing currency, selling, buying, eating in restaurants, attending meetings, walking or riding through the streets, all going their separate ways, every head full of thoughts without discipline or direction. And he stood there on the mountain knowing how well he could direct them all and unite their wills.

Except that he lacked the necessary power. He might stand up here above Zürich, or be lying in that grave, but change Zürich he could not. He had been living here for more than a year, and all his efforts had been in vain, nothing had been done.

Three weeks ago this city had been revelling in its idiotic carnival: bands barging through the streets in clownish costumes, squads of zealous drummers and earsplitting trumpeters, characters on stilts, others with oakum hair a yard long, beak-nosed witches and bedouins on camels, carts carrying merry-go-rounds, shops, dead giants, cannon shooting soot, tubes spitting confetti—how many thousands of idlers had sat up at night preparing for this, making costumes, rehearsing, what an abundance of well-nourished manpower, released from the threat of war, they had squandered on it!

If only half as much manpower could be thrown into a general strike!

In a month's time, after Easter, there would be the 'farewell to winter' festival (there were more holidays than you could count in this country), and yet another procession, this time without masks and make-up, the craftsmen of Zürich on parade, just like last year: outsize sacks of outsize grain, outsize work-benches, bookbinders' benches, grinding wheels, tailors' irons, a brick-roofed forge on a float with smiths plying the bellows and hammering as it went along; hammers, axes, pitchforks, flails (stirring unpleasant memories of how his mother had once tried to make a farmer of him, at Alakayevka— he loathed those pitchforks and flails); oars carried over the shoulder, fish strung on poles, shoes on banners, children with baked loaves and pretzels—yes, indeed, they might well boast of all this labour, if they had not lapsed into bourgeois degeneracy, if only they did not so doggedly proclaim their conservatism, if it were all something more than a defiant clinging to the past, which must be destroyed without trace. If behind the craftsmen in leather aprons there were no horsemen in red, white, blue and silver tunics, violet tailcoats and cocked hats of all colours; no marching columns of old men in old-fashioned frock coats carrying red umbrellas, no learned judges with outsize gold medals, not to mention marchionesses and countesses in velvet dresses and white wigs—the guillotines of the great French Revolution had failed in their task! And once again trumpeters by the hundred and bands by the dozen, and mounted brass bands, and horsemen in helmets and breastplates, halberdiers and infantry of the Napoleonic period—the last time the Swiss had been at war—how merrily they played at war, since there was no need to march to the slaughter-house, and the traitorous social patriots would not call on them to turn about and start a civil war!

What sort of working class was it, anyway? When their landlady in Bern, a proletarian who took in ironing, learnt that they had cremated Nadya's mother instead of burying her, that they were not Christians—she had turned them out. Another landlady had turned them out simply for switching on the electric light in the day-time, to show the Shklovskys how bright it was.

No, there was no hope of raising them in rebellion.

What could a handful of foreigners do, however sound their ideas might be?

He turned away from the avenue and took a steep path up towards the forest.

The clouds were thinning to a tender primrose colour, so that you could guess where the evening sun was.

Now he was in the forest. It was untended, but there were little avenues here and there. Interspersed with the firs were trees with greyish-white trunks, but not birches or aspens. The damp earth was thickly carpeted with dead leaves. It was muddy and you could slip, but in the mountain boots which were so ridiculous on city pavements he was quite at home here.

He climbed steeply, working his legs hard. He was alone. No neatly dressed couples took their walks in this damp and muddy place.

He stopped to get his breath.

On the bare trees the damp-blackened bird-boxes were still empty.

There is no harder climb than that from illegality to legality. *Underground* means just what it says: you keep out of sight, do everything anonymously, and suddenly you must climb up to a high place and say: Yes, here I am! Take up your arms, I will lead you! Which was why 1905 had proved so difficult for him, while Trotsky and Parvus had seized complete control of the Russian revolution. How important it is to reach the scene of revolution in good time! If you are one week late you lose everything.

What would Parvus do now? I should have given a more friendly answer!

Shall I go then? If the news is fully confirmed, shall I go?

Just like that? Abandon everything? And fly through the air?

Beyond the first ridge the ground fell away to a dark damp grove of firs, and the road there was churned-up mud. But you needed no path to walk along the ridge itself—it was dry, with grass and scattered pines growing on it.

Up another hillock.

From here the view opened out again more spaciously than ever. You could see a large stretch of unruffled leaden grey lake and all Zürich under the inverted basin of a sky never shattered by shellburst, never rent by the cries of a revolutionary crowd. And there was the sun, already setting, not down below but almost at eye-level, beyond the gently sloping line of the Uetliberg.

As though he was awaking from healing oblivion, the thing which had driven him so unseasonably, in the middle of a working day, out into the damp air on the mountain surfaced again in his mind: the unease and agitation he had experienced in the Russian reading room, the chorus of sheep bleating that the revolution had started.

How credulous they were, all these professional revolutionaries, they would fall for any fairy tale.

This was just the time to show the greatest distrust and caution.

He moved on along the dry pathless ridge, over brown grass and dry twigs. Here on the mountain squirrels often ran up the trees, and sometimes young mountain goats, the size of a dog, could be glimpsed in the distance darting across the road.

High up in the silence and the clear air the pressure in his head eased, the cramping iron band was removed. All irritations, all irritating people, were cancelled, forgotten, left down below.

This last winter had been a hard one, and had thoroughly exhausted him. It was impossible to live under such strain, he must take care of himself.

But what was the point? If he was to do nothing, why take care?

In any case he would not live long. Something was wrong with his head. Seriously wrong.

The ridge along which he was walking ended abruptly where a gravel road ran across it. Here was a place he recognised—the obelisk. A path led down to it. It commemorated the two battles of 1799 in which the revolutionary French and the reactionary Austrians and Russians had fought for Zürich.

Lenin sat down on a damp bench facing the obelisk. He was tired.

Yes, indeed, there had been shooting here too. It was a frightening thought that Russian troops had been even here.

That even this place had been within reach of the Tsar's paw.

The clop-clop of hooves on the hard ground reached him from above, from beyond the brow of the road. Out of the dark wood in the fading afterglow appeared first a woman's hat held by a ribbon, then the woman herself, dressed in red, then a chestnut horse. The horse was walking, the woman sitting erect in the saddle, and there was something in her bearing, in the carriage of her head, which made him think... Inessa?!

He shuddered, saw, believed!—although it was quite impossible.

She came nearer—no, of course it wasn't—but there was a certain resemblance. That awareness of herself, that way of carrying herself like a rare and precious object.

She came out of the dark thicket, all in red, and rode by in the damp, clean, noiseless evening.

Of the two the horse was the more conscious of its beauty. Its glossy hide was a light chestnut, almost yellow, it wore an ornate bridle, and it stepped daintily on its neat little hooves.

The horsewoman seemed apathetic or perhaps sad as she sat looking straight ahead down the sloping road, without a sideways glance either at the obelisk or at the shabby man (or mushroom?) squat on the bench in a round black hat.

He sat very still studying her face and the hair like a black wing peeping under her hat.

If he could suddenly liberate his mind from all the work that needed to be and must be done—how beautiful this would seem! A beautiful woman!

Her only movement was the swaying of shoulders and hips as the sway of the horse lifted her toe-caps in the stirrups.

She rode on downhill to a turn in the road—and there was nothing but the rhythm of hooves for a little while longer.

She rode on, carrying a little part of him away with her.

L-2

Lenin had made a close study of many earlier revolutions and attempted revolutions—since revolution was what he was born for and had lived for he naturally knew more about it than anything else—and had his favourite personalities, episodes, methods and ideas. He had seen for himself only one revolution, and not from the beginning, not all of it, nor had he been in the main centres of action. He had indeed taken no part in it, had through no wish of his own merely observed it, drawn his conclusions, and later amended them.

But there was another revolution in another country, while he was a babe in arms, with which he felt a fateful affinity, which made his heart beat faster like the sound of a beloved name, an ineluctable passion which was both love and pain: he suffered for its mistakes more than for his own, he anxiously scanned each of its seventy-one days as though they were the sublimest, the decisive days in his own life, its name was for ever on his lips: the Paris Commune!

In the West, the one thing on which people wanted his views and considered his opinion important was the Russian revolution of 1905, and he gave regular talks on it, particularly on January 9th, the most notable date in Western minds. (He had done so this year, too, in the Zürich Volkshaus, warning his audience that 'Europe is pregnant with revolution!' with Switzerland mainly in mind.) But it was boring for him to talk about a revolution which had been filched from him (and the jealous conclusions he had drawn in his rivalry with Parvus and Trotsky were best kept to himself for the time being).

About the Paris Commune no one ever asked him, there were many people who could talk about it with greater authority, but he yearned towards it, as though if one lacerated breast, one wound, were pressed against another they might help each other to heal. And when one by one all the participants and non-participants in the 1905 revolution were forced to flee secretly, surreptitiously from a Russia where all was lost, in the damp Geneva winter of 1908, despondent, at loggerheads with all his old comrades, exasperated to the point of nervous collapse, he had sought relief in his lonely work on the lessons of the Paris Commune.

In the course of this last anxious winter the cliquish tittle-tattle of the Skittle Club had worn him down, and he felt a physical dread of speaking in a large crowded hall, but he accepted with the greatest alacrity a sudden invitation, arranged by Abramovich, to lecture on the Paris Commune at La Chaux-de-Fonds on March 18th, the anniversary of the rising. (Many French refugees had lived round La Chaux-de-Fonds since Huguenot times. Refugee *communards* had joined their fellow countrymen, and descendants of both groups still lived there.)

Then the news of revolution in Russia had dropped from the sky and from day to day was gradually disentangled.

It was less than three days since that first unconfirmed report from Russia—three twenty-four-hour days, since he had not slept for three nights; but most surprisingly his head no longer ached, he no longer felt ill at all after this powerful injection of fresh energy—yet in those seventy hours how many feelings and thoughts had rushed and blazed and roared through his breast and his head, as though through the flue of a great furnace! Knowing so little, piecing the fragments together, he had made picture after picture of what was happening there. And had taken decisions to suit every variant. Experienced as he now was, his decisions were all impeccably correct, but the picture itself was always delusive, because subsequent dispatches refuted or modified earlier ones. He had no reliable information *of his own* from Russia, had never had any, and could have none.

As time goes by you get to know yourself. Even without intellectual soul-searching you cannot help noticing certain

[185]

characteristics in yourself. Inertia, for instance. At forty-seven you aren't quite so nimble. Even when you see the right political steps to take you cannot get up speed all at once. And when you do, it's just as difficult to stop.

The tremendous news from Russia had not immediately diverted him from his previous course, not instantly taken possession of him—but it was more and more powerfully obsessing him now. The first night had passed in a torment of regret: why, oh why, had he not moved to Sweden a year ago, as Shlyapnikov had urged him to do, as Parvus had suggested? Why had he stayed in desperately stupid bourgeois Switzerland? All through the war years it had seemed so obvious that he must not leave Switzerland at any price, that he must sit it out here to the end. But now it was just as obvious that he should have left in time! Whether to split the Swedish Party, or just to be close to events in Russia—Stockholm was the place! From Stockholm too it would be possible to send for someone from Russia, one of the Bolshevik members of the Duma for instance, if they came back from Siberia.

Earlier on it would have been possible to do it quite inconspicuously, through Germany of course, the only sensible way. But now, with everybody alert, in a fever of excitement, endlessly discussing—it was no longer possible to slip away. Damn it all!

It was, however, equally impossible to postpone action a minute longer: whatever the prospects of success, he must begin to act at once! So as soon as he awoke on the morning of the 16th he exerted himself and by a well-tried route sent off a photograph for a transit visa—to Hanecki. (Poor old Kuba had also been having a hard time: he had been arrested in January for illegal trading, and deported from Denmark.) He followed it with a telegram explicitly stating (in case they didn't think of it themselves—he shouldn't have been so careless and impatient) that *Uncle*'s photograph should be forwarded at once to Sklarz in Berlin, at No. 9 Tiergartenstrasse.

He must make peace with the whole crew immediately. Nobody else could help to get him out.

The morning of the 16th also brought fresh reports. The Tsar was supposed to have abdicated!!! (Could he have done so in such a hurry? Without putting up a fight at all?? What could possibly have made him do it??? No, this was a trap of some sort. Who was replacing him? That was the thing. If there was no Nicholas there would be somebody else, somebody cleverer.) And apparently a Provisional Government had been formed (but were the Tsar's ministers in safe custody?) including Guchkov, Milyukov and even Kerensky. (Shades of the contemptible Louis Blanc! How your pseudo-Socialist loves sticking his behind into a bourgeois ministerial chair.)

The émigré blabberers would be in ecstasy: not one among them would shut his pink bleating mouth from morning to night. But when you thought of it, Petersburg was awash with the blood of workers for a whole week, and then, as always in European history, as in 1830, as in 1848, the eternally credulous masses had surrendered power pure and unalloyed to that bourgeois scum, to all those Shingarevs and Milyukovs. The old hackneyed pattern!

The crows in the émigré library might gawp and gush, but a true revolutionary must prick up his ears, strain every nerve, keep a sharp look-out! Back *there* they would make a mess of things, surrender everything in a spirit of maudlin Christian charity, because there wasn't a real tactical mind amongst them. It rankled that he was not there himself, that it was impossible to intervene, impossible to direct them.

He hadn't thought of Kollontai all winter, but in the last few days she had become one of his most important correspondents. The centre of events had shifted to where she was. As soon as he had posted the photograph to Hanecki he sat down to write to Aleksandra Mikhailovna: to explain to her what *we* must do now. Our slogans of course remain the same: convert imperialist war into civil war! That the Cadets are now in power—that the fatheads have leapt into the middle of it—is simply too marvellous. Let's see how the darling boys will provide the freedom, bread and peace they've promised the people. While we wait and see. While we arm ourselves and wait. Arm ourselves and prepare for the higher stage of the revolution. No confidence in Chkheidze and the Socialists of the centre! No merger with them! We will act independently of all others! Always independently! We will not allow anyone to involve us in attempts at unification. In fact, it will be extremely unfortunate if the Cadet government permits a legal workers' party at all. That would greatly weaken us. It is to be hoped that we shall remain illegal. But if legality is thrust upon us we must preserve an underground section: the underground is where our strength lies, we must never completely abandon the underground! We must wrest *all* power from the swindling Cadets. Only then shall we have the 'great and glorious' revolution! I am furious, absolutely furious that I cannot come to Scandinavia immediately!

But early on the morning of the 17th new information put things in a different light: the Cadet government's victory was far from assured, the Tsar hadn't abdicated at all, only run away, and no one knew where he was, but from the usual pattern of European revolutions it was perfectly obvious: he was gathering a counter-revolutionary host, preparing his Koblenz. Even if he did not succeed in this, he could try some other trick, yes, that's it—he might for instance flee abroad and issue a manifesto about a *separate peace* with Germany! Nothing could be simpler! They were so very cunning, the Romanovs. (In *his* place that would be the best thing to do, a brilliant step: become the peasants' Tsar-Peacemaker!) He would immediately win the sympathy of the Russian people, the Cadet government would totter and take flight, and Germany —Germany would cease to be the ally of the revolutionary party because it would be of no more use to her ... (Oh dear, dear, we have quite a while to wait before we go to Russia, there's nothing for us to do there yet. So why did I send that telegram to Hanecki? How stupid of me to leave a trail.)

Aleksandra Mikhailovna, we're afraid that we shan't manage to leave this wretched country very soon, it's a very complicated business. We can best help by advising you from Switzerland.

Well then, the comrades who were going from Stockholm to Russia must be given a precise tactical programme. It could be presented in the form of theses ... his hand was already writing them... The most important thing for the proletariat to do is to arm itself, that will help, whatever happens: first they must crush the monarchy, and then the predatory imperialist Cadets ... Ah, Grigory! Sit down and help me ... The new government won't be able to give the people bread, and without bread freedom is no use to anybody. The only way to

[188]

get bread is to *take it by force* from the landlords and capitalists. And this can only be done by a workers' government (by us) ... Oh yes! I must write a postscript to Kollontai telling her to acquaint Pyatakov and Evgenia Bosh with these theses. (The time had come when he could no longer scorn even the piglets. Nobody was to be scorned at a time like this. The really useful person to have around just now would be Malinovsky! What a shame they had blackened the man beyond hope of rehabilitation. He was doing very positive work in the prisoner-of-war camps. They had issued another statement in his defence in January. He must be saved, must be brought back.) Next ... and this is important: we must not neglect to stir up the benighted domestic servants against their employers—this will be a great help in establishing the power of the Soviets. What does genuine freedom mean today? First of all, the election of new officers by the soldiers. And in all contexts, general assemblies and elections, elections to every office in the land. The complete abolition of bureaucratic interference in everyday life, in the schools, in ... Russia's present freedom is very relative. But we must know how to use it for the transition to the higher stage of revolution. Neither Kerensky nor Gvozdev can offer the working class a way out ... Right, the post office will be closing shortly, I must get the letter off now.

But look at this, Grigory, they've proclaimed an amnesty. A general amnesty must mean freedom for all the parties of the left? Can they really have brought themselves to do it? This is bad. Very bad. Now that he's legitimate Chkheidze and his Mensheviks will spread themselves and occupy every position before we have a chance. Will they leave us standing yet again?

No, no, we mustn't sit idly by, we must be ready with something. And quickly! We won't go, of course, the revolution may still be rolled back, it's happened so often before, you can never be sure of anything—but we must prepare the way just in case. I tell you what ... Yes, that's it ... Is it Saturday today? That's bad. Never mind, you hurry off back to Bern, yes, you must go back immediately, there's nobody else: try and catch Weiss at home, late this evening would be best, he always goes off somewhere on Sundays. And tell him to go straight to the German Embassy. On Monday! We must break out of this vicious circle. Why is Romberg himself saying nothing, why doesn't he send somebody? It's surprising. They ought to be more interested than we are. We can at least contemplate travelling via England, whereas they have no other way out. Make Weiss understand that he must in no circumstances mention you and me in particular, but must say that a lot of people, including us, would like to go. In that way we can sound them out and see what the chances are. What should we ask for? Suppose Germany publicly announces that it is prepared to let through all those who ... all those whose love of freedom draws them home to Russia. That's it. As far as we're concerned such a declaration would be a fully acceptable basis.

Another thing! All these diplomats are blockheads, they don't begin to understand who's who and what's what in the revolutionary movement. So let Weiss build us up a bit. Let him hint that the revolutionary movement in Russia is *completely* controlled from Switzerland. That every important action has to be decided on first of all in Switzerland. That in Russia, quite literally, not a single important step is taken without instructions from us. So that in the present circumstances ... Got it? Right, get going, I too have an early train to catch tomorrow, to La Chaux-de-Fonds, for my lecture.

All the enthusiasm he had felt for the Paris Commune three days ago had turned to dust.

Next morning, in his haste and absent-mindedness, he put on a completely worn-out cap by mistake, and at La Chaux-de-Fonds the chairman of the trade union took him for a tramp and wouldn't believe that he was the expected lecturer.

On Sunday afternoon in the Watchmakers' Club he gave a lecture in German entitled 'Will the Russian Revolution go the same way as the Paris Commune?' without a written text, improvising from brief notes, before a gathering of two hundred people. He had no real feel for his listeners, no idea what interested them and what they expected. He seemed to have lost his sensitivity, he no longer saw the auditorium or felt the paper in his hand, he let slip all sense of time. What was more, his affection for his early love, the Commune, deserted him, he was imperceptibly drawn further and further afield, and not so much in precise formulations as in stray thoughts, he began fusing the two revolutionary experiences—the Commune, and this other which had flowered so suddenly: is it fraudulent, or the greatest event which life has in store? We must not repeat the Commune's two fundamental mistakes: it failed to seize the banks, and it was too magnanimous: instead of shooting the hostile classes wholesale it spared their lives, imagining that it could re-educate them. This is the greatest danger which threatens the proletariat—this magnanimity in the middle of a revolution. It must be taught not to be afraid of ruthless mass methods!

He didn't know what the La Chaux-de-Fonds watchmakers made of it all, but he himself was in the grip of a growing anxiety: time was running out! While this lecture was going on here in La Chaux-de-Fonds, there in Petersburg opportunities were slipping away irrecoverably, and some pathetic and unworthy person was steadily tightening his hold on power.

A French lecturer replaced him on the platform. Abramovich had assembled all the local Russians, and since there were still twenty-five minutes or so to wait for the train, Lenin gave them too a sort of lecture, and of course on the same subject, but this time without analogies, speaking straightforwardly about things which preoccupied them as much as himself, and ending with this forthright statement: 'If need be we shall not be afraid to hang eight hundred bourgeois and landlords on lamp-posts!'

Rocked by the train, he thought and thought. There was no real *power* in Petersburg. Power meant the Tsar and his bureaucratic machine, but they had been thrown out. Power meant the army, but it was chained to the front. The Cadets had no power at all. The Soviet of Deputies carried little weight. What could it do? And there was a great danger, in fact it was almost certain, that Chkheidze's Mensheviks would presently seize control of it. In Petersburg and in the Soviet there was a vacuum, and he felt its suctional pull demanding that he fill it with his own power. If he succeeded in taking Petersburg he could challenge both the army and the Tsar.

Should he go then? Should he make up his mind at last and go??? ...

Shaken by the speed of the train, Lenin sat by a window in

the second class, his image reflected in the darkness outside together with the bright interior of the carriage, fixedly staring, absently surrendering his ticket for a first and a second inspection, not hearing the passers-by or the names of stations —thinking.

Should he go? ...

He was in that state of mind when he neither saw nor heard whether there was anyone else in the carriage. Because he was alone at the window, alone in the train, Inessa was not at Clarens, but travelling at his side. How good it was—they hadn't talked like this for a long time.

It's like this, you see—it's quite impossible for me to go. And just as impossible not to. I tell you what—perhaps you should go on ahead for the time being? There's no risk in it for you. And nobody will bar your way. (This was quite sincere, there was no contradiction in it: the person you love is the one to send ahead, because if you feel concern for her you naturally share with her your concern for the Cause. That was always the way of it, and how could it be otherwise? And if she didn't refuse outright it meant that she agreed.)

It was nearly a year since they had seen each other and their relationship was gradually breaking down ... But on this auspicious, this happy Commune anniversary, rocked by the train side by side with Inessa, he had the old warm and joyous feeling of closeness, the same urgent need for her, yearned to say a couple of words to her in reality here and now, tomorrow would be too late!

He jumped out at one station to buy a postcard, and posted it at another.

... Dear Friend! ... I have read about the amnesty ... We are all dreaming of going home ...

Yes, dreaming—that defines it exactly! A dream is precisely what it is.

... If you want to go, come and see me. We'll have a talk about it ...

No, really, we must see each other ... If only for a second! Do come! ...

... I would like you to do something for me—find out on the quiet in England whether they would let me go through ...

England, of course, wouldn't want to let him through: he

was an enemy of the war, an enemy of the Entente. But perhaps there was some way of deceiving the English?

Anyhow, going via France, England and Norway might take as much as a month. In that time the new regime would become firmer, find its feet, get into its stride, and there would be no hope of shaking it, of diverting it. He must hurry, before it hardened.

It was the same with the war. People would get used to the war continuing in spite of the revolution, and think that it must be so.

Then there were the German submarines. Now that the long awaited moment had arrived, how could he take risks? Only a fool would do so.

That night, at home in the Spiegelgasse, he slept only fitfully. Sleeping or waking, he was more and more tormented by the nagging question: should he go? Go at once?

Morning brought reports which all said the same thing, without contradictions. The Tsar had indeed abdicated! No doubt about it! And not only he, but Michael too, the whole dynasty, the whole gang of them had renounced the throne.

There would be no restoration!!

The only burning question now was how to return. By what route? By what means? It must be quick! There mustn't be an hour's delay now! He must get there at once! Before it was too late! Must seize the helm! Correct the course, set a new one, immediately!

Weiss is seeing Romberg today. Good. But for the moment that is ... just exploring the ground, a tentative enquiry ... My hasty remark three days ago, to Hanecki again, about the '*Swedish deaf-mute*', wasn't serious. More important is the passport photograph. (A good thing I sent it.) Could it possibly reach Sklarz today? No, of course not. The day after tomorrow. Then the matter will be considered by the Ministry, and by the General Staff. *They* surely won't delay, they should have thought of it for themselves, should have been quick off the mark and sent somebody to suggest it. Not a word from them. Blockheads. Everything has to go up the bureaucratic ladder.

Or perhaps they are holding out for a higher price? If so, they are politically beneath contempt. For some distance along the road they can look forward to a solid alliance and a separate peace. (Though later on ... The Prussian Junker brain cannot of course follow the spiral paths of the dialectic. How can they see beyond today's trenches? What do they know of the world proletarian revolution? Later on, of course, we shall outsmart them, because we are cleverer. But for the time being all they need think of is making a separate peace and detaching the Baltic provinces, Poland, the Ukraine, and the Caucasus. All that we'll readily give them—we've said so all along.)

Siefeldt hasn't turned up either. Not a sign of life from Moor.

But what about Parvus? The unfailingly clever Parvus! What can he be doing? Izrail Lazarevich! Here I sit in this wretched Switzerland as if in a corked bottle! No one knows better than *you* how important it is to be in time for a revolution! Why is nobody offering me a chance to go? Is anything at all being done?

The room in the Spiegelgasse was a rat-hole. The sun never shone through the window.

Where was I, then? There's no time to think properly, you're bound to miss something. What are they doing there in Petersburg—Kamenev and Shlyapnikov? Kamenev bears a great historical responsibility. The *theses* have filtered through to them, but that was before ... Yes, that's it: I must summarise them again in a telegram. A telegram to Stockholm won't break the Party bank. Nadya, Moisei, will one of you go and send a telegram? Our tactics: *No confidence in the new government! No rapprochement with any other party! Your sole duty to arm, repeat arm, yourselves!* ... Put your headscarf on, you've got bronchitis! ...

All the same, just in case the Germans are too slow we must also make preparations to travel through England. Tell Karpinsky, for instance, to get a transit visa in his own name, and we can put my photograph on it. Me in a wig, though, or else they'll recognise me by my baldness. Must write to him at once! An express letter to Geneva! Who'll post it? Very well, I'll run down myself.

The wind was blowing harder and colder along the narrow back streets, and whenever a stronger gust met him head on it stopped him in his tracks. But it's good to walk in the teeth of the wind, to fight your way against it! It's a lifelong habit, I've always walked against the wind—and I don't regret it. I wouldn't want a different life!

The same wind carried him up the steep street and home—just in time: he was called to the telephone on another floor. Who could it be? Hardly anyone knew this number, he used it only in exceptional circumstances.

Up the dark stairs.

It was Inessa!! All the way from Clarens! Her voice was like the modulations of the piano under her fingers.

'Inessa, it's so long since I heard you! ... My dearest! ... Only yesterday, while I was on a journey, I sent you a post-card ... We must go at once, we must all go! I'm working on a number of possibilities, one of them is bound to come off!! Apart from everything else we must reconnoitre the English route. Perhaps the most convenient thing would be for you to ... What? It isn't convenient? ... Well, I never insist, you know that ... You're not sure whether you'll go at all? Not go at all?? Can't make your mind up?' (They were out of tune, at cross purposes. When you don't meet for a long time it's always the same, you are never attuned to each other—and the telephone doesn't help.) ... 'Why ever not? How can you bear not to go! ... I was absolutely certain! It never entered my head ... Yes, of course, it's your nerves ... I know, I know ...' (Let's not discuss our nerves over the telephone, at a franc a minute.) 'Well, all right ... I'll try something else ...'

She would have done better not to ring, it had only depressed him ... spoilt his mood and his plans ...

Where their relationship had gone wrong he couldn't guess. Or why. What was there to spoil it? When had he ever tried so hard to please, when had he deferred to anybody as he did to her? ...

He had been surprised that with the three of them it had held together so long. But now it had collapsed ...

The memory of this telephone call rankled, and he couldn't force himself to work. He sat down to write by the window where it was lighter, with the action programme for the Petersburg comrades on his knees—left to themselves they would never ... The wind was simply roaring outside and blowing through cracks he had never noticed before. It was March, but maybe he should light the stove? The landlady and her husband would say they were wasting coal. He draped his overcoat over his shoulders.

He must begin by analysing the situation. What precisely the situation was he did not know, and he could not reconstitute it from the meagre scraps in the papers, but in a general theoretical way he understood it well enough and knew that things could not have gone otherwise in Petersburg... Is what has happened in Russia a miracle? There are no miracles, in nature or in history, they are just a philistine illusion ... The corruption of the Tsarist gang, the brutality of the Romanov family, those organisers of pogroms who have inundated Russia with the blood of Jews and workers ... An eight-day revolution ... But it was rehearsed in 1905 ... Awash in blood and mud, the cart of the Romanov monarchy is overturned ... This is in effect the beginning of that great universal civil war to which we have long summoned you ...

The things left unsaid in his conversation with Inessa prevented him from working. Her telephone call had excited him —and left him unsatisfied. They had misunderstood each other, riled each other again.

It is *only natural* that revolution has broken out in Russia first. That was to be expected. We did expect it. Our proletariat is the most revolutionary in the world... Apart from that the whole course of events shows clearly that the British and French embassies and their agents were the immediate organisers of the conspiracy, together with the Octobrists and the Cadets ...

Are we to go then while she stays behind? Stays behind for good? Events can separate people, part them for ever ...

Milyukov is in the new government merely to make honeyed professorial speeches, while the decisions are made by henchmen of hangman Stolypin... The Soviet must try to ally itself not with the peasantry at large but first and foremost with the agricultural labourers and the poorest peasants, separating them from the more prosperous. It is important to split the peasantry right now and set the poor against the rich. That is the crux of the matter.

What a hurricane! And there seems to be a dash of snow

[196]

with it. It's dark even by the window now, I need the lamp
again.

No, I shall have no peace until I've written to Inessa ...
Why don't I do it at once?

'I cannot conceal my deep disappointment from you. We
should be galloping home, but people keep "waiting" for
something ... If I go via England under my own name they
will simply arrest me ... I was certain that you would rush
off there! ... Perhaps your health won't let you? ... At least
let Krylenko try, so that we can find out what the procedure
is.'

Now that his ache had eased he was seized and carried away
by the sudden thought that he could use this letter for another
purpose.

'Here's something just to think about: so many social patriots and Russian patriots without party live near you, some
of them rich! Why shouldn't the obvious idea of going home
via Germany occur to *them*? *They* could easily ask for a carriage to Copenhagen. *I* can't do that—I'm a "defeatist". But
they can. If only I could teach that scum, those idiots, some
sense. Perhaps you can put them up to it? You think the Germans won't give them a carriage? I'm willing to bet that they
will! I'm certain of it! Of course if it came from *me* or from
you it would immediately spoil the whole thing ... But there
must be fools in Geneva who would serve the purpose? ...'

The whole problem has come down to this: there is no
point in reconnoitring the route through France and England
—Germany is the only way to go, of course, but it must look
as though the idea had originated not with *us* but with somebody else.

If anyone doubts it, we must argue along these lines: your
misgivings would make a cat laugh! Can you see the Russian
workers believing for a minute that old and tried revolutionaries are truckling to the German imperialists? Are you afraid
they'll say that we've 'sold ourselves to the Germans'? People
always have said this sort of thing about us internationalists
anyway, simply because we don't support the war. We shall
prove by our deeds that we are not German agents. In the
meantime all we must think of is going home, if necessary
with the help of the devil himself!

But someone—who?—must be induced to take the initiative. Otherwise even if there's an opportunity I shan't be able to go. We cannot be the only ones or the first to suggest it as *our own idea*—that would cause difficulties in Russia.

So the day rolled by, bringing no decision, offering no way out. So much might have happened in Russia, so many blunders could have been made in that one day!

Press your head to the dark window-pane and stare out into the howling darkness—and you could imagine that those were bullets flying! It must be just like this in Petersburg now. There was a furious howling in the chimney, and that banging somewhere on the roof was new—the wind must have torn something loose. What a blizzard!

I feel as if we're missing our very last chance. Must write, and keep writing.

'Milyukov and Guchkov are puppets in the hands of the Entente ... It is not for the workers to support the new government, but for the government to "support" the workers ... Help the workers to arm, and freedom in Russia will be invincible! Teach the people *not to believe mere words*! ... The people will not want to go hungry, and will soon realise that there *is* bread in Russia and that it can be *taken by force* ... And so we shall win through to the democratic republic, and after that to socialism ...'

He felt wound down and his arms and legs ached for exercise. That's it—he would go out into the storm and walk till he could walk no more! If he didn't he wouldn't get to sleep anyway. Let the wind buffet him, blow right through him.

At the foot of the stairs he buttoned himself up to the chin and rammed his old cap on firmly. (The chairman of the La Chaux-de-Fonds trade union had asked 'Who's the pilot?')

Once outside he was buffeted and bowled along—a real hurricane! But it was dry underfoot, with only a little snow. The street lamps were all visible, but the sky was dark. A crash and tinkle of glass from a shattered lamp. There was a rattle of loose tiles—something might fall on your head here.

The narrow, narrow, narrow streets of the old city; turn where you would it was a labyrinth. You could wander like a lost mouse, and never break through to the spaciousness of Petersburg squares.

Russia used to be governed by 40,000 landlords. Surely we can muster as many supporters and govern rather better?

On the Niederhofstrasse, the street for nocturnal pleasure-seekers, there were hardly any passers-by. They had all taken refuge behind the brightly lit windows. And there, floundering helplessly in the great wind, huddled, bent double, came a familiar limp and flabby figure ... Grigory!

From the station? Back again already?

'Vladimir Ilyich, there's a lot to tell you, so I decided to come instead of writing.'

'What about Weiss? Did he see Romberg?'

'Yes, today. I'll tell you right away.'

They staggered this way and that, fighting off the wind with their arms, clutching at their caps. They started trudging back. Talking was difficult, but they could not wait.

At Bern the émigré Committee for Return to the Homeland had been in session all day long, with Grigory representing the Bolsheviks. Come on then, how did it go?

'Talk, talk, talk, they went over every possible way of going —via the Allied countries or via Scandinavia. Then Martov suggested going via Germany!'

'Martov??'

'Yes—via Germany!!'

'Martov did???'

He could not get his breath to shout.

'Yes! In exchange for German prisoners of war in Russia!'

'Ma-artov????'

'Said we should get the consent of the Provisional Government—and negotiate with the Swiss authorities through Grimm ...'

What a stroke of luck! *What* a stroke of luck! The suggestion had come from good old Yuly, not from us! So that's what we'll call it—the Martov Plan! As for us, we are merely falling in with it.

The first word has been spoken.

Documents

(Nos. 18, 19, 20, 22, cited by Werner Hahlweg:
Lenins Rückkehr nach Russland 1917)

23 March

*(Baron Romberg, German Ambassador in Bern, to the Ministry
of Foreign Affairs. In cipher. Top secret.)*

Prominent revolutionaries here wish to return to Russia
via Germany, since they are afraid to go via France because
of U-boats.

23 March

*(Zimmerman, Secretary of State, German Ministry of Foreign
Affairs, to the Staff of the Supreme High Command.)*

Since it is in our interests that the influence of the radical
wing of revolutionaries should prevail in Russia, it seems
appropriate to authorise transit.

25 March

*(Staff of the Supreme High Command to Ministry of Foreign
Affairs.)*

No objections to transit of Russian revolutionaries travelling as a group and reliably escorted.

26 March

*(German Ministry of Foreign Affairs to Ambassador Romberg.
In cipher.)*

Group transport under military surveillance. Date of departure and list of names must be submitted four days in
advance. Objections on part of General Staff to particular
individuals unlikely.

27 March

*(Ambassador Romberg to Imperial Chancellor Bethmann Holl-
weg. Top secret.)*

From a thorough discussion with our Russian confidential
agent Weiss I have ascertained how we can support the revolution in Russia ... We must avoid anything which might be
exploited by the warmongers in Russia and the countries of
the Entente. The partisans of peace in Russia will prevail ...
I replied that if Germany had clung above all to the ruling
dynasty, it was because in earlier times she had met with
understanding and support for her peace-loving policy only

in this quarter. If we now meet with the same goodwill on the extreme left this will suit us just as well.

As regards peace terms he said that his party would not go to war for Courland and agreed to the detachment and neutralisation of Poland.

He explained to me that the Cadets, in alliance with the Entente, possess unlimited means for propaganda, whereas the revolutionaries have great difficulties in this matter. Weiss has hitherto claimed only very small sums, fearing that it would arouse suspicion in his own party if he were seen in possession of larger funds. But these objections are no longer valid. The larger the funds we can make available to him, the more active he will be in the cause of peace. I should like to recommend very emphatically that in any case we put 30,000 francs at Herr Weiss's disposal for the month of April, which he wants to use in the first place to enable his most important party comrades to travel to Russia. I believe that it would be unwise at this decisive moment to restrict him too much and so antagonise him. May I also promise him further subsidies?

L-3

Since that evening of March 19th, when the storm had hit
Zürich and battered the old city all night long, then at dawn
had brought a heavy fall of snow, shortly followed by rain,
then sleet, then snow again, then more rain, then towards
evening more snow, and only in the course of the following
night, when it had whitened the whole city, had it blown itself
out—ever since that night and day of storm, pacing and racing
about the cramped cell-like little room from dining table to
half-dark window, imprisoned in his Swiss cage, confined to
his room by bad weather, his leaping passion to enter the fray
almost bursting his ribcage, Lenin had decided, or rather it
was decided for him, that since he was detained he must without delay write and send to the Petersburg Bolsheviks a programme of action, write and send letters and half-written
apologies for letters, and as soon as he had finished get someone to run to the post with what he had to show for that day,
while he plunged into the newspapers—he bought them all
now, the whole room was littered with them—and picked out
scrap by scrap whatever myopic Western correspondents had
spotted and seized on and feeble bourgeois minds had selected
as suitable for their press—pick it out, snap it up, bring the
searching light of his Bolshevik intellect to bear on it, unravel
it, explain it to the uncomprehending, the bewildered, the
stupid. 'Defend the new Russian republic'? A fraud, decep-
tion of the workers. 'Now overthrow your Wilhelm!' A
fallacious slogan, all efforts must be concentrated on overthrowing the bourgeois government in Russia! The Pro-

visional Government is a government aiming at restoration of the monarchy, an agent of British capital! Better a split with any of our own comrades than collaboration with Kerensky or Chkheidze, or the slightest concession to them!

In this process of analysis and elucidation he discovered for himself missing links and forged for the Party new plans of organisation. In response to the magnificent manifesto of the Bolshevik Central Committee (Kamenev's work for sure, he had a head on his shoulders) which was issued in Petersburg on March 13th, and reached him much abbreviated in a newspaper he happened to read ten days later, he must suggest and explain how they should organise *now* (his advice was different from that he had given in 1905). This time the whole mass of the people must be armed. The people's militia must take in every single member of the population from fifteen (to draw adolescents into political life!) to sixty-five, both sexes alike (to pluck women from the stultifying kitchen atmosphere!), and this militia must become the basic organ of state administration! Only thus, *with weapons in everyone's hands*, could they ensure perfect order, the speedy distribution of bread, and shortly thereafter peace and socialism!

Between Tuesday 20th and Friday 23rd four such 'letters from afar' were dashed off and immediately expressed—once written they become more and more urgent, you can't hold them up, can't hold them back—to Hanecki—who else?—to that splendid, clever, efficient Kuba, who would make arrangements to send them on to Petersburg. (Copies went immediately to Inessa, who wrote to Usievich, who wrote to the Karpinskys, who wrote back to Lenin. All this was extremely important for concerting tactics.) Somebody was always tripping up, which meant another dash to the post office, then a hunt round the kiosks and reading rooms for unread newspapers, and then once again analysis and conjecture, projecting new points in the programme like rays of light into the future. First Lunacharsky tries to wriggle out of attacking Chkheidze—let him feel an admonitory chill. Next, Gorky, the half-wit, comes poking his nose into politics: with his greetings to the Provisional Government, and his bedtime stories about 'an honourable peace', a terribly damaging statement, he must be rapped on the knuckles. (If you can't stick to the Party line, don't butt in where you aren't wanted, get on with your pretty pictures.) Then there's all that unpleasantness with Chernomazov in Petersburg: not satisfied with Malinovsky, they are out to swamp the whole Party with buckets of filth. Kollontai is on her way to Russia, lucky thing! While we're stuck here, there might be time to get the five hundred pages of my *Agrarian Programme* retyped—who'll take it on? Another thing, I absolutely must write some leaflets for Russian prisoners of war, there are two million of them: 'Loudly declare that you will return to Russia not as the Tsar's army but as the army of the revolution,' (they could very easily be used against it!) 'and we will hurry home and send you food and money from Russia ...' Oh yes, as I leave, I simply must write a farewell letter to the Swiss proletariat, brand the chauvinists once again, point the way once again. (That's dangerous though, it might hinder my departure. I know— I'll write it and leave it behind, then set off the fuse with a telegram from Russia telling them to print it.) Meanwhile ...

Meanwhile I'm not happy about Inessa. She is hurt. Angry. She's staying on in Clarens. (Or perhaps she was no longer there? Their correspondence had broken down, so perhaps she had already left?) She was angry with him, but, as women always do, she had twisted it into something different, irrelevant, pretending that there were 'theoretical disagreements', capriciously raising objections to things which a child would find obvious. How badly he needed her there at his side! What a time she had chosen! Surely this was no time for female sulks? There was nobody to collect and systematise all the reports from Russia, he could easily miss something enormously important! Not only was she unwilling to try out the English return route, she wouldn't even come to Zürich for one little day! In 1914 she had abandoned her children and travelled from the Adriatic to Brussels for him, yet now that she was only in Clarens and had no children on her hands she hadn't once come over.

There was no knowing whether she would go home with them at all.

But all these things, even his troubles with Inessa, were eddies on the face of the water, while the big events were silently gliding like great fat dark fishes near the bottom.

A cryptic signal from Hanecki: 'It's *coming*!' But waiting was torture. Counting the days, you would think the passport could have been prepared in Berlin and sent—but it hadn't arrived.

And the all-powerful Parvus said nothing.

Of course, he had every right to be offended. And it was quite possible that he was testing Lenin's nerves, and holding out to strengthen his own position.

But they had no escape from each other: events were forcing them together.

The Germans had paid him millions for a mirage, but now there was something worth paying for.

And there would be someone to receive money now. Now at last it was needed.

Meanwhile the noisy 'Repatriation Committees', even where Zimmerwaldists predominated, were all clinging to legality, waiting for permission from the venal Guchkov government, which had already sent 180,000 francs privately collected for the return of their dear compatriots, only of course through Allied countries (with German submarines sinking the convoy of fools on the way), and this money was already the centre of intrigues: the Bolsheviks might be denied their share, and the meetings almost came to blows.

Ilyich of course did not attend, but he was told about these sessions in detail. As these quarrels became more and more heated—and the mood of the émigrés in Switzerland was only a pale reflection of what was to come in Russia—he realised that in his haste he had slipped up badly: it was impossible to obtain an individual passport and travel alone.

So on the 23rd, a week after sending the photograph, he telegraphed Hanecki to call it off: 'Official travel arrangements for individuals unacceptable.'

That was that. They'd refused.

However, Weiss had called several times on Romberg, who assured him that urgent letters were being exchanged with Berlin, some of them by special messenger. Gradually, out of the darkness, out of the future, out of the unknown emerged the contours of the great design—like a mighty locomotive out of the mists, though as yet its wheels were turning very, very slowly, if indeed it was moving at all.

Behind it there was a carriage.

Emerging from the darkness—a carriage.

Not at all bad. Acceptable.

But for the time being I hope that as far as those windbags on the Repatriation Committees are concerned ... these conditions are not public knowledge?

No, no. Oh no. That's all at the official level. Our business with you is confidential.

Good, good. So gradually, putting a few heads together, by our joint efforts, we're getting things a bit clearer, finding our way. It's a bit less vague. (But how it dragged on! Not like the Germans, this! They should be feeling the heat more now that the Provisional Government had announced that it was continuing the war.)

They began preparing a list of those who would go. They asked their own supporters all over Switzerland, but secretly, that was important—they didn't want any foreign bodies. At the same time—this too was important—they told everyone the opposite: England won't let us in, and it can't be done through Germany. They loudly discussed anecdotal attempts: Valya Safarova had petitioned the British consulate, somebody had wired a protest to Milyukov, and Sara Ravich had had the idea of a fictitious marriage with a Swiss citizen, which would give her the right to travel direct. Lenin laughed, and recommended an 'eligible old party'—Akselrod, who could no longer be of use to the revolution in any other way.

With the Germans things dragged on slowly, though sometimes the wheels seemed to turn too fast. Or rather one machine ground away independently of another. On the evening of March 27th he gave the Swiss in the Volkshaus a two-and-a-half-hour lecture on the Russian revolution, telling them that the second, the true revolution, was still to come, that a suitable form for the revolutionary state already existed in the Soviets, and that it was necessary to prepare immediately for an uprising against the bourgeoisie. The lecture refreshed him by diverting his thoughts from all those exasperatingly inconclusive plans of departure. He was quite happy to walk home in the pleasant evening air. When he got up to his room he exclaimed in surprise: a thin little man with grey wavy hair and a corner of handkerchief sticking out of his pocket sat there smiling, as though expecting a joyous reunion, and was self-importantly slow to rise and shake hands.

Sklarz!!!

Without a word of reproach—or of praise—Lenin advanced with a piercing, quizzical look—the look which always frightened people—on Sklarz, who lost his self-assurance and rose, whereupon Lenin wrung his hand as though he wanted to tear it off.

'Well? What have you brought?'

No traveller's tales, no preambles, no gush—just tell me what you've brought.

This businessman who was becoming more and more at home in the high politics of great Germany, who was received with respect by prominent generals and in ministries, and whose mission today was to bestow generosity, was none the less taken aback by that cutting gaze from slit eyes, by the unfriendly curve of eyebrows and moustaches, taken aback as though a football had bounced in his face, forgot his smile, the amiably verbose prelude with which he had intended to amuse, even his carefully prepared jokes, and immediately told his big news.

He did not sit down.

Lenin did not sit down.

Only Zinoviev sat and snuffled.

It was like this. Sklarz had come not just from Parvus, although Hippohead had begun the whole thing (of his own accord, before Lenin's request reached him, as soon as he had heard of the Petersburg revolution, believing that he knew what to do quite as well as Lenin). Sklarz had brought all the necessary documents from the General Staff authorising transit through Germany, together with assurances that the German Consul in Zürich, and if necessary the German Ambassador in Bern, would assist their departure. Sklarz had brought the documents all signed and sealed, and there they lay—a miracle, except that miracles never happen—on the faded oilcloth in the circle of yellow light from the paraffin lamp.

Here you are. Herr Ulyanov. Frau Ulyanov. All in order. And Zinoviev? ...

Of course. And Frau Lilina. All in order.

Yes, well ... and what of ...?

Yes, there's one more, five altogether, yes, here it is: Frau Armand.

The genius Parvus had not lost his touch, he had thought of everything.

Inessa too ...

That was it, then! All problems solved! Not another hour of waiting: no more manoeuvres, diplomatic play-acting, fretting, dispatching messengers, waiting for news, being at everyone's mercy. All he need do was to pack his belongings— and a revolutionary has none!—and go, tomorrow evening if he felt like it! It's only twelve days since the Tsar abdicated, and in three days' time we shall be in Petersburg and switch the Russian revolution in the right direction! Could things have gone more quickly, in the middle of a world war? Nobody could possibly spoil things now—he would burst upon the first great meeting in Petersburg before anyone else, beating even the Siberian exiles to it, he would turn the Soviet of Deputies against the squalid Guchkov government, he would create a people's militia embracing all citizens of both sexes from fifteen to sixty-five, he would do whatever he pleased!

The documents lay where they were, with their Gothic flourishes, with the German eagle stamped all over them, and with Lenin's photograph, which had come in useful after all, already gummed on to them—those precious documents, in the light of the paraffin lamp, on the cheap oilcloth with threadbare patches.

Documents which could not be drawn up until the Chancellor himself said 'Yes'.

Parvus had made up for his old misdemeanours.

The lumpish Zinoviev smirked and reached for the documents. Lenin turned on him like an enemy, and he froze.

Alas, the lesson had been learnt long ago: the hand carelessly thrust into the flame of revolution gets burnt.

Nervously rubbing his almost scorched palms above the documents, Lenin snatched them away and clasped them behind his back.

A deal like *this* could not remain hidden. It would be impossible to make it look respectable. The threads would be relentlessly unravelled until they led right back to Parvus, and it would be no good trying to hide behind his glorious revolutionary past, you would be daubed with the same mud, and the rudder of revolution wrested from your hands.

Perhaps that was it: perhaps Parvus was going to so much trouble simply so that Lenin would be tarred with the same brush? Perhaps Parvus had arranged this individual and family journey to slip a noose on him and then take him in hand? Dictate conditions, tell him how to conduct the revolution?

Only Lenin had spotted the trap in time!

'But you put in the order yourself, Herr Ulyanov! Nothing is more insulting to a businessman than to hear good merchandise called inferior.'

'I ordered them, yes. But I was wrong. Circumstances have shown me my mistake.' Lenin spoke gloomily, still on his feet, his voice betraying none of the tension in his mind, dictating like a ventriloquist. 'There must be a large group. About forty people. A whole carriage. A sealed carriage with extraterritorial status.'

He raised his eyes and scrutinised Sklarz very closely, and this time there was a gleam of sympathy and even of good humour. (He had remembered that this man could get through to the German government within twenty-four hours. It was an excellent thing that he had come. Thank you, Parvus! We'll just modify the plan a bit, it'll only take a few days.)

Sensing that Lenin was a little more friendly, Sklarz relaxed and smiled. He was unaccustomed to such treatment even in the most exalted circles, and had done nothing to deserve it.

'Izrail Lazarevich asks us to hurry,' he reminded Lenin. 'In case this *government enjoying the people's confidence* makes peace!'

'It won't, it won't.' Lenin's slit eyes twinkled merrily.

He made Sklarz sit down and sat facing him across the table, and not so much with his words as with his eyes hypnotically instilled his instructions so that the other would remember and carry them out exactly.

'Go and tell them straight. We've been working along other lines for a very long time. They must clearly understand that we cannot compromise ourselves, and they must not put us in a compromising position. They must not restrict the right to go, exclude people fit for military service and so on.'

(Lenin for one was fit, but had never been called up because he was the oldest son in the family: he owed his exemption to his brother's execution.)

'Nor must they enquire into attitudes to the war. They mustn't arrange any individual checking of passports. We go out as we came in—not a crack in the eggshell, you understand? And not a word in the press.'

It must all be done suddenly. The carriage must be let through like an artillery shell. The public must have no time to hear of it and discuss it.

'There's another thing.' Sklarz had just remembered the most delightful bit. 'The German government will meet all the expenses of the journey.'

'What next!' Lenin's eyes flashed angrily. 'It would look very strange if we travelled on those terms. How stupid your people are. We absolutely must pay for ourselves!' More calmly he added, 'Third-class fare.'

He hadn't finished yet. 'You come to see me, and you can't manage to dress discreetly. You may have been noticed by some of the comrades. You will, therefore, stay on for a day and keep to your hotel, while Dora comes here. Without any documents, of course. She can tell some cock-and-bull story, and I shall say no. Only then will you leave. And as soon as the Germans agree you must let us know immediately!'

When Sklarz had got the message, collected the documents, shaken hands with deferential gratitude and gone away, the feeble Zinoviev put his surprise into words.

'How can *we* put conditions to *them*?' he asked, his flabby shoulders shifting uneasily.

Lenin gave him a sharp squint.

'They can't get out of it. It's more important to them than to us.'

'We'd better conceal Sklarz's visit.'

'No, we'll tell Platten. It'll be worse if he finds out for himself. Platten and Münzenberg we mustn't lose.'

Also, for safety's sake—an immediate letter to Hanecki (who might show it around): 'I cannot, of course, use the services of people connected in any way with *The Bell*' ... Not forgetting to mention 'your plan for travelling via England ...'

The more erratic his movements, the more false trails he laid, the safer his burrow.

Take Romberg's offer of a carriage. This carriage must be talked out into the open, helped to emerge into the mind of the public like a chicken from an egg. They must mention it casually in speech and in writing.

'Perhaps the *Swiss* government will get us a carriage ...'

'Maybe the *British* government will let the carriage through?'

'How do you mean?'

'From port to port, of course. Why shouldn't the British let a sealed carriage go through? With Comrade Platten, for instance, and a few others, it doesn't matter who or how many, irrespective of their views on war and peace?'

'What do you mean—Britain's an island, and we're talking about a railway carriage?'

'Yes, well, it would go by a neutral ship. With the right to inform all, repeat all, countries of its sailing schedule.' (In case a German submarine knowing no better sank its friends.)

No one could talk of anything but the journey. Several émigré committees and all the party directorates had asked Grimm to negotiate with the German Ambassador. (Since Martov's proposal to release one German prisoner of war for every émigré repatriated.) Excellent, excellent. The Martov Plan was working!

And Grimm had taken it on! (Better still.) But he was not just the Zimmerwald leader, he was also a member of the Swiss Parliament, and it would have been unwise for him to take such a step without the sympathy of the government, of Foreign Minister Hoffmann, for instance. (This meant that there must have been consultations. Why should Switzerland be against it, anyway? The Swiss themselves wouldn't mind sending that rowdy bunch packing. Switzerland itself was in an uncomfortable position with the war on every side.) Grimm went to see Romberg again and again, negotiating *in absolute secrecy*; not a word must filter through to the press, there must be no stain on Swiss neutrality—but he didn't mind reporting to the main representatives of each party (Natanson, Martov, Zinoviev). 'We're all in the know.'

It was going at a snail's pace. But never mind, never mind.

Romberg said 'Yes' to everybody, and Grimm considered that he had made light work of it. If he says yes, it's yes. All that remains is for you, comrades, to request permission from your Provisional Government.

Oh, thank you! Excuse us for not taking off our caps to you! And after that we spend our lives kow-towing to Louis Blanc-Kerensky?

Through all these anxious days the rogue Radek was missed terribly: they summoned him by telephone from the Davos sanatorium where he was recuperating, but even for the Russian revolution he wouldn't come immediately. Before he arrived, though, he had understood the situation, and thought up yet another diversionary *démarche*—through a German correspondent in Bern. Romberg had given him the same answer as all the others: yes, yes, of course, we will let through all those who wish to go.

Still the German frontier would not open, and all those *desirous* of travelling had got no further than making enquiries, comparing notes, asking the Provisional Government's permission in telegrams to Kerensky, and mostly just dithered.

Everyone had agreed—and nothing had begun to happen. These old-world diplomatic methods were so clumsy.

Nothing could begin to happen until the great dark fish in the depths had finished their run.

Until Sklarz had reported Lenin's counter-proposals in Berlin.

Until the German General Staff said its final yes.

Until the German Ministry of Foreign Affairs took fright: by now there had been much public discussion of their return and Prince Lvov had told the Swiss minister frankly that the speedy departure of the émigrés from Switzerland was undesirable. So that they must hurry—who could be causing the delay?—Germany would never have another chance like this.

On Saturday March 31st Ambassador Romberg in Bern at last received instructions to inform Lenin as quickly as possible that his proposals concerning extraterritoriality had been accepted, and that there would be no individual checks or discriminatory conditions.

On Saturday—and 'immediately!' So that there was no question of lazily putting it off over Sunday. Breaking all the laws of discretion, and using the emergency line, the German Ambassador started ringing around, and finally found the German Socialist Paul Levi in the Volkshaus: 'Please inform Lenin as quickly as possible that ...'

Another ring called Ulyanov to the neighbours' telephone at home in the Spiegelgasse, and he went along in some agitation thinking it might be Inessa.

But no—it was his answer!!!

At long last the way was open! At last they could fix the departure of a group of forty for the day after tomorrow, giving the comrades just time enough to pack, return their library books, put their financial affairs in order, assemble from Geneva, Clarens, Bern, Lucerne, and buy provisions for the journey. They could be away by Tuesday, and the following Saturday—a week later than if he had accepted Sklarz's first proposal—take a hand in the Russian revolution!

While he was still in the gloom of the musty staircase, and then in the dim daylight of his cell-like room—heavy snow with intervals of sleet had been teeming down all day long—gripping the revers of his waistcoat to prevent his hands from flinging themselves prematurely into action, soothed by the greatcoat-like weight of his greasy old jacket—Lenin forced himself not to rush off and announce the news to someone, but to think. Think. Think, rapidly pacing.

A strong man never loses his head in defeat and despondency. But losing your head in moments of success is easy, and for a politician this is the greatest of dangers.

The way was wide open—and still it was impossible to make use of it: there must be no explaining afterwards by whom and how it had been arranged that the leading Bolsheviks alone should suddenly be provided with a carriage, and why they had taken it.

A few more baffling and misleading moves must be made first.

There was no room here to stretch his legs, he couldn't go out in such weather (and reading rooms were long since forgotten). His restless pacing made him dizzy, and fiery spirals bored into his brain.

[213]

The way was open—but where to? To a forced wait on the Finnish frontier? Or to one of the Provisional Government's gaols? It was easy to imagine how the gales of chauvinism were howling in Russia by now! To present petit-bourgeois ways of thinking what he was doing was 'treason'. Even here in Switzerland the Mensheviks, the SRs, and the rest of the invertebrate émigré riff-raff would cry treason.

No!

No.

No ...

It was one thing to be restrained by circumstances—but how difficult it was to restrain *yourself* when you were set free and longing to go.

The next thing to do was to ... was to ...

The events which had glided like heavy dark fish near the seabed must now be seen passing over the surface like little white sailing boats.

The negotiations are *concluded*? So now's the time to *begin* them! Let's make it appear that we're only beginning today!

What more suitable personage for this task than guileless trustful Platten?

Obviously a group must be got ready. And a list already exists.

(Inessa! Won't you go even now? It's monstrous! You won't go with us? To Russia! To the great day we have waited for so long? You want to stay in this putrid place? ...)

Forty people can hardly be accused of treason. If there are forty the blame will be spread too thin to matter. We could of course pick up a few Maximalists and a mixed bunch of desperate characters, and it would all look a little more inno-cent. But ... it's better not to take outsiders along, not to have unnecessary witnesses of every move we make—and who knows what may happen? Anyway, what profit is there in transporting our enemies by our own efforts, in our own carriage, to Petersburg, just to fight them there? No! Every detail, including the date and time of departure, must be kept secret until the last moment.

Only the fact that negotiations are going on must be public. Without an agreement already in your pocket you couldn't possibly begin such negotiations. What a humiliation it would be if they failed! But now that we have an agreement, we can go ahead.

Like all proletarian business, like every step in the proletarian cause, this journey needs to be highly organised. Bind them with hoops of iron. Can't have some turd slithering out of it afterwards. We must all be in the same boat. No one must be able to evade responsibility, no one must be able to say: 'I had no part in it! I never suspected what was going on!'

Every one of them, then, must sign his name to it. As though he were taking a solemn oath. Like bandits kissing the knife. So that no one can break ranks later on and rush to 'expose' us. It's a very serious responsibility and all forty of us must share it.

(Surely Inessa will come? ...)

He had already sat down to draw up such a pledge. On his chair by the window, in the half darkness with a snowstorm outside, he balanced the paper on his knees and wrote—his slanting handwriting, bigger than usual in these days of agitation, tumbling over itself as it pursued his thoughts obliquely across the page—sketching out points which might be included. 'I confirm that I have been informed of the conditions proposed by the German Embassy to Comrade Platten ... and that in agreeing to conform to them I accept full political responsibility for the possible consequences ...'

Suddenly out in the corridor he heard Radek's pleasantly sharp, mocking voice. He had come, then! No guest or assistant could be more welcome just then! Karl, Karl, how are you, take your coat off, oh dear, the snow's got under your collar. You'll never guess what news we have for you!

The little yelps, the flashing teeth which his upper lip could not cover, the crop of curls, the halo of whiskers—Radek the mischievous, chuckling schoolboy.

Come on then, let's draft it together. And draw up equally firm conditions for Romberg.

'*You* make conditions for *them*?'

'Yes. What of it?'

'That's delightful!'

Radek was just the man for this sort of prank. His advice was as good as his jokes, he was inspired and yet circumspect.

[215]

Only smoking wasn't allowed in this room, he had to suck an empty pipe. And ...oh, no ...

'Vladimir Ilyich! What do we do about *me*! Surely you wouldn't think of not taking me?'

'Why shouldn't we take you?'

'Well, if we say here "Russian émigrés". I'm an Austrian subject.'

So he was, damn it! Damn it all! They'd got used to thinking of him as one of themselves—he was a 'Polish comrade' only for form's sake. But how could they not take him? A Radek couldn't be left behind.

Radek had already seen a way out. If Platten made a written agreement with Romberg—and if there was only a verbal understanding it would be still easier to confuse the issue— he must leave out the word 'Russian' and put in 'political émigrés'. Since only they were under discussion the Germans would put their fist to it without a second thought.

Normally tricks would be impermissible at such an enormously important juncture, in such an extremely serious matter, and the German General Staff was not a partner to joke with. But for Radek—that irreplaceable, that incomparable fount of ingenuity—for sharp, caustic, impudent Radek, perhaps he should risk it?

'But will Platten agree to handle the negotiations? Will he want to go?'

'There's nobody else. So he will agree.'

'What if Münzenberg were to go? He's a bit firmer.'

'Willi? No, he counts as a German deserter. How can he deal with the Ambassador? Or travel through Germany?'

'All the same'—Radek rattled his pipe-stem against his teeth—'all the same Platten is Party Secretary here, how can he travel with émigrés? Besides, he will be worried to death that it may somehow harm his Switzerland.'

'How can it? Switzerland can only benefit.'

No, Lenin had no doubts on this score. Platten as a rule sheepishly deferred to Grimm, but in the most important things he would go along, once he saw the point. He was a working man, a proletarian to the marrow. Of the discussions with Parvus he knew, and would know, nothing.

Whereas Radek knew it all, whether you told him about

Parvus or not. Radek had a quite indecent admiration for Parvus: in the taverns of Bern he might revile Parvus, as his international duty obliged him to, for his rash step towards the chauvinists, his wealth, his shady deals, his dishonesty, his love life—but he gaped and drooled so that you could see he thought Parvus a fine fellow and longed to be like him! ...

'As for Sklarz, I've told Platten that he's a twopenny-halfpenny errand-boy of the German government, and that I threw him out! I shall say about Grimm that there's something suspicious in his behaviour, he's holding up our departure, seeing what's in it for himself. But we can wait no longer, the revolution calls! Let's act like proletarians, openly, without secrets—and apply directly to the German Embassy! And he'll do it!' Lenin spoke with assurance.

What should they instruct him to say to Romberg? A completely new text was required. 'In Russia things are taking a turn which endangers the cause of *peace*. Russia must be wrested from the British and French warmongers. We shall of course endeavour in return to liberate the German prisoners of war. (Hold us to it if you can! ...) But we must be insured against embarrassment, and have guarantees that we shall not be pestered on the journey ... We are prepared to travel in locked compartments, with the blinds down if necessary. But we must be sure that the carriage will not be stopped ...'

Lenin dominated the room, pacing rapidly along its diagonal, three paces this way, three paces that, with one hand behind his back and flourishing the other, while Radek wrote, steadying the page with his empty pipe.

Radek always stirred in new ideas: if we're taking a step like this it might help to collect supporting signatures from Western Socialists ... Socialists, of course, but why not some eminently respectable people too? Where can we find them? ...

'Romain Rolland, for instance?'

What a brainy fellow! Just the thing!

It was high time to cast the hook. Who would dangle it in front of Rolland for them?

Since Radek's arrival Lenin had ceased to feel as though his head were bursting with a searing eddy of thoughts. He had an outlet for his ideas, he could express them and receive an answer. Here was another ... If they demonstratively started fresh negotiations through Platten, should they not just as demonstratively break with Grimm?

Break with a loud snap!

'Taking care to shift all the blame on to him!'

'And giving the blackguard a bit extra for what we owe him! Make him regret postponing the Swiss Congress!'

The way to do it was first to publish all the confidential information on his secret negotiations!

That hurts every time—the sudden publication of confidential matters. Leaves the enemy simp-ly stunned.

So why not immediately, without further ado, prepare such a publication?

'Dotting all the i's ...'

'And publish it tomorrow!'

Yes, with Radek the most strenuous work turned into a merry game! That was what he particularly liked about Radek—the way he entered into the spirit of things!

They were both sitting now—Radek writing, worrying his empty pipe with his teeth—no time for a smoke in the corridor—occasionally laughing and bobbing up and down on his chair as he thought of a neat phrase, while Lenin sat beside him and gave advice. Radek was the only person to whom Lenin could completely surrender his pen, and sit by with nothing to do but laugh. There had never been a cleverer pen in the whole Bolshevik Party. Bogdanov, Lunacharsky, Bukharin were all poorer writers.

'Another important thing is that it will look as though it's the Swiss who are negotiating, because they want to get rid of us. It's none of our doing!'

He was so clever, so quick, simply priceless!

'We'll get it published right away, tomorrow, by Nobs or ...'

'Tomorrow's Sunday. But I tell you what!' Sparks danced behind Radek's glasses. 'As it's Sunday tomorrow we'll send Grimm a telegram immediately. Right now, on Saturday evening!' Radek grinned and bobbed up and down as though there were splinters in his chair.

Lenin too bounced happily in his seat.

They talked and talked, interrupting each other, correcting each other, and Radek wrote it all down:

'Our party has decided ... to accept unconditionally ... the proposal to travel through Germany ... and to organise this journey at once ... We are *absolutely* unable to take responsibility ... for further delay ... emphatically protest ... and *will travel alone*!'

'Beautiful,' said Radek, scratching behind his ear. 'We'll coat it with chocolate for him. "We *earnestly* request you to reach an immediate agreement ..." Reach agreement tomorrow, on a Swiss Sunday! What's more, tomorrow is also April 1st, Western style!'

'April 1st?!!' Lenin hadn't laughed so much in a long time. All the tension of the last few weeks burst from his breast in loud, harsh, liberating spasms of laughter. 'This will be a nice box of chocolates for the centrist swine!'

'"Reach immediate agreement ... and *if possible* tomorrow." While all of Switzerland is snoozing!'

'"Inform us of the decision! ... Gratefully yours ..."'

It was like when in a game of chess you make a well thought out move and then see that it is even more effective and promising than you had calculated. This bit of fun—Grimm's Sunday chore on April Fool's Day—was typical of Radek the jester.

'And if he doesn't do it on Sunday—on Monday we shall be free to act ourselves!'

'On Tuesday, anyway ...'

Ah, but Radek had an even better idea. 'Vladimir Ilyich! What about Martov? We must write to Martov, particularly as he's the initiator of the *Plan*!?' Radek was choking with laughter.

'Write what to Martov?' Even Lenin's mind couldn't work quite so quickly.

'To tell him that we accept immediately *Grimm's proposals for us to travel via Germany*! That way we can do the dirty on Grimm by making it look like *his* proposal!!! Tell the whole world it comes from him! That the Swiss Socialists are shoving us out! A member of the Swiss Parliament!'

Now, this really was a stroke of genius! Bravo, Radek! Grimm would set up a howl! Make frantic excuses! But it's always easier to spit than to wipe it off. You have to learn to spit first and at the right moment.

'The scoundrel will wish he'd printed my pamphlet after all ...'

'It's getting late, though. We shall have to post it at the Fraumünster.'

'I can run down, Vladimir Ilyich.'

'Let's go together now we're in the mood.'

In that case they must look around and think what else needed to be done. Of course, a letter to Hanecki in Stockholm—'Urgent that you wire three thousand crowns for travel expenses!'

(Must also write to Inessa: 'Don't worry about money ... we have more than we thought ... The comrades in Stockholm are giving us a lot of help ... I hope that we shall have you travelling with us?')

Another thing—he must draw out the hundred francs he had deposited in the cantonal bank as a condition of residence in Switzerland. No point in pampering the lackeys' republic.

Lenin put on his iron-heavy quilted greatcoat and Radek the thin summer coat in which he ran round all through the winter, with his pockets crammed with books.

He filled his pipe and had his matches ready.

Lenin said out loud: 'That's fine. What can Platten's negotiations with Romberg amount to? Romberg will just take the documents out of his desk drawer. But we had to fling these few days in the chauvinists' ugly faces.'

Radek, lightfooted and pleased with himself, danced about like an adolescent.

'My hands itch, my tongue itches! I can't wait for the wide open Russian spaces, can't wait to start agitating!'

And, letting Lenin go in front, holding a match ready to strike in the corridor, he said:

'It comes to this, Vladimir Ilyich: six months from now we shall either be ministers or we shall be hanged.'

Documents

(Nos. 30, 31, cited by Werner Hahlweg:
Lenins Rückkehr nach Russland 1917)

31 March. Berlin
*(Memo by an official of the Foreign Ministry with the General
Staff.)*

... Above all we must avoid compromising the travellers
by excessive attentiveness on our part. It would be very
desirable to have some sort of declaration from the Swiss
government. If we suddenly send these restless elements to
Sweden without such a declaration it may be used against us.

31 March
*(Assistant Secretary of State von Stumm to Ambassador
Romberg in Bern. In cipher.)*

Urgent! The journey of the Russian émigrés through Germany should take place very quickly, since the Entente has
already started counter-measures in Switzerland. Speed up
the negotiations as much as possible.

2 April
*(Count von Brockdorff-Rantzau, German Ambassador in Copen-
hagen, to the Ministry of Foreign Affairs. Top secret.)*

... We must now definitely try to create the utmost chaos in
Russia. To this end we must avoid any discernible interference in the course of the Russian revolution. But we must
secretly do all we can to aggravate the contradictions between
the moderate and the extreme parties, since we are extremely
interested in the victory of the latter, for another upheaval
will then be inevitable, and will take forms which will shake
the Russian state to its foundations ...

Support by us of the extreme elements is preferable, because
in this way the work is done more thoroughly and achieves its
results more quickly. According to all forecasts we may count
on the disintegration being so far advanced in three months
or so that military intervention by us will guarantee the
collapse of Russian might.

Author's Note
Those who are surprised by V. I. Lenin's choice of words, his way of thinking and acting, may read more carefully those of his works which have been used here.

V boevoy komitet pri Sankt-Peterburgskom komitete (To the Combat Committee of the St Petersburg Committee). Sobranie Sochinenii (4th edition) Vol. 9, p. 315

Zadachi otryadov revolyutsionnoi armii (Tasks of units of the revolutionary army). *Op. cit.*, Vol. 9, p. 389

O lozunge 'razoruzheniya' (On the slogan 'disarmament'). *Op. cit.*, Vol. 23, p. 83

Rech' na s'yezde shveitsarskoy s-d partii 4 ii 1916 (Speech at the Congress of the Swiss Social Democratic Party). *Op. cit.*, Vol. 23, p. 110

Zadachi levykh tsimmerval'distov v shveitsarskoy s-d partii (Tasks of the left Zimmerwaldists in the Swiss Social Democratic Party). *Op. cit.*, Vol. 23, p. 126

Tezisy ob otnoshenii shveitsarskoy s-d partii k voine (Theses on the attitude of the Swiss Social Democratic Party to the war). *Op. cit.*, Vol. 23, p. 138

Printsipial'nye polozheniya k voprosu o voine (The war question: statements of principle). *Op. cit.*, Vol. 23, p. 141

Otkrytoye pis'mo k Sharlyu Nenu (Open letter to Charles Naine). *Op. cit.*, Vol. 23, p. 212

Dvenadtsat' kratkikh tezisov o zashchite G. Greilikhom zashchity otechestva (Twelve short theses on G. Greulich's defence of defence of the fatherland). *Op. cit.*, Vol. 23, p. 247

Nabrosok tezisov 4 (17) Marta 1917 (Draft theses of 4 (17) March 1917). *Op. cit.*, Vol. 23, p. 282

Pis'ma iz daleka (Letters from afar). *Op. cit.*, Vol. 23, p. 289

Pis'ma Lenina voennykh let (1914–1917) (Lenin's wartime letters), Sobranie Sochinenii (5th edition), Vols. 48, 49

I consider it my duty to mention four recent studies which have particularly helped me in writing these chapters. They are:

Werner Hahlweg: *Lenins Rückkehr nach Russland 1917.* Leiden 1957

Z. A. B. Zeman and W. B. Scharlau: *The Merchant of Revolution*. London 1965.

Willi Gautschi: *Lenin als Emigrant in der Schweiz*. Köln 1973

Fritz N. Platten Jun.: *Von der Spiegelgasse in den Kreml. Volksrecht*, 13iii–17iv.67

I must express my gratitude to these writers for their close attention to events which determined the course of the twentieth century, but which have been carefully concealed from history, and which because of the direction taken by the development of the West have received little attention.

Author's Index of Names

Abramovich, Aleksandr E. (b. 1893) Native of Odessa. Member of the RSDRP from 1908. In Switzerland from 1911: studied in Geneva, worked in La Chaux-de-Fonds Watch Factory. Returned to Russia with Lenin's group. Some indications that he was a Soviet agent in the Bavarian Republic in 1918. On the staff of Comintern.

Armand, Inessa Teodorovna (1874–1920) Born in Paris, into a French theatrical family. Brought up in Russia by an aunt who was employed there as a governess. Married the factory owner Armand, by whom she had four children, then left him for his younger brother and gave birth to another son (in Switzerland). During the 1905 Revolution was connected with the SR group in Moscow, was subsequently banished, then emigrated. After her second husband's death studied at the Sorbonne, met Lenin in 1909, and thereafter supported the Bolsheviks. Was Lenin's intimate friend, with short breaks, until her death, and was throughout this period among his closest collaborators. Visited Russia in 1912, was gaoled for a short time, but released thanks to her first husband's intercession. Took part in the Kienthal Conference with the Bolshevik delegation. Returned to Russia with Lenin's group. After the October Revolution was for a time Chairman of the Moscow Provincial Economic Council, later Head of the Women's Department of the Central Committee of the Party.

Bagotsky (Polish), Sergei Yustinovich (1879–1953) A Pole from Russia. Doctor. Was in Cracow with Lenin, followed him to Switzerland. At that time was Lenin's assistant in practical and financial matters, and in maintaining conspiratorial contacts through intermediaries with the Germans. As an émigré in Switzerland lived in style and spent freely (Nobs's testimony). From 1918 representative of the Russian Red Cross in Switzerland.

Bogdanov (Malinovsky), Aleksandr Aleksandrovich (1873–1928) Son of a physics teacher, educated at the Tula High School, in 1899 entered the Medical School of Kharkov University. 'Parted company' with the local group of Social-Democratic intellectuals 'over the question of morals, to which they attached unconditional importance.' Doctor, sociologist and philosopher. Light sentences of banishment on various occasions (Tula, Kaluga, Vologda). Sided with Lenin in 1904 and became a member of the first Bolshevik leadership. Theoretician of armed uprising, organiser of tactical assaults, expropriations, schemes for raising Party funds. Arrested together with the whole Petersburg Soviet in 1905, but soon released. During the revolutionary years 1906–1907 lived with Lenin at Kuokkala. Consistently adhered to the Bolshevik line of boycotting parliamentary and legal activity, which Lenin abandoned in

1907. Finding Bogdanov's presence in the leadership a nuisance, Lenin attacked his philosophical ideas (in *Materialism and Empirio-criticism*, 1909), and drove him right out of the Party. After that Bogdanov never held an important Party or Soviet post. Called up during the war, served as a doctor at the front. Published many works on political economy, philosophy, the organisation of science and of the economy, as well as two novels of fantasy. Died as the result of a dangerous experiment in blood transfusion.

Bosh, Evgenia Gotlibovna (1879–1924) Native of Ochakov. Married at sixteen to the son of a factory owner, left her husband when she was twenty-one and plunged into Social-Democratic politics (in Kiev). Bolshevik. Mistress of Pyatakov. Banished to Irkutsk Province in 1913, escaped with Pyatakov via Vladivostok. Was in Switzerland for a short time, then in Scandinavia. After the February Revolution Chairman of the Kiev Provincial Party Committee, urged the Guards Corps to advance on Kiev and overthrow the Rada, the Ukrainian nationalist government. Member of Kiev War-Revolutionary Committee. In the first Communist government of the Ukraine (Kharkov 1918) as 'People's Secretary for Internal Affairs'. During the Civil War assigned to punitive operations at provincial level (Penza, Astrakhan, Gomel), Commissar of the Caspian-Caucasian Front. Accused of Trotskyism in 1923. Committed suicide in 1924.

Brilliant See Sokol'nikov.

Bronski (Warszawski), Moisei (1882–1941) Native of Lodz, Polish Social Democrat, then Bolshevik. Emigrated to Switzerland in 1907. Close assistant of Lenin who introduced him into the Kienthal Conference. After the October Revolution worked for a time on the editorial staff of *Pravda*; Deputy People's Commissar of Trade and Industry; 1920–1922, Political Representative (Ambassador) in Austria. Held no important post after Lenin's death.

Bukharin, Nikolai Ivanovich (1888–1938) Most considerable theoretician and lost leader of the Bolshevik Party. Born into the family of a schoolteacher. Had a mixed upbringing—amongst intellectuals and ordinary people. Educated at Moscow High School No. 1, joined the Bolshevik Party at eighteen, co-opted to the Moscow Committee of the Party as a twenty-year-old student. Briefly detained on various occasions. Escaped abroad from his place of banishment. Emigré from 1911, studied intensively, began writing. Returned to Russia in 1917 by way of America, Japan and Siberia. From summer 1917 member of the Central Committee. Led the 'Left Communist' opposition to the Peace of Brest-Litovsk—instead of reinforcing Germany by a separate peace Russia should aim at world revolution. Published a great deal in the Soviet period (on economics, on politics, works of popularisation). Was a member of the seven-man leadership (Politburo) after Lenin's death,

[225]

and was used by Stalin to destroy it. Trotsky, Kamenev and Zinoviev were routed with his help, after which he and his supporters Rykov and Tomsky were eliminated. On the threshold of the thirties seems to have understood the criminality of Stalin's policies, which spelt ruin for the peasantry and for the general health of the nation's economy, but was unable to oppose them firmly and effectively. Shot after a show trial with the usual 'confessions'.

Burtsev, Vladimir L'vovich (1862–1942) Revolutionary, member of the People's Will Party in the 'eighties, terrorist at the end of the nineteenth century. Arrested, escaped. Called for the assassination of Alexander III in the British press—and even under English law incurred a prison sentence of eighteen months. Also expelled from Switzerland for terrorist propaganda. Specialised in exposing police spies in the Russian revolutionary movement. During the 1905 and 1917 revolutions edited the journal *Byloe* (*The Past*), from 1911–1914 the newspaper *Budushchee*, (*The Future*) which he sent from abroad to the Tsar, to Grand Dukes, ministers, and the library of the State Duma. At the beginning of the First World War became a patriot, gave himself up at the Russian frontier, was tried, banished and amnestied (1915). Under the Bolsheviks arrested on various occasions, resumed publication of *Byloe*, then published *Obshchee Delo* (*Common Cause*) under the Whites. Reemigrated.

Chudnovsky, Grigory Isaakovich (1848–1918) Social Democrat. Menshevik. Spent many years abroad. Returned to Russia with Trotsky, joined the Inter-District group, then the Bolsheviks. He and Antonov-Ovseenko were in charge of the assault on the Winter Palace. Military Commissar of Kiev. Killed in the Ukraine.

Greulich, Herman (1842–1925) Native of Breslau, book-binder. One of the founders of the Swiss Social Democratic Party and its newspaper *Berner Tagwacht*. Most popular of Swiss working-class leaders ('Papa Greulich'). Member of the Swiss Parliament from 1902 until his death.

Grimm, Robert (1881–1958) Printer, mechanic. One of the leaders of the Swiss Social Democratic Party. From 1905 Trade Union Secretary in Basel. From 1919 Secretary of the Party and editor-in-chief of *Berner Tagwacht*. From 1911 member of the Swiss Parliament, from 1946 its Chairman. Initiator and Chairman of the Zimmerwald and Kienthal conferences. One of the organisers of the '2½ International' (to the left of the Socialist International, but more moderate than Comintern).

Guilbeaux, Henri (1885–1938) French Social Democrat, internationalist. Opposed the war, in Geneva from 1915, published the journal *Demain* from 1916. Took part in the Kienthal Conference. On the staff of Comintern, but lost sympathy with the USSR in the thirties.

Hanecki (Fürstenberg), Jacob (1879–1937) Came of a wealthy Warsaw family. Joined the Social Democrats at the end of the nineteenth century. Attended the Second Congress of the RSDRP as a member of the Polish Socialist delegation. Was for many years simultaneously a member of the Polish and of the Russian parties. Briefly detained on various occasions, never sentenced for a long term. As a conscript abused his regimental commander, but was excused because of his 'excitability'. Twice escaped from places of banishment. Before the war joined Radek in splitting the Polish Social Democratic Party (in opposition to Rosa Luxemburg). From 1912 an intimate collaborator of Lenin, with him in Cracow, then in Switzerland, whence he moved in 1915 to work with Parvus in Scandinavia as director of his agency. In March 1917 he, Radek and Vorovsky were left by Lenin in Stockholm disguised as the 'Foreign Bureau of the Central Committee' to ensure the uninterrupted transfer of funds from Parvus for the reinforcement of Bolshevik organisations and the Bolshevik press in Russia, and also to carry on Bolshevik propaganda directed at the West. After the October Revolution was in the People's Commissariat of Finance (as Chief Commissar for Banks). Took part in negotiating the 'Supplementary Agreement' with Germany in August 1918, by which Russia's obligations under the Brest–Litovsk treaty were expanded to include increased supplies of foodstuffs and *materiel* to Germany on the eve of that country's defeat. Took part in important diplomatic discussions in 1920–1925. Many dark patches in his biography. After Lenin's death People's Commissar for Foreign Trade, various minor posts. Arrested and shot in 1937 together with his wife and son.

Inessa, see Armand

Kamenev (Rosenfeld), Lev Borisovich (1883–1936) Educated at Tiflis High School and Moscow University (Law Faculty), where he began his revolutionary career and was expelled. After a brief period of detention went abroad, where he joined the Bolsheviks in 1903. Returned to Russia several times, was briefly detained twice. Active as propagandist in the revolutionary years, prolonged residence abroad from 1908, became a member of Lenin's new entourage. Posted to Russia after Malinovsky's exposure in 1914 to lead the Bolshevik group in the State Duma from outside (when war broke out—from Finland). In November arrested while secretly conferring with them near Petersburg, tried in 1915, made things easier for himself by rejecting Lenin's defeatist line, which the Bolshevik faction in the Duma had accepted. Returned to Petrograd after the February Revolution, and since he enjoyed Lenin's confidence more than others in Petrograd, led the Party until his return. The only member of the Party who spoke out against the April Theses. When the Bolsheviks seized control of the Second Congress of Soviets on the night of their coup he became Chairman of that body and of the new Central Executive Committee. Took part in the negotiations with Germany at Brest-Litovsk. He was one of the ailing Lenin's three deputies—

the others being Rykov and Tsyurupa—in 1922. He and Zinoviev were constant companions in failure in the struggle against Stalin. Already doomed, he demanded at the 1934 Congress that the Party should not engage in ideological debate with the 'Kulak opposition' group led by Ryutin but shoot them. He was shot himself after the 1936 trial.

Kamo (Ter-Petrosyan), Semyon Arshakovich (1882–1922) Native of Gori in Georgia, son of a wealthy contractor. Expelled from school for expressing free-thinking views in scripture lessons. Influenced by his older compatriot Dzhugashvili (Stalin). Resourceful and skilful in illegal activities under arms, successfully carried out expropriation operations on Stalin's instructions, including the famous Treasury raid (Tiflis, June 1907). While travelling to Berlin to carry out his next raid was arrested by the German police with a case full of explosives. Avoided being handed over to the Russian government by successfully pretending for years to be violently insane. Was, however, finally handed over, but saved from execution by a German press campaign in defence of 'a man well known to be sick'. Escaped from prison hospital to join Lenin abroad. Returned to the Caucasus in 1912, was wounded and arrested during another interrupted mailbag robbery and sentenced to death. A liberal procurator, however, delayed implementation of the sentence until promulgation of the amnesty on the tercentenary of the Romanov dynasty, and so saved his life. Released from prison by the February Revolution. Lenin sent him to a mountain resort in the Caucasus for his health. Then Kamo served in the Cheka in Baku. Carried on underground activity after the establishment of the Menshevik government in Georgia. Rejected Lenin's suggestion that he should enrol in the Academy of the General Staff. Died after being run over by a car.

Karpinsky, Vyacheslav Alekseevich (1880–1965) Social Democrat from 1898, Bolshevik from the time of the split. Continuously resident in Geneva as an émigré from 1904. Lenin used him for minor editorial and practical tasks. In the Soviet period Doctor of Economic Sciences.

Kesküla, Alexander Eduard (1882–1963) An Estonian from Tartu. Took part in the 1905 Revolution. Arrested, but amnestied. Emigrated. Before the war studied unsystematically in Switzerland. In 1914 put himself at the disposal of the German Ambassador in Switzerland, Baron Romberg, tried to obtain German support for the Estonian liberation movement. Romberg used him for liaison with Russian revolutionary émigrés of various factions, including Lenin. To give him greater scope, he was transferred by the Germans to Scandinavia. There he sent agents to Russia and financed Bolshevik publications (Bukharin, Pyatakov, etc.) without disclosing the source of his funds. Acted as channel of communication between the Bolsheviks in Scandinavia and those in Switzerland.

Kharitonov, Moisei M. (1887–1948) Social Democrat from 1905. Studied law in Switzerland from 1912. Close to Lenin, returned to Russia in his group. After the October Revolution head of the Petrograd Militia. In the twenties secretary of provincial Party committees first in the Urals, then at Perm, then at Saratov. Supported the Zinoviev-Kamenev opposition in 1925, then their bloc with Trotsky. Occupied no important post after this.

Kollontai, Aleksandra Mikhailovna (1872–1952) Daughter of a (Ukrainian) general and a Finnish peasant woman. Brought up in a rich landowning milieu, not allowed to attend high school or Bestuzhev courses, where she might come into contact with revolutionary elements. Studied privately with professors of history and literature. An early marriage to escape parental control did not last long. Joined cultural and educational societies, all concerned with aid to revolutionaries. Studied economics abroad. Social Democrat from the end of the nineteenth century. Witnessed the shooting on Palace Square on January 9th 1905. Wrote proclamations for both Social Democratic factions. 'I felt a greater affinity for Bolshevism, with its intransigence'—but until 1915 she was a Menshevik, favoured general reconciliation in 1914, and was only gradually converted to Lenin's 'civil war' and so to Bolshevism. Before and during the war Shlyapnikov's mistress. People's Commissar for Social Insurance in the first Bolshevik government. Then for many years Soviet Ambassador to Norway and Sweden.

Kozlovsky, M. Yu. (1876–1929) Social Democrat, Petersburg lawyer, had clandestine links with Parvus's agency. Member of the Executive Committee of the Petrograd Soviet in 1917. Arrested in July, together with some leading Bolsheviks, after the revelations about Bolshevik dealings with the Germans. (They were all released at the time of the Kornilov mutiny.) After the October Revolution, Chairman of the Extraordinary Commission of Investigation in Petrograd and Chairman of the Little Sovnarkom. Later People's Commissar of Justice for Lithuania and Belorussia.

Krasin, Leonid Borisovich (1870–1926) Native of Tobolsk province, revolutionary from student days (influenced by political exiles). Received a technical education, periodically interrupted by arrest and banishment, became an engineer. This decided his future role in the Party: as its expert on conspiratorial techniques, the making of explosives, armed attacks. It was Krasin, too, who established contact with the factory owner Savva Morozov, and arranged regular financial help for the Party from this source. From 1903 a Bolshevik, and even became a member of the Central Committee. At the height of his revolutionary career he was simultaneously in charge of the whole Petersburg lighting grid. Emigrated in 1908, ousted from the Bolshevik leadership in 1909, gave up politics. Worked as an engineer in Berlin, returned to Russia, where he held managerial jobs. Rejoined the Party in 1917. Took part in the Brest-

Litovsk negotiations and in the 'Supplementary' talks in Berlin (August 1918—see Hanecki). Went to see Ludendorff at Staff Headquarters in a vain effort to persuade the Germans not to detach the Caucasus and Turkestan. (Ludendorff's plan was frustrated by the arrival of the American expeditionary force in France.) Held several important economic posts; was People's Commissar of Foreign Trade, then of Roads and Railways; from 1920 Ambassador in London; took part in other diplomatic negotiations, including the Genoa and Hague Conferences.

Krupskaya, Nadezhda Konstantinovna (1869–1939) Daughter of a court official. From 1897 Lenin's wife (the marriage was formalised in church so that she could go to Siberia with him). Shared his whole life, performed routine tasks for the Party. Tried to write original works on education, but achieved nothing of significance. After the October Revolution was amongst those in charge of the People's Commissariat of Education. In 1925 joined Zinoviev and Kamenev in their unsuccessful opposition to Stalin. Thereafter, during Stalin's dictatorship, had nothing to say for herself.

Levi (Hartstein), Paul (1883–1930) German Social Democrat, lawyer. As an émigré in Switzerland member of the Zimmerwald Left, later in Germany a Communist. Reverted to the Social Democratic Party in the twenties.

Litvinov (Wallach), Maksim Maksimovich (1876–1951) From a well-off family in Poland. Attracted to Marxism while performing military service as a volunteer. Arrested with the Kiev Committee of the RSDRP in 1901, escaped from imprisonment in Kiev in 1902 and fled abroad. A Bolshevik from 1903. In 1905 made an unsuccessful attempt to transport arms from Britain to Russia. Continuously in emigration except for short trips to Russia. In London from 1907. Represented the Bolsheviks in the International Socialist Bureau (2nd International). After the October Revolution was the first Soviet Political Representative (Ambassador) in London, was arrested in retaliation for Lockhart's arrest in Moscow and exchanged for him. Successful diplomatic career, Deputy People's Commissar, then from 1930–1939—i.e. in the peak years of the Stalin terror—People's Commissar for Foreign Affairs and herald of PEACE in the West; his speeches flooded the pages of Soviet newspapers and were popular. Demoted during the years of Soviet friendship with Hitler Germany. From 1941–1943 Ambassador to the United States. 1943–1946, again Deputy People's Commissar for Foreign Affairs.

Lunacharsky, Anatoly Vasil'evich (1875–1933) Prolific journalist and lecturer, feeble dramatist and writer (his choice of pen-name—Voinov, from '*voin*', warrior—indicates the level of his talent). Native of Poltava, from the family of a civil servant with radical leanings. Studied Marxism from the age of fifteen, agitator amongst workers at the age of seventeen.

When he left high school went to Zürich University. Returned to Russia in 1899, engaged in propaganda. Three short periods of imprisonment— a few months at a time—banished to Kaluga, Vologda, studied intensively, published first works. Emigrated in 1903, joined Bolsheviks and visited all émigré groups to popularise their position, agreed to speak on the principles of armed uprising at the Third Congress of the Party. During the 1905 Revolution active as journalist, underwent one month's detention and emigrated until the next revolution. Contributed to many Bolshevik publications. Pupil of Avenarius, differed with Lenin on philosophical questions in 1908–1909. Made an unsuccessful attempt to found a distinct party (the Vperyod—'Forward'—group). In the Trotsky–Martov group during the war. Returned to Russia via Germany with the second émigré party, was for a few months a member of the Inter-District group until they merged with the Bolsheviks in July 1917. In this way he came back to Lenin. Imprisoned for a short time by the Provisional Government, together with certain leading Bolsheviks, on a charge of treason—collaboration with the Germans. 'Both before I went to gaol and while I was there my life was in extreme danger on various occasions.' Released a month later. After the October Revolution People's Commissar for Education until 1929. During the Civil War paid many visits to the fronts and to forward areas, incessantly haranguing the troops. Equally well known in Moscow as an irrepressible lecturer. In 1923 published a book on the leaders of the Revolution without mentioning Stalin. This mistake earned him many years of disfavour and brought him into real danger. Died en route for Spain to take up his appointment as Ambassador.

Malinovsky, Roman Vatslavovich (1876–1918) Pole, native of Plock. Tailor, then metalworker. Three convictions for larceny. While performing military service became an informer for the secret police. Originally a Menshevik, went over to the Bolsheviks in 1910. Co-opted to the Central Committee by Lenin, appointed Chairman of the Russian Bureau (i.e. Director of the Party on Russian soil). Split the Social Democratic group in the Duma on Lenin's instructions and became leader of the Bolshevik faction. Conducted its work and composed his speeches under the simultaneous guidance of Lenin and the Police Department. But in 1914 a new head of the Police Department decided that it was self-defeating for the State to use a prominent member of the Duma as an informer, discharged Malinovsky and ordered him to give up his work in the Duma. (The situation is reminiscent of the way in which the police themselves exposed Azef.) Malinovsky resigned his parliamentary position without explanation and vanished. Rumours that he was a provocateur began to circulate, but Lenin, Zinoviev and Hanecki exonerated him in 1914 and again in 1917: 'The leading organs of the Party are absolutely sure of Malinovsky's political honesty. The accusations are absolute nonsense.' During the war was in the army and taken prisoner by the Germans. In 1918 decided to return to Russia after Lenin had promised him personal safety. (According to rumours a written guarantee signed by Lenin was taken from Malinovsky at the frontier.) He was tried by a tribunal on November 5th 1918 in Lenin's presence. Malinovsky defended himself in a six-hour speech. He was shot immediately.

Martov (Tsederbaum), Yuly Osipovich (1873–1923) Began revolutionary career as a student, was expelled and arrested on various occasions. In Vilna in the 1890s he formulated the ideology of the Jewish Bund, but he soon became an opponent of that party. Arrested together with Lenin in Petersburg in 1896, banished for three years. Unlike Lenin he had no strings to pull and so served his sentence in the Turukhan Territory. Emigré from 1901. Leader of the Mensheviks. Could not stand Bolshevik unscrupulousness. Favoured the development of Social Democracy by legal means. At the beginning of the war was against defence of the fatherland but also against converting the war into civil war. Returned to Russia via Germany with the second émigré party in May 1917. Was for a Socialist coalition government and against the seizure of power. At the Congress of Soviets in October spoke against the assault on the Winter Palace. Protested strongly against the dissolution of the Constituent Assembly, and, while the Red Terror was raging, against the death penalty. In 1920 with Lenin's permission left for Germany, where he published *Sotsialisticheskii Vestnik* (*Socialist Herald*). One of the founders of the '2½ International' ('for dictatorship of the proletariat, but without terror'). Died of tuberculosis of the throat.

Moor, Karl (1852–1932) Swiss Social Democrat. In 1892–1906 member of the editorial team of *Berner Tagwacht*. Well-to-do. During the war a double agent for German and Austrian secret services (code name 'Baier'). Was very helpful to Lenin. Took care of Münzenberg while he was in gaol in Switzerland, and of Platten in gaol in Lithuania, rescued Radek from gaol in Berlin (1919). Carried out secret diplomatic missions for the Soviet government. After the October Revolution an honorary citizen of the Soviet Union, and lived mainly there till 1927. Spent his last years in Berlin.

Münzenberg, Wilhelm (1889–1940) Native of Erfurt. Emigrated to Switzerland in 1910. There he became Secretary of the Socialist Youth International and editor of its organ *Jugend Internationale*. Organised workers' demonstrations in Zürich during the war. Took part in Kienthal Conference. From 1916 among the leaders of the Swiss Social Democratic Party. In 1917 the German authorities gave him travel facilities (although he was a deserter from the German army). Also in 1917 was responsible for bloody street fighting in Zürich. Arrested as a result of this, and again in 1918. Deported to Germany at the end of the war.

Secretary of the Communist Youth International 1919–1921. Visited Lenin in Moscow in 1920. In 1924 set up as a publisher of left-wing newspapers. Communist deputy in the Reichstag till 1933, when he emigrated to France. Summoned to the USSR by Stalin but refused to go. Found hanged in the forest near Grenoble in the summer of 1940.

Nobs, Ernst (1886–1957) Son of a tailor. Teacher. From 1915 editor-in-chief of the Party organ *Volksrecht* and other Socialist publications. From 1916 Chairman of the Party organisation in Zürich. From 1917 one of the leaders of the Swiss Party. From 1919 member of the Swiss Parliament, from 1943 to 1951 member of the government, in 1948 President of Switzerland.

Parvus (Helphand), Aleksandr (Izrail) Lazarevich (1867–1924) Native of Minsk province (Berezino), spent his childhood in Odessa. Completed course at Odessa High School in 1885, Basel University in 1891. Began successful career as a journalist in the German left-wing press ('the journalistic revolution'), intermediary between the German and Russian Social Democrats (Plekhanov, Potresov). Organised the publication of *Iskra* (*The Spark*) in Leipzig and contributed articles to it. Expelled from various German *länder* for his journalistic activities, moved to others. Real leader of the Petersburg Soviet in 1905, spent some months in the Kresty and Petropavlovsk prisons, administrative exile for three years to Siberia, escaped en route, returned to Petersburg, went abroad. Sharply attacked the 'Russian course' (policy of rapprochement) adopted by the German government from 1907. From 1910 to 1915 he was in Turkey and the Balkans, where he became extremely rich. Acted as financial adviser to the Turkish and Bulgarian governments when they came into the World War. From February 1915 entered into negotiations with the German Ministry of Foreign Affairs. Undertook to bring Russia out of the war by starting a revolution there. Under cover of trading operations sent German money to Russian revolutionaries—after the February Revolution exclusively to the Bolsheviks, enabling them quickly to reinforce their press and their membership, which were low and ineffectual in February 1917. After the revelations of July 1917, which were not followed up, he fiercely attacked Kerensky in the German press. In 1917 he obstructed concerted socialist efforts to end the war and influenced the German government to await the collapse of Russia into anarchy and then neutralise it. Wanted to return to Russia after the October Revolution (he had no confidence in Bolshevik organising abilities, and condemned Lenin's 'concessions' to the peasants). Lenin refused to have him. Parvus began attacking Lenin only when the Soviet government assigned two million roubles to 'support revolution in Europe'. He thought that it would be very dangerous if the Bolsheviks made Russia a great military power. Left for Switzerland after the German revolution of November 1918, settled in a villa by the lake at Zürich. His orgies

[233]

there, together with the scandals around Sklarz in Berlin (he had bribed members of the Social Democratic government), led to Parvus's expulsion from Switzerland. He built himself an opulent residence on the island of Schwanenwerder in Germany and lived there for the rest of his life.

Platten, Fritz (1883–1942) Metalworker, then draughtsman. Secretary of Swiss Social Democratic Party, took part in Zimmerwald and Kienthal conferences, where he sided with Lenin. When Lenin's group went home he was not allowed into Russia by British frontier controls. Returned to Switzerland, established contact with Baron Romberg to arrange further emigré echelons. ('We must increase the number of firm partisans of peace in Petersburg by bringing them in from abroad.') Member of Swiss Parliament from 1917, founded the Swiss Communist Party in 1918. At this time made a number of visits to Moscow, was one of the prominent figures at the inaugural meetings of Comintern (1919), was a member of the Bureau of Comintern. Secretary of the Swiss Communist Party until 1923, from then until his death lived in the USSR. Died in place of banishment.

Plekhanov, Georgy Valentinovich (1856–1918) The first important Russian Marxist. Founded the Marxist 'Liberation of Labour' group in Geneva in 1883. For many years leader of the Russian Social Democratic movement—until the split with Lenin in 1903. At the Second Congress, where the split took place, he still declared himself in favour of revolutionary dictatorship. Later he again allied himself with Lenin in a futile attempt to regain the leadership of the Party. In 1914 he took up a patriotic position, to which he clung more and more fervently in his remaining years. In 1917 he returned to Russia via England, arriving a few days before Lenin. Because of the fragmentation of the Social Democratic Party he had long ceased to lead the Mensheviks, and controlled only the 'Edinstvo' ('Unity'—i.e. *national* unity) group, which tried to ally itself with the Cadets and was smashed as a result of the October Revolution.

Potresov, Aleksandr Nikolaevich (1869–1934) Gentleman, son of an artillery colonel. Inherited compassion for the people from his mother. Graduated in science, began studying law, but succumbed to the lure of politics. First visited Switzerland in 1892 and made contact with Plekhanov and the 'Liberation of Labour' group. Became Plekhanov's publisher in Russia. Exiled to Vyatka province 1898–1900: produced the plan for *Iskra* together with Lenin and Martov—the three of them exchanged letters from their places of banishment—and in 1900 went to Switzerland to carry it out. Dropped out because of illness in 1901–1903. One of the first to return to Petersburg in 1905 to take part in the revolution, cooperated with Parvus and Trotsky in publications. After the suppression of the revolution refused on principle to emigrate. Plek-

[234]

hanov attacked Potresov from abroad in reply to his critical articles and Lenin took advantage of this. (The term 'Liquidator' originated in this polemic.) Potresov believed that the underground could not express the interests of the workers and that Socialists should concentrate on legal organisations. He felt that the 1914 war was the beginning of the end for Russia. Supported Guchkov's War-Industrial Committee. Acknowledged leader of the 'Menshevik-Defensists'. Strongly opposed to a separate peace, lived underground after the Bolsheviks came to power, arrested by the Cheka, released thanks to the efforts of old acquaintances. In February 1925, suffering from spinal tuberculosis, allowed to leave for treatment in Berlin. Bedridden until his death.

Pyatakov, Georgy Leonidovich (1890–1937) Son of an engineer. As a fifteen-year-old pupil of a Modern School took part in street meetings, and was expelled. At sixteen conducted anarchist propaganda, took part in an 'expropriation', trained himself for terrorist activity. Social Democrat from the age of twenty. In 1913 banished to Siberia, from there went via Japan to Europe (Switzerland, Sweden). After the February Revolution Chairman of the Kiev Committee of the Bolshevik Party, then also of the Kiev Soviet of Workers' Deputies. Took an active part in the October rising in Kiev; underground work in the Ukraine; from the end of 1918, first head of the Soviet government in the Ukraine. For most of the Civil War was a Commissar; did not shrink from punitive operations. In 1920 joined Trotsky's attempt to create a Labour Army (prototype of the labour camps) in the Urals. In 1922 chairman of the tribunal which tried the SRs in Moscow. From 1923 member of the Central Committee. He was concerned throughout with the administration of the economy, and by 1930 was the real overlord of heavy industry. Arrested, tortured, shot after a show trial.

Radek (Sobelsohn), Karl Berngardovich (1885–1939). A brilliant journalist and an audacious and resourceful politician. Native of Galicia, Polish Social Democrat. Emigrated, returned to Warsaw for the 1905 Revolution, again emigrated to Berlin. Opponent of Rosa Luxemburg in the Polish Social Democratic Party, expelled from the German Social Democratic Party for unseemly behaviour. At the beginning of the war left Germany for Switzerland to avoid the call-up. Attended Zimmerwald and Kienthal conferences, was sometimes at odds with Lenin, sometimes his ally and his favourite. Travelled through Germany with Lenin's group, stayed behind in the Bolshevik Foreign Bureau in Stockholm for the rest of 1917 (see Hanecki). Took part in the Brest-Litovsk negotiations. At the end of 1918 went to Germany to help start a proletarian revolution, was arrested, visited in gaol by prominent politicians. Released. Was in Germany on various secret missions (seeking an alliance against Poland, etc.) In 1923 sent there again to foment revolution (did not succeed). Member of the Central Committee, member of the Executive Committee of Comintern. In 1923–1925 shared the discomfiture of the opposition leaders, and ceased to hold prominent Party posts. For many years the most effective writer in the Soviet press. At the show trial of January 1937 made incriminating statements about others. He was not shot, but died in confinement shortly afterwards in unknown circumstances.

Rakovsky, Christo Georgievich (1873–1941) Son of well-to-do Bulgarian parents, and member of a family which played a considerable part in the fight for independence from Turkey. Involved in political disturbances as a fourteen-year-old schoolboy, emigrated at the age of seventeen to Geneva, where he came under Plekhanov's influence and made the acquaintance of the international Socialist Democratic movement. Connected with Russia by marriage, travelled there. Published articles in the left-wing press (pen-name 'Insarov'). An émigré for many years in Western Europe, persistent revolutionary activity in Roumania and Bulgaria. Took part in Zimmerwald Conference. Liberated from prison in Roumania by the February Revolution, went to Petersburg, joined the Bolsheviks. After the October Revolution a commissar in South Russia (of a naval unit, the Odessa Extraordinary Collegium etc.). On instructions from the Soviet government discussed with Skoropadsky and the Germans the separation of the Ukraine from Russia and a peace treaty between the two. None the less, when the Bolsheviks occupied and reoccupied the Ukraine it was always Rakovsky who became Chairman of its Council of People's Commissars, and in fact he governed the Republic until 1923 (combining this office with many military-political and economic-administrative posts). Went to Britain as Political Representative in 1923, to France in 1925. From 1919 in the Central Committee of the Party and a member of the supreme leadership. Fell together with the leaders of the first anti-Stalin oppositions. Condemned at the 1937 show trial. Died in gaol in unknown circumstances.

Ravich, Sara Naumovna (1879–1957) Social Democrat from 1903; in Geneva from 1907. Was arrested in Munich while changing money stolen from the Russian Treasury in Tiflis. Returned to Russia with Lenin's group, became a member of the Petrograd Committee of the Bolshevik Party. Apparently arrested in 1938, but survived the camps. Wrote a novel about the Decembrists.

Ryazanov (Goldendakh), David Borisovich (1870–1938) In the revolutionary movement from the age of seventeen, 'almost the first to become a Marxist in Odessa'. Following his theoretical and bookish inclinations, became a historian of Marxism. Arrested several times, made several trips abroad. From 1907 in emigration, writing a history of the First International, published certain works of Marx and Engels for the first time, became the leading expert on their literary remains. Attended Zimmerwald Conference. Returned to Russia via Germany with the second party of Russian émigrés. In 1917 joined the Bolsheviks. Lecturer, founder and director of the Marx-Engels Institute. Expelled from the party in 1931. Died at place of banishment.

Safarov, Georgy Ivanovich (1891–1942) Social Democrat from 1908, émigré in Switzerland from 1912, sided with Lenin and left for Russia with him. Chief editor of *Leningradskaya Pravda*, active member of the Zinoviev–Kamenev opposition in 1928. Expelled from the Party as a Trotskyist in 1927. Arrested in 1935.

Semashko, Nikolai Aleksandrovich (1874–1949) Son of a gentleman in Orel province. Nephew of Plekhanov, educated at Yelets High School, and (with interruptions when he was in detention or rusticated) in the Faculty of Medicine at Kazan University. During the 1905 Revolution was conspicuous at meetings in Nizhny Novgorod, was arrested, released on bail, emigrated. Close to Lenin in Geneva and Paris. After the October Revolution People's Commissar for Health. (Many hospitals in the USSR, and many streets with hospitals in them, are called after him, just as many streets with post offices are called after Podbelsky.)

Shklovsky, Georgy L'vovich (1875–1937) Social Democrat from 1898, emigrated to Switzerland in 1909. Chemist. Helped Lenin in routine matters (treasurer etc.). Returned to Russia in summer 1917 with the third party of émigrés. In 1918 in charge of the Soviet office in Bern, then held other diplomatic posts. In 1927 demoted as a Trotskyist. Committed suicide during the Great Purge.

Shlyapnikov, Aleksandr Gavrilovich (1885–1937) From a family of Old Believers in Murom. His father, an artisan, died early leaving a wife and four children. He had three years of elementary education, dreamt of becoming a skilled workman, and eventually became a highly qualified fitter and turner. Originally a staunch adherent of the Old Belief, he succumbed to the spirit of the time and was converted to Social Democracy. Worked in Sormovo, then Petersburg. Arrested on various occasions, never held for more than a year, but either amnestied or released against sureties. From 1905 a Bolshevik. Emigrated in 1908, worked in several Western European factories. During the war crossed the Russian frontier from Scandinavia several times, and was the only one in the whole Bolshevik Party to provide a real channel of communication between the emigration and the homeland: he delivered literature to Russia, and put life into the Party organisations in the capital and the provinces (of which he made a clandestine tour). From 1915 Chairman of the Russian Bureau of the Central Committee, i.e. formally and in fact in charge of the whole Party on Russian soil, while all other well-known leaders were lying low during the war years and the majority of Party committees did nothing. The February Revolution found Shlyapnikov in Petersburg. He became one of the Bolshevik members of the Executive Committee of the Soviet, created the Red Guards, made the arrangements to welcome Lenin on his return. But he was soon pushed into the background as former émigrés began arriving in large numbers. Was chairman of the Metalworkers' Union for many years, People's Commissar for Labour in the first Soviet government. When the government fled to Moscow was given the job of organising an orderly evacuation of Petersburg. Led the 'Workers' Opposition' (1921) which accused the Party leaders of forgetting the interests of the workers, and of political degeneracy. Furiously attacked by Trotsky, Lenin and the majority of the Central Committee: he was never forgiven for his role in this opposition. Thereafter held only secondary posts. He was hemmed in by informers, and in 1929 Stalin used to ring Shlyapnikov at night and demand that he slander himself. Expelled from the party in 1933, banished, arrested a year later. Under investigation for three years, would not give an inch, so that it was impossible to bring him into court in a show trial. Shot in September 1937. Rehabilitated by the Procurator's office in 1956, but still denied posthumous reinstatement in the Party: a *workers' opposition* is unforgivable.

Siefeldt, Artur Rudolf (1889–1938) An Estonian from Tallin. Sampled nearly all revolutionary factions, finally joined the Bolsheviks in Zürich from 1913 to 1917. Helped Lenin in his communications with Kesküla. Left Switzerland in 1917 with the second émigré group to travel through Germany.

Sklarz, Georg (b. 1878) Businessman, expressed no political opinions. From the beginning of the war in 1914 an agent of German Intelligence and the Naval General Staff. Worked in Parvus's agency, then made big deals on his own account, in war supplies to begin with, and continued his operations in ruined Germany after the war. Accused at a scandalous trial of bribing certain leading German Socialist politicians—Scheideman, Noske, Ebert—and high-ranking officers.

Sokol'nikov (Brilliant), Grigory Yakovlevich (1888–1939) Son of a doctor, high school education in Moscow. Bolshevik from 1905, member of 'Military-Technical Bureau' which organised armed raids. Emigrated in 1909 from his place of banishment on the Yenisei. Graduated from Faculty of Law in Paris. During the war vacillated between the *Nashe Slovo* group (Martov–Trotsky) and the Bolsheviks. Returned to Russia with Lenin's group. From July 1917 in the Bolshevik Central Committee, editor of *Pravda*, member of the Politburo when the October Revolution took place. Organised the seizure of the banks, became their Commissar General. Signed the Brest-Livovsk Treaty as head of the Soviet delegation, took part in the supplementary discussions in Berlin. In charge on the political side of operations to put down the workers' risings at Izhevsk and Votkin and the peasant risings in Vyatka province. Then in charge of punitive operations on the Don which provoked the Don rising. Army commander during capture of Rostov and evacuation of Whites from Novorossiisk. In 1920 he, Safarov, Kaganovich and Peters were in charge of operations to subdue Turkestan. Occupied an unfortunate position in the Party discussion on trade unions. From 1921 to 1926 People's Commissar for Finance. From 1929 Ambassador in London, from 1934 Deputy People's Commissar for Foreign Affairs. A defendant at one of the Moscow show trials. Died in confinement.

Tsivin, Evgeny (known to German and Austrian intelligence services as 'Weiss', and 'Ernst Kohler'). Russian revolutionary who worked in Switzerland during the war in contact with the Austrian and later also with the German intelligence services.

Uritsky, Moisei Solomonovich (1873–1918) From a merchant family in the town in Cherkassy. Educated in Belaya Tserkov' High School, Law Faculty of Kiev University. Took part in Social-Democratic movement, had no difficulty in escaping from places of banishment and going abroad. A Menshevik. During the war with Trotsky in the *Nashe Slovo* group, was Parvus's channel of communication with the Inter-District group in Petersburg. Went with them when they merged with the Bolsheviks, and immediately became a member of the Central Committee. Member of the Military-Revolutionary Committee, which directed the uprising in October 1917. 'Commissar of the Constituent Assembly'— and dispersed it. Head of the Cheka in Petrograd, organised the Red Terror in the former capital. Killed by the student Kanegisser.

Weiss, see Tsivin

Zinoviev (Apfelbaum), Grigory Evseevich (1883–1936) Native of Elizavetgrad. Uneducated. In his youth an office boy. Joined the Social Democrats at eighteen, emigrated at nineteen without having been arrested. Met Lenin in 1903 and joined him for good. Tried studying at Bern University, first in the Faculty of Chemistry then in the Law Faculty, but abandoned the attempt. During the 1905 Revolution complained of heart trouble (at the age of twenty-two), was forbidden by a specialist to 'take any part in politics' and went abroad again. Once the major revolutionary events were past he recovered and returned to Russia. In 1908 he was arrested for the first time, was released after a few months as a result of representations on his behalf, and this time went abroad to stay. From 1907 on he was a permanent member of the Bolshevik Central Committee. When Lenin changed his entourage in 1908 Zinoviev became his closest assistant, and co-editor of all his publications. He followed Lenin to Galicia, and back to Switzerland, was taken by him to the Zimmerwald and Kienthal conferences. Throughout the war years the 'Central Committee' meant Lenin, Zinoviev and anyone they cared to co-opt. He returned to Russia via Germany in Lenin's group, was fully informed on the connections with Parvus and the question of German aid. After the press revelations in July 1917 he went into hiding with Lenin (on the Finnish Gulf) to escape possible trial.

Remained in hiding until the October Revolution. After the Revolution Chairman of the Petrograd Soviet of Workers' Deputies, Chairman of the Council of People's Commissars of the Union of Communes of the Northern Region—i.e. after the flight of the Soviet government to Moscow in March 1918 he was virtual dictator of Petrograd and North-West Russia. The terrorist operations of 1918–1919 were carried out under his direction. From 1919 head of Comintern. In 1923–1924 he helped Stalin to defeat Trotsky and entrench himself as Secretary General. In 1925 he and Kamenev led the 'Leningrad Opposition', which tried to seize power in the Party but was defeated by Stalin in alliance with Bukharin. After this he tried acting in alliance with Trotsky, but they could not recover lost ground. After 1926 lost all his main posts, and all importance. Tried twice—in 1935 and 1936—before he was shot. Is said to have kissed the boots of the Chekists who led him out to be shot, pleading for mercy.

Translator's Footnotes

Chapter 22

1 July 16th–17th 1914.
2 'very truly' is in English in the original.
3 'One shot for every Russian!'

Chapter 47

1 *Epitaph for a Living Friend* appeared in *Nashe Slovo* in mid-February 1915.
2 That is to say, January 22nd by the Western European, Gregorian, calendar. At this point the Julian calendar was still in use in Russia.

Chapter L-1

1 The dates used throughout this and subsequent chapters are those of the Western, Gregorian, calendar.

Translator's Glossary

The following notes may be helpful in providing additional information on some of the proper names mentioned in the text.

Adler, Friedrich (Fritz) (1879–1960) Son of Victor Adler, Secretary of the Austrian Social Democratic Party, 1911–1916. During the war exhorted the Austrian proletariat to remain 'neutral'. Assassinated Prime Minister Sturgk on 21 October 1916. Sentenced to death. The sentence was commuted to a long term of imprisonment, and he was set free by the 'Austrian revolution' in 1918. Lenin finally decided that the assassination was 'the act of a despairing Kautskyite'. Adler was Secretary of the Executive Committee of the Socialist International from 1923 to 1940, emigrated to the USA on the eve of the Second World War, and spent his last years in Switzerland.

Adler, Victor (1852–1918) One of the major figures in the Austrian Social Democratic movement. In Leninist terms a 'revisionist', and during the First World War, a 'social chauvinist'. Lenin owed his release from prison in Poronin to Adler's success in persuading the Austrian authorities that his anti-Tsarist activity might help the Central Powers.

Akselrod, P. B. (1850–1928) A co-founder with Plekhanov of the first Russian Marxist party, the 'Liberation of Labour' group, formed in Switzerland in 1883. Influential as a theorist. One of the leaders of the Menshevik wing of Russian Social Democracy from 1903. A Liquidator (q.v.) after 1905. A centrist in the First World War. Staunch supporter of the Provisional Government. Left Russia after the October Revolution, died in Berlin.

Alakayevka A village in Samara province. Lenin's mother bought a house at Alakayevka in 1889, and Lenin spent his summers with his family there until 1893.

Aleksinsky, G. A. (1879–1966) Bolshevik in 1905–1907. Member of the Duma in 1907. Became a Recallist (q.v.) and joined the Vperyod group (q.v.). Patriot in the First World War. Co-operated with the Provisional Government's intelligence officers in publishing documents concerning Lenin's relations with the Germans (July 1917). Left Russia in 1918.

Bauer, Otto (1882–1938) One of the leaders of the Austrian Social Democratic Party, prominent figure in the Second International. Preferred Mensheviks to Bolsheviks. Minister of Foreign Affairs in November 1918–July 1919. An 'opportunist' and 'reformist' (in Leninist terms) throughout his active career, he became in his last years (spent in Czechoslovakia and France) an admirer of Stalinist Russia.

Bazarov, V. A. (real name Rudnev) (1874–1939) Philosopher and economist. Social Democrat from 1896. Bolshevik from 1904. Translator (with Skvortsov-Stepanov) of Marx's *Capital*. Became a Machist (q.v.) and God-Builder (q.v.). Menshevik in 1917–1919. Worked in Soviet planning organs after 1921.

Bebel, August (1840–1913) Dominant figure in the German Social Democratic Party. Highly esteemed by Marx and Engels. One of the founders of the Second International. Under his leadership the German Social Democratic Party became the strongest in Europe. Combated 'revisionism', but resisted demands for expulsion of revisionists. Incorrectly, in the Leninist view, distinguished between aggressive and defensive wars.

Bernstein, Eduard (1850–1932) German Socialist. Orthodox Marxist, then 'revisionist' theoretician. 'Movement is all, the final goal is nothing.' One of Lenin's favourite targets.

Black Hundreds Extreme right-wing monarchist organisations which sprang up during the 1905 Revolution, the most important being the 'Union of the Russian People' and the 'Union of the Archangel Michael'. With the encouragement and sometimes the assistance of police their rank and file members sought to stamp out revolution by counter-violence. Their targets included not only members of revolutionary parties but on occasions liberal politicians. Their anti-semitic outrages seriously damaged the reputation of the Tsarist government in Western Europe.

Blanc, Louis (1811–1882) French Socialist historian, theorist and politician. Joined the Provisional Government in the revolutionary year of 1848, and was therefore in Lenin's eyes the prototype of the Socialist demagogue who encourages reformist illusions among the masses.

Bloody Sunday 9 January 1905 (22 January New Style). On this day a procession of workers 150,000 strong, led by the priest Father Gapon, attempted to present a petition to the Tsar at the Winter Palace. (He was not in fact in residence.) The Governor-General of St Petersburg, Grand Duke Vladimir, ordered troops to open fire on the demonstrators, of whom more than a thousand were killed and several thousands wounded. This event was the signal for the general strike which grew into the 1905 Revolution.

Bonch, V. D., (Bonch-Bruevich) (1873–1955) Social Democrat, ethnographer, historian. Bolshevik from 1903. From 1907 worked on various legal Social-Democratic journals, while simultaneously pursuing his research into Russian religious sects. Useful to Lenin in contacts with sympathisers outside the Party.

Branting, Karl Hjalmar (1860–1925) Swedish Social Democrat leader, prominent figure in the Second International. In Leninist terms a 'revisionist' and 'class collaborator with the bourgeoisie'. During the First World War worked for the eventual restoration of international

Social-Democratic unity. Ridiculed the Zimmerwald Conference. After the October Revolution condemned the Bolsheviks as extremists 'out of touch with reality'. Admired Kerensky. First Socialist Prime Minister of Sweden in 1920.

Cadets ('Kadety', a nickname composed from the initial letters in Russian of their original party title—Constitutional Democrats.) The most important of Russian liberal groups, who formed themselves into a political party in 1905, to participate in elections to the first Duma. Also known as the 'Party of People's Freedom'.

The Development of Capitalism in Russia Work written by Lenin in 1896 which contributed to the success of Marxism against Populism. Published at St Petersburg in 1899 under his pseudonym of Ilin.

Duma Representative legislative assembly established by the Tsar after the 1905 Revolution. There were four successive Dumas between April 1906 and October 1917:

> 1st Duma: 27th April to 8th July 1906; 18 SD delegates; the Bolsheviks boycotted the elections:
>
> 2nd Duma: 20th February to 2nd June 1907; 65 SDs, including 18 Bolsheviks;
>
> 3rd Duma: 1st November 1907 to 9th June 1912; 19 SDs, including 6 Bolsheviks;
>
> 4th Duma: 15th November 1912 to 6th October 1917 (dissolved by the Provisional Government).

Economists Russian Social Democrats in the 1890s who held that in Russian conditions Marxists should for the time being not attempt to form a Socialist political party but support the liberal opposition to the autocratic system, while simultaneously assisting the proletariat in its 'economic' struggle for higher wages and better conditions.

Expropriations Euphemism for robbery with violence as a means of raising Party funds, practised during and immediately after the 1905 Revolution both by the Bolsheviks and by the Maximalists (q.v.). (Even the biggest Bolshevik coup—the Tiflis Treasury raid—was less spectacular and lucrative than the Maximalist raids on the Moscow Merchant Mutual Credit Bank and the Petersburg Treasury in 1906.) Lenin regarded such raids as a form of 'partisan warfare', and the Stockholm Congress of the Bolshevik Party (April 1906) while condemning expropriation of 'private capital' approved raids on government agencies. Hostile publicity in the Socialist press abroad—including criticism from the Mensheviks and from Trotsky—and the Stolypin government's success in repressing revolutionary activity forced the Bolsheviks to abandon this practice.

God-Builders A literary-philosophical group who sought to endow Marxism with a religious appeal. In their teaching 'God' did not exist, but was to be constructed by the collective self-perfection of the human species. Through its most important members (Lunacharsky, Bazarov and Gorky—see separate entries) the group had personal and ideological links with the Machists (q.v.). Lenin held that any form of 'religion' was incompatible with Marxism, and saw this jejune mystification as essentially an attempt to win back 'petit-bourgeois intellectuals' disillusioned by the abortive revolution on 1905.

Gorky, Maksim (A. M. Peshkov) (1868–1936) The only major Russian writer in the Social Democratic camp. Joined the Bolshevik Party in 1905. His ideological instability (i.e. receptivity to new ideas) troubled his relations with Lenin, who however showed unusual patience in his efforts to win the errant writer over: he was not only an ornament to the movement, but useful in spreading its influence and swelling its funds. Gorky was an associate of Bogdanov (q.v.) and a God-Builder (q.v.) in the years immediately before the war. He returned from emigration to Russia in 1913, and founded the journal *Letopis* (q.v.) in 1915. In 1917–1918 his articles in *Novaya Zhizú* (*New Life*), highly critical of the Bolshevik party and the new régime's policies, greatly annoyed Lenin. From 1918–1921 he occupied himself mainly in attempting to resuscitate Russian cultural life. In 1921 he left Russia, revisited the country in 1928 and 1929, and re-immigrated in 1931.

Grigory See Zinoviev (Author's Index).

Grishka See Zinoviev (Author's Index).

Grütlian Reformists Members of the Grütliverein, a Swiss educational society for workers and artisans which existed from 1838 to 1925. (According to tradition the three cantons sealed their alliance against the Hapsburgs on the Field of Grütli in 1307.) Attacked by Lenin as disseminators of petit-bourgeois reformist illusions amongst workers. Merged with the Swiss Social Democratic Party in 1925.

Guchkov, A. I. (1862–1936) Moscow property owner and industrialist, politician, in the Duma period one of the leaders of the moderate conservative Octobrist Party ('Union of October 17'—the date in 1905 on which the Tsar promulgated his manifesto promising an elected Duma). Highly critical of the Tsarist government's military preparations before the First World War, and its conduct of the war. Minister of War and of the Navy in the Provisional Government. Shared Milyukov's views on Russia's war aims, and resigned with him in May 1917. Emigrated in 1918. Remained an active opponent of Bolshevism.

Gvozdev, K. A. (b. 1883) Member of the SR party, 1903–1907. Strike leader in 1905. During the war a 'defensist', organised working-class support for the War-Industrial Committee. Held office in the Provisional Government (Deputy Minister, then Minister of Labour). Abandoned politics in 1918, subsequently worked in the cooperative movement and economic planning bodies. For Lenin, a prototype of the working-class leader who sells out to the bourgeoisie.

[245]

Haase, Hugo (1863–1919) German Social Democrat. Close associate of Kautsky. Reichstag deputy, 1897–1907 and 1912–1918. Spoke in support of war credits for the German government in August 1914. Presided, jointly with Ebert, over the anti-revolutionary Social Democratic government after Germany's defeat in 1918.

Hilferding, Rudolf (1877–1941) One of the leaders of the Austrian and German Social Democratic parties. A Marxist theorist of some importance. Lenin drew heavily on Hilferding's *Finance Capital* (1910) in writing his own *Imperialism*. 'Opportunist.' Held ministerial office in Germany in the twenties. Hostile to Soviet Russia. Emigrated to France in 1933. Handed over to the Germans by the Vichy government. Died in gaol.

Huysmans, Camille (1871–1968) Belgian Social Democrat. Secretary of the International Socialist Bureau, 1904–1919. Helped Russian revolutionaries to purchase arms in Belgium in 1905–1906. 'Centrist' during the First World War.

Ilyich See Vladimir Ilyich.

Imperialism (Full title *Imperialism as the Highest Stage of Capitalism.*) This is an ambitious attempt by Lenin, completed in 1916, to provide a theoretical foundation for his views on war and revolution. Amongst other things, it purports to explain why reformist Social Democracy is based on illusions, and why the first proletarian revolution may occur in one of the less highly developed capitalist countries.

Inter-District group (Russian *Mezhrayontsy*) A Social-Democratic group formed in St Petersburg in 1913, consisting to begin with of adherents of Trotsky or Plekhanov, who wanted the Party to rise above the Bolshevik-Menshevik squabble. During the war conducted anti-war propaganda in the Russian army. Played an important part after the February Revolution, when several prominent returning Social Democrats, including Trotsky and Lunacharsky, joined them. Incorporated in the Bolshevik Party in August 1917.

International The Second International, founded in 1889, was long divided over socialist attitudes to war and did not survive the First World War. After the war the following appeared: the Bern International, uniting the right wing (1919); the Communist International or Comintern (1919–1943); the Vienna International or '2½ International', uniting the Centre with the anti-Bolshevik left.

In 1923 the Second International was reborn from the merger of the Bern and Vienna Internationals.

Iskra (The Spark) Russian Marxist journal and organisation founded by Lenin at Munich, 24 December 1900, in collaboration with Plekhanov, Akselrod, Vera Zasulich, Potresov and Martov. Lenin's attempts to gain control of *Iskra*, which he wanted to see become the Party's organisational centre, led to the split of the Bolsheviks from the Mensheviks at the Second Congress (Brussels, 30th July 1903). The bone of contention between the two factions of the RSDRP, *Iskra* eluded the Bolsheviks in November 1903. It continued to appear, with a Menshevik slant, until October 1905.

Jaurès, Jean (1859–1914) French politician. An ardent pacifist, he vainly proposed to the Congresses of Stuttgart (1907), Copenhagen (1910) and Basel (1912) that they should adopt a resolution urging the Socialists to combat the threat of war by every means including a general strike and a rising. Assassinated on the eve of war.

Jouhaux, Leon (1879–1954) French trade union leader. Secretary General of CGT, 1909–1940, 1945–1947. Patriot (in Leninist terms 'chauvinist') during the First World War. Member of French delegation at Versailles. Vehement critic of Soviet Russia and Comintern, described by Lenin as 'one of the vilest of social-traitors'. After the Second World War active in the movement for European unity.

Kautsky, Karl (1854–1938) One of the leaders and theoreticians of German Democratic Socialism and of the Second International. Graduated to Marxism in the '80s. Editor of *Neue Zeit*, 1883–1917. Centrist.

Kienthal Conference International socialist conference, 24–30 April 1916, to concert views on war and peace. Though the Zimmerwald Left failed to carry the vote on any of the major issues discussed, the conference was in Lenin's view a further step towards the creation of a new, revolutionary Socialist International.

Klara See Zetkin.

Koba A romantic Caucasian outlaw, hero of the Georgian novelist Kazbegi's story *The Patricide*. Joseph Dzhugashvili used this *nom de guerre* until in 1912 he began styling himself Stalin, and old Caucasian cronies were allowed to call him 'Koba' even when he became dictator.

Kommunist Short-lived journal published by Lenin in Geneva. One double number appeared in September 1915, including three of his articles. He hoped to make this the international journal of the Social Democratic left, but his disagreements with other editorial contributors (Bukharin and Pyatakov) precipitated its collapse.

Konovalov, Aleksandr Ivanovich (1875–1948) Industrialist. Member of the Fourth Duma (Progressive Party). Vice-Chairman of Central War-Industrial Committee, 1915–1916. Minister of Trade and Industry in the Provisional Government of 1917.

Krylenko, N. V. (1885–1940) Bolshevik from 1904. Active at various stages as propagandist in the armed forces. Briefly Commander-in-Chief and Commissar for Defence after the October Revolution. Then worked in court system. Prosecutor at state trials, 1918–1931. Commissar for Justice, 1936–1940.

Kuba See Hanecki (Author's Index).

Ledebour, Georg (1850–1947) German Social Democrat. Lawyer.

Reichstag deputy, 1900–1918, 1920–1924. Member of the 'rightist' (anti-Leninist) majority at Zimmerwald. From 1917 leader of leftist groups which broke with the old Social Democratic leaders, but refused to join the Communists.

Letopis A literary, scientific and political journal founded by Gorky (q.v.) and published in St Petersburg from December 1915 to December 1917. Its eminent contributors included Blok, Mayakovsky and Pavlov. Lenin disapproved of its editorial policy, set by Mensheviks and members of the Vperyod group (q.v.), but Bolsheviks including Krupskaya used it as a vehicle for legal publication.

Liebknecht, Karl (1871–1919) Son of Wilhelm Liebknecht, one of the founders of the German Social Democratic Party. Lawyer by profession. Social Democrat from 1900. Close associate of Rosa Luxemburg in her anti-revisionist and anti-militarist campaigns. Enthusiastic propagandist for the Russian revolution of 1905. Elected to the Reichstag in 1912. To preserve Party unity voted—against his conscience—for war credits in August 1914, but shortly declared his opposition to the war. Called up in 1915, but continued to make anti-war speeches in the Reichstag. Expressed what was also Lenin's attitude to the war in a letter to the Zimmerwald Conference. Expelled from the Social Democratic Party in 1916. Arrested for organising an anti-war demonstration in Berlin on May Day 1916, sentenced to four years and one month imprisonment. Released in October 1918. Joined Rosa Luxemburg in founding the newspaper *Rote Fahne* (November 1918) and the German Communist Party (December 1918), and was murdered with her in January 1919.

Lilina, Zinka Zinoviev's mistress

Liquidators A name given by their enemies to those (mainly Mensheviks) who, after the revolutionary wave of 1905–1907 had receded, urged Russian Socialists to concentrate on the battle for reforms within the Duma and for the legalisation of the workers' movement—in effect, to abandon revolutionary activity. Lenin succeeded in fusing in his own mind this hostile trend to his right with his foes on the left—Recallists and Ultimatists.

Longuet, Jean (1876–1938) French Social Democrat. Son of Marx's daughter Jenny. Close collaborator of Jaurès. During the war a 'centrist-pacifist'. Condemned by Lenin as a 'French Kautskyite'.

Lozovsky, A. (real name Dridzo) (1878–1952) Social Democrat, Bolshevik from 1903. In emigration, 1909–1917; member of French Socialist Party. A 'conciliationist' (i.e. favoured reconciliation between Bolsheviks and Mensheviks). Back in Russia, expelled from Bolshevik Party in December 1917, readmitted in 1919. Was at various times a trade union organiser, diplomat and professor in the Higher Party School. Perished in the purge of 1952.

Luxemburg, Rosa (1871–1919) Born in Zamość (Poland), emigrated to

Switzerland 1889, graduated from Zürich University. Outstanding leader of the left wing of Polish Social Democracy (the Social Democratic Party of the Kingdom of Poland and Lithuania), which through her friend and one-time lover Leon Jogiches (Tyszko—q.v.) she continued to dominate even after 1898, when she made Germany the main sphere of her activities. Her major theoretical works, particularly *The Accumulation of Capital*, were unacceptable to Lenin. In spite of her misgivings about Bolshevik élitism, and her awareness that Bolshevik organisational principles might lead to the establishment of a personal dictatorship, she sided with Lenin on various occasions, most notably at the Fifth Congress of the RSDRP in 1907, and at the Stuttgart Congress of the Second International in the same year, when their joint amendment to a resolution seemed to have committed international Social Democracy to the use of an eventual European war as the occasion for revolutionary 'overthrow of the bourgeoisie'.

During the First World War, together with Karl Liebknecht (q.v.) and Klara Zetkin (q.v.) she led a left-wing group in the German Social Democratic Party which became known as the Spartacus League. Her 'anti-war' policy ('struggle for peace without annexations', 'war on war') fell short of the radical demands of Lenin and the left minority at the Zimmerwald Conference. Whereas Lenin throve on splits, she did her best to preserve the organisational unit of the massive German Social Democratic Party, while working for its ideological conversion from within: it was the Party majority which in the end expelled her left-wing group from its ranks. In gaol at the time of the Bolshevik Revolution, she hailed it with enthusiasm, though Lenin's opportunist agrarian policy and the summary dismissal of the Constituent Assembly perturbed her. In December 1918 she was one of the founders of the German Communist Party. During the rioting in Berlin in January 1919 she was murdered while under arrest.

Lyadov, M. N. (real name Mandelstam) (1872–1947) Revolutionary, historian. Bolshevik from 1903. Bolshevik representative at Amsterdam Congress of the Second International, 1904. Member of the Party's Moscow Committee during the 1905 Revolution. Emigrated 1908. Became a Recallist (q.v.) and in 1909 joined the Vperyod group (q.v.). Lectured in the Vperyod schools on Capri and at Bologna. In 1911 broke with Vperyod and went to work in Baku. In 1917 editor of the Baku *Izvestia*. Supported the Mensheviks until 1920, when he moved to Moscow and was readmitted to the Bolshevik Party. Rector of the Sverdlov Communist University 1923–29. Author of the first outline history of Russian Social Democracy (1906) and of many subsequent works on the subject.

Machists Followers of the Austrian physicist and philosopher Ernst Mach (1838–1916). His re-examination of the basic concepts of Newtonian physics prepared the ground for Einstein's work, and his influence as a philosopher can be seen in the development of twentieth-century neo-positivism. He aspired to replace explanatory with purely descriptive procedures, in which only empirically verifiable data were admissible, and rejected as metaphysical such conceptions as absolute space and time, substance, 'thing'. Lenin regarded Mach's teaching as subjectivist and idealist, and, less questionably, saw it as incompatible with traditional Marxist materialism. In his only extended philosophical monograph (*Materialism and Empirio-criticism*), Lenin attacked Bogdanov and others who sought to reconcile Machism with Marxism. It is unlikely that he would have devoted so much effort to an enterprise for which he lacked all qualifications if the Machist deviation had not coincided with a threat from the same quarter to his position as Party leader.

Manuilsky, D. Z. (1883–1959) Ukrainian, Social Democrat. Educated at Petersburg University, imprisoned for his part in organising the naval mutinies of 1906, escaped. Graduated in Law from the Sorbonne, 1911. Member of Vperyod (q.v.) and Recallist (q.v.) groups. Worked underground in Russia, 1912–1913. In France during the war. Internationalist. Returned to Russia in May 1917, joined the Inter-District group, entered the Bolshevik Party with them. After the October Revolution held important posts in the Ukraine, and in Comintern. Led the Ukrainian delegation to the United Nations, 1945, and to the Paris Peace Conference, 1946. Academician.

Materialism and Empirio-criticism In this work (1909) Lenin attempted to defend orthodox Marxist materialism as he understood it against Machist (q.v.) revision.

Maximalists An extremist group which broke away from the Socialist Revolutionaries in 1904. Distinguished by its fanatical belief in 'propaganda by the deed'—i.e. political assassination and robbery ('expropriations'). A majority of the group, by then much reduced, decided in 1920 to dissolve it and seek membership of the Bolshevik Party.

Menzhinsky, V. R. (1874–1934) Graduate of St Petersburg University (Law), revolutionary from 1895. Member of the Military Organisation of the Petersburg Committee, 1905. Emigré in Belgium, Switzerland, France and America. In 1917 member of the Bureau of the Military Organisation of the Bolshevik Central Committee, editor of the Bolshevik paper *Soldat*. Best remembered as Dzerzhinsky's deputy, 1923–1926, and successor, 1926–1934, as head of OGPU.

Michael, Grand Duke (1878–1918) Mikhail Alexandrovich was Nicholas II's morganatically married younger brother. The Duma politicians who forced Nicholas to abdicate in February 1917 expected him to name his young invalid son Alexis as his successor, with Michael as Regent. Nicholas, however, also renounced the throne on behalf of

Alexis, and designated Michael as his successor. After a brief attempt to find a *modus vivendi* with the new régime Michael also withdrew. He was shot by the Bolsheviks in Perm in July 1918.

Milyukov, P. N. (1859–1943) A major Russian historian, and leader of the Constitutional Democratic Party (Cadets). Duma deputy from 1907 onwards. Sharply criticised the Tsarist government in the First World War from a patriotic position. Minister of Foreign Affairs after the February Revolution of 1917, determined to carry on the war against Germany to final victory and the achievement of Russia's original war aims. Forced to resign in May by Menshevik and SR hostility to his policies. Left Russia in 1920, lived mainly in Paris, wrote many historical and topical works, remained active in émigré politics. After the German attack on the USSR in 1941 his Russian patriotism prevailed over his hatred of Bolshevism, and he greeted Soviet military successes with enthusiasm.

Mimiola, Giulio (1889–1916) Italian Social Democrat.

Moisei See Bronski (Author's Index).

Morozov, Savva Industrialist. Contributed to Bolshevik funds through L. B. Krasin.

Nadya See Krupskaya (Author's Index).

Naine, Charles (1874–1926) Lawyer, one of the leaders of the Swiss SDs. Editor of *La Sentinelle* and *Volksrecht*. Internationalist (Kienthal) during the war. In 1917 moved to the centre, then to the right of the Party. 1919–1921, a founder of the '2½ International'.

Nashe Slovo (Our Word) A newspaper published in Paris from January 1915, on the initiative of Antonov-Ovseenko, then a Menshevik, but in 1917 and afterwards one of the outstanding Bolshevik military leaders. *Nashe Slovo* opposed the war and denounced 'social patriotism', but was less narrow and dogmatic in its editorial policy than Lenin's *Social Democrat*. Its contributors included Radek, Rakovsky, Kollontai, Uritsky (see separate entries), the future Soviet Commissar for Foreign Affairs Chicherin, and above all Trotsky, who represented the paper at the Zimmerwald Conference.

Natanson, M. A. (1850–1919) Russian revolutionary. One of the outstanding leaders of the Populist movement from 1869 onwards. Joined the Socialist Revolutionary Party in 1905 and became a member of its Central Committee. Was an internationalist during the war, took part in the Zimmerwald and Kienthal conferences. After the October Revolution was one of the leaders of the Left SRs who briefly collaborated with the Bolsheviks. Described by Lenin as 'a revolutionary Communist, quite close to us, almost at one with us'.

Nevskaya Zastava A district in St Petersburg.

One Step Forward, Two Steps Back A polemical work written by Lenin in 1904, denouncing Menshevik ideas on party organisation.

[251]

Octobrists A moderate Russian conservative party founded in 1905, which unlike the liberals and all parties to the left, regarded the concessions made by the Tsar in his Manifesto of 17 October 1905 as a satisfactory basis for cooperation between government and Duma in the reconstruction of Russia after the 1905 Revolution. See also Guchkov.

Pannekoek, Antoni (1873–1960) Dutch Social Democrat. Astronomer by profession. Leftist. Sided with the Zimmerwald Left during the war. One of the founders of the Communist Party of the Netherlands in 1919. Here too deviated leftwards, attacked Lenin as an opportunist, withdrew from the Party and from politics in 1921, concentrated on his researches into the Milky Way.

Recallists (Russian '*Otzovisty*') A dissident group within the Bolshevik Party which in 1908 opposed Lenin's tactics of 'temporary retreat' and of 'using all legal possibilities', including participation in the Duma, of reinforcing the Party's political position. The Recallists, whose members included Bogdanov (q.v.) and Lunacharsky (q.v.), demanded the 'recall' of Bolshevik deputies from the Duma, and the total withdrawal of the Party into the underground to prepare the next armed uprising.

Roland-Holst (Roland Holst van der Schalk), Henrietta (1869–1952) Dutch writer, poetess, Social Democrat. Left the Social Democratic Party in 1912, headed the Revolutionary Socialist League in 1915. At Zimmerwald supported Trotsky's intermediate position, but later sided with the Zimmerwald Left and published articles in its journal, *Vorbote*. After the war joined the Communist Party of the Netherlands. Withdrew from it in 1927 and became editor of the Flemish Trotskyist organ *De Vlam*. Active in the Dutch resistance movement during the Second World War.

Rolland, Romain (1866–1944) French writer, musicologist and Socialist. In Switzerland during the First World War. Eloquent anti-war propagandist. Friend of Lunacharsky, and later Gorky. Reacted enthusiastically to the February Revolution. Showed some initial misgivings about Lenin's regime, but from the late twenties onwards became an increasingly fervent and uncritical admirer of the USSR.

Rosa See Luxemburg.

Rozhkov, N. A. (1869–1927) Social Democrat and a historian of some note. A Bolshevik from 1905. Joined the Liquidators in 1910 while in Siberian exile, and in 1917 was active in the cause of reunification of Bolsheviks and Mensheviks. Held office in the Provisional Government in May–July 1917. Hostile to the Bolsheviks after the October Revolution, but in 1922 broke with the Mensheviks and reconciled himself to the new régime.

RSDRP Russian Social Democratic Workers' Party. Founded in March 1898 at the First Congress at Minsk. At the Second Congress, Brussels–London (1903) it split into two factions, Bolsheviks and Mensheviks, and at the Sixth Pan-Russian Conference (Prague 1912) it broke up. From March 1918 the Bolshevik faction took the name of Russian Communist Party.

Shingarev, A. I. (1869–1918) Physician by training, liberal politician, one of the leaders and most talented orator of the Cadet Party. Minister of Agriculture (February–May), Minister of Finance (May–July) in the Provisional Government, 1917. Imprisoned by the Bolsheviks in November 1917, transferred to hospital in January 1918, there murdered by anarchist sailors.

Shmidt, Nikolai Pavlovich Nephew of Morozov (q.v.), he was a rich student who committed suicide in prison after bequeathing his fortune to the RSDRP (1906). His younger sister Elisabeth Pavlovna, made a fictitious marriage with a Bolshevik which gave her legal authority to make her inheritance over to the Bolsheviks.

Shushenskoye See Yenisei.

Social Democrat Bolshevik newspaper. After the police confiscated its first number, brought out in Russia in 1908, it was published in Paris until 1914, and then in Geneva. It provided Lenin with a platform for his campaigns against Bolshevik deviationists, and for his propaganda during the war.

Spilka A Ukrainian Social Democratic nationalist group established in 1904 which entered the Menshevik party as an autonomous section.

SR The Socialist-Revolutionary Party was born at the end of 1901 out of the merging of the Populist groups. Adept at terrorism. In 1917 it supported the Provisional Government (Kerensky and Chernov were SRs). Fought against the Bolsheviks during the Civil War, and did not survive the Bolshevik victory.

Stolypin, P. A. (1862–1911) Prime Minister of Russia from 1906 until his assassination in 1911. Believed that given two decades of peace Russia could be made stable and prosperous. To this end he tried to reinforce the government by an understanding with the Duma, and to create a class of loyal and contented smallholders by agrarian reform. He had more success in his stern endeavours to repress revolutionary activities by summary trial and execution. Was scarcely less unpopular with the court clique than with revolutionaries. His assassin was loosely connected both with the SR Party and with the secret police.

Sumenson, Evgenia Employee of the Fabian Klingsland company in Petrograd, which had dealings with Hanecki's firm. Said to have acted as Hanecki's intermediary in transferring German money to Kozlovsky (q.v.). Arrested together with Kozlovsky in July 1917 when the Provisional Government published its materials intended to confirm rumours that Lenin was a German agent.

Two Tactics of Democratic Socialism in the Democratic Revolution, 1905. Work in which Lenin shows that the union of the workers

[253]

with the peasants under the workers' direction is the decisive pre-condition for a victory of the bourgeois democratic revolution and its transformation into a socialist revolution.

Tyszka (or Tyszko), Jan (real name Leon Jogiches) (1867–1919) Born in Vilna. Member of revolutionary organisations from the age of eighteen. Co-founder of the Social Democratic Party of the Kingdom of Poland and Lithuania. Close collaborator of Rosa Luxemburg, and for some years her lover. Took part in the revolutionary events of 1905 in Warsaw, arrested in 1906 and sentenced to eight years' imprisonment. Escaped, and from 1907 controlled the SDKPiL from Berlin. Inter-nationalist during the First World War, prominent member of the German Socialist left. Led the Spartacus group while Rosa Luxemburg was in gaol, and until his own arrest in March 1918. Secretary of the Central Committee of the German Communist Party at its foundation in December 1918. Arrested in March 1919, murdered in prison.

Ultimatists A dissident Bolshevik group which shared the general views of the Recallists (q.v.), differing from them only on minor questions of tactics.

Ulyanov Lenin's real name.

Usievich, G. A. (1890–1918) Became a revolutionary Social Democrat as a student at St Petersburg University in 1907. Escaped abroad from exile on the Yenisei in 1914, was interned in Austria, then went to Switzerland late in 1915, where he met Lenin. Returned with him to Russia in 1917. Killed in battle in Siberia, August 1918.

Valentinov, N. V. (real name Volsky) (1879–1954) Social Democrat (Menshevik) journalist, philosopher and memoirist. His Machist (q.v.) revision of Marxism outraged both Lenin and Plekhanov. Withdrew from active politics in 1917. In the twenties worked on the *Trade and Industrial Gazette* published by the Supreme Economic Council. His published reminiscences of Lenin, of the Russian Symbolist poets, and of Soviet economic mandarins are eminently readable and historically valuable.

Vandervelde, Emile (1866–1938) Belgian Social Democrat. From 1900 chairman of the International Socialist Bureau of the Second Inter-national. A revisionist, and in the First World War a patriot ('social chauvinist'). Visited Russia after the February Revolution to urge continued Russian participation in the war, and in 1922 to assist in the defence of the SR leaders brought to trial by Lenin. Belgian Minister of Foreign Affairs, 1925–1927.

Vladimir Ilyich Lenin's forename and patronymic. The patronymic Ilyich used alone indicates affectionate respect.

Volodya Affectionate diminutive of Lenin's forename.

Vorbote Theoretical journal published by the Bureau of the Zimmerwald Left, of which only two numbers appeared (in January and May 1916).

The first included Lenin's article on 'Opportunism and the Collapse of the Second International', and the second his theses on 'Socialist Revolution and the Right of Nations to Self-Determination'.

Vperyod (Forward) group Extreme leftish Bolshevik schismatics, whose views Lenin considered a 'caricature of Bolshevism'. This alliance of Recallists, Ultimatists, and Machists attracted (sometimes, as in the case of Krasin and Gorky, only briefly) many past and future luminaries of Bolshevism who in the years 1909–1917 found Lenin's policies timid, opportunistic, and unrevolutionary, and his behaviour within the Party intolerably highhanded. Among its members were Bogdanov, Lunacharsky, Lyadov, Aleksinsky, Manuilsky (see separate entries). The group was loosely held together by common disapproval of participation in the Duma and other legal organisations, by eagerness to precipitate a fresh armed uprising in Russia (which Lenin in 1908–1914 rightly thought had no chance of success), and by its demands for complete freedom of thought within the Party. Its numbers were steadily reduced by internal quarrels and defections. In 1917 its remnants fused with the Inter-District group (q.v.) and so were carried back into the Bolshevik Party in August of that year.

What Is to be Done? One of Lenin's most seminal works, published in 1902. Attacking Economism (q.v.) the main Russian variant of revisionist Marxism, he argues that the spontaneous development of the workers' movement can produce only a (non-revolutionary) trade-unionist mentality, and that the movement must be led by a tightly organised party of professional revolutionaries.

Yenisei One of the great Siberian rivers. The Yenisei region was used as a place of exile, remote and primitive, from the seventeenth century onwards. Lenin spent the years 1897–1900 in banishment there (at Shushenskoye); Krupskaya joined him in May 1898.

Zemlyachka, R. S. (real name Zalkind) (1876–1947) Bolshevik from 1903. Secretary of the Moscow Bolshevik Committee during the Moscow rising in December 1905. Then worked underground in Petersburg; was imprisoned, 1907–1908; continued underground activity in Baku; emigrated in 1909. Returned to Russia in 1913. After the October Revolution held many important posts in the Party apparatus. Deputy Chairman of the Council of People's Commissars, 1939–1943.

Zetkin, Klara (Clara) (née Eisner) (1857–1933) Prominent figure in the German Social Democratic Party, the Second International, and in the international women's movement. Close friend of Rosa Luxemburg, whose line she supported in the First World War. Perhaps influenced by her Russian émigré husband, she was less inclined than Rosa to criticise Russian comrades. Joined the infant German Communist Party early in 1919. Took a very active part in the work of the Communist International, where, in spite of occasional vacillations, she always ended in support of the current Soviet leadership. As the oldest serving deputy made the opening speech in the Reichstag in August 1932, calling for a united front against Fascism—until this late date the German Communists had been intent on combating Social Democrats in the first place. Died near Moscow. Her remains were immured in the Kremlin wall, near the Lenin Mausoleum.

Zimmerwald Conference International socialist conference, 5–8 September 1915, intended to re-establish international socialist links after the collapse of the Second International. The 'right', most effectively represented by Akselrod (q.v.) and Ledebour (q.v.), dominated the conference. From Lenin's point of view its value was that it enabled him to identify and attach to himself a staunch leftist minority. 'The development of the international socialist movement,' he wrote, 'is moving slowly ... but definitely in the direction of "a break" with opportunism and social chauvinism.'